The Lost
Treasure of the
CONCEPCIÓN

The Lost Treasure of the CONCEPCIÓN

The Story of One of the World's Greatest
Treasure Finds and Burt Webber—
the Man Who Never Gave Up

by John Grissim

WILLIAM MORROW AND COMPANY, INC.
New York
1980

BOOK DESIGN BY SALLIE BALDWIN, ANTLER & BALDWIN, INC.

Library of Congress Cataloging in Publication Data

Grissim, John, 1941–
    The lost treasure of the Concepción.

    1. Concepción (Ship) 2. Treasure-trove—Silver
Bank. 3. Webber, Burt, 1942– 4. Adventure and
adventurers—United States—Biography. I. Title.
G530.C74G74   909′.096363   80-14653
ISBN 0-688-03635-X

Printed in the United States of America

First Edition

1 2 3 4 5 6 7 8 9 10

To the men of Operation Phips I and II, and those
who believed in them, and to all who dare
to live the dream of finding treasure

Preface and Acknowledgments

In the spring of 1978, while researching an article on treasure hunting for *Playboy* magazine, I spent several weeks in Florida with camera and tape recorder documenting the ongoing search for the treasure of several Spanish galleons. The historical background of these legendary ships was fascinating, but no less intriguing were the men and women who today devote their lives to the pursuit of an underwater Eldorado. After probing the waters off Marathon Key with treasure hunter Robert Marx (in search of the *San Fernando*) and watching Mel Fisher scour the ocean floor thirty miles west of Key West for artifacts from the *Atocha*, I, too, began dreaming of one day participating in a treasure hunt in the warm clear waters of the Florida Keys or the Caribbean.

Some months later the opportunity to fulfill that dream was provided by Burt Webber, Jr., who was preparing an expedition to the Silver Shoals to find and salvage the *Nuestra Señora de la Concepción*. Webber agreed to my joining the expedition to chronicle events. The experience turned out to be an extraordinary and rewarding adventure that contained all the ingredients of a classic tale of a search for sunken treasure. It was a great privilege to have been involved in a rare moment of living history. My hope is that the pages to follow have in some measure captured the character and passion of that moment.

A great many people have helped make this book possible. I am indebted to Burt Webber, Warren Stearns, and Stanley Smith—the Seaquest International A-Team—for their essential contributions and goodwill on so many levels. Thanks, too, to my agent John Brockman and to Susan Hanger for first-rate editorial judgment and sustaining enthusiasm.

I am extremely fortunate to have had the superb assistance of Judi Mackesy who transcribed a mountain of interview tapes and typed the manuscript, and whose encouragement and kindly critical eye were a tremendous asset. Her conscientious commitment to the project was an inspiration for which I will be forever grateful.

For introducing me to the reality and sometime hilarity of the hunt in Florida, many thanks to Mel and Deo Fisher, Bleth McCaley, Claudia Linzee, Ashley Simmons, and Robert Marx. Thanks, too, to Key West's Don Kincaid, an outstanding underwater lensman, for photographic advice, and to Elmer Collett and Kirby Ferris for the use of much-appreciated photo equipment. In Scott Tye, a veteran diver for the National Park Service, and the good people at Marin Skin Diving in San Rafael, California (Debbie Jemison, George Gregor, Jean Gregor, and Richard Gallagher), I found a source of generous support, good advice, and good deals on all matters relative to scuba diving. Thanks to all of you. No less a debt is owed to my favorite travel agent Jackie Hazelrigg of Small World Travel who time and again found a way to "get me there" on very short notice.

For much-needed contributions I am grateful to Stan Waterman, Don Summers, and John Berrier, to historians Jack Haskins, Peter Earle, and John Potter, Jr., as well as to designer/cartographer Jon Goodchild for his splendid rendering of the treasure maps in this book. Last but hardly least, I am indebted to Stephen Staples, Milan Melvin, Nick Gravenites, Anna, and Nancy Sullivan for support and favors too numerous to mention.

December, 1979   JOHN GRISSIM

Contents

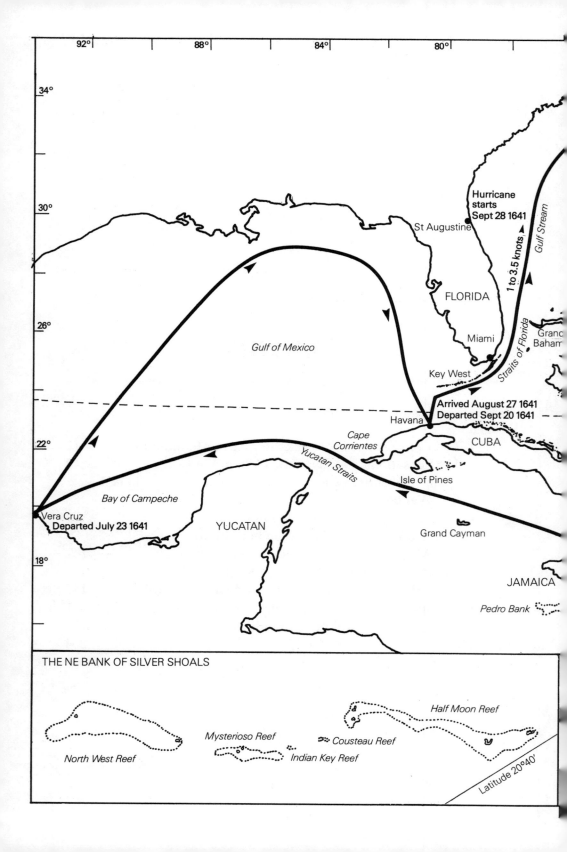

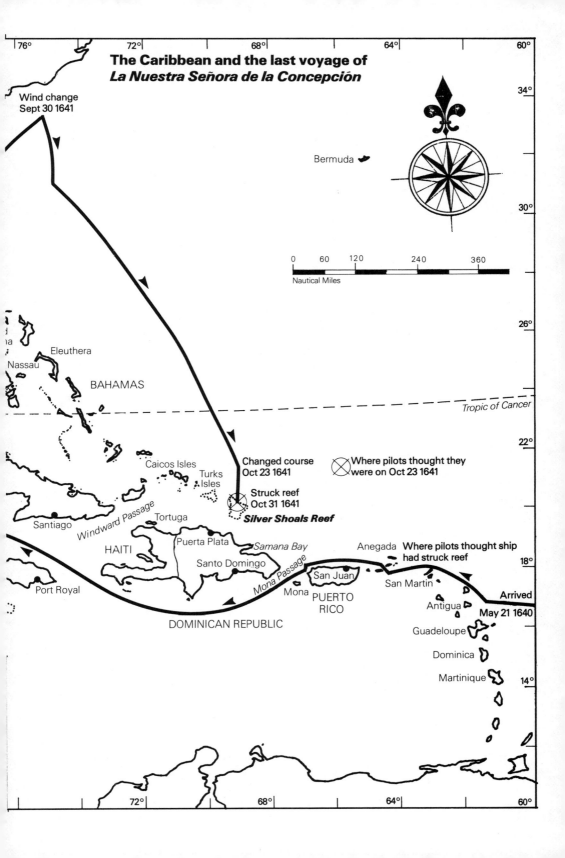

*There are few things as powerful as treasure
once it fastens itself upon the mind.*
—JOSEPH CONRAD

Prologue

It was a day at sea that ended with a flourish. The sun took refuge behind distant clouds, dazzling the sea beneath with long rays reminiscent of old-time religious prints, reappeared momentarily in molten orange, then slipped languidly beneath the horizon, leaving behind towering clouds suffused with red and pink. A light breeze gave way to a warm stillness and the cyan-blue water turned calm. Here in the nether reaches of the Atlantic Ocean somewhere north of the Dominican Republic nature was in one of her most benign moods.

The setting was nearly as empty as it was vast, for nowhere was there to be found any point of land or sign of man—save one. Still visible in the failing light, a fair-sized motor yacht bobbed gently on a mooring, the light from her portholes casting a warm glow. Her elegant lines might have suggested a chartered vessel on a pleasure cruise were it not for the ES/88 painted in bold red naval lettering on her sides and the two inflatable boats that floated astern. As the evening stars appeared, a figure emerged from the starboard hatch and tossed some table scraps over the side, then paused by the rail to savor the night, its silence broken only by the distant drone of a generator below.

Inside the vessel's wardroom a dozen men sat in canvas deck chairs by a long galley table finishing the evening meal. Normally, at this time a few might have left the table to read or play chess or backgammon or perhaps take a turn topside. But this night, November 25, 1978, was anything but normal. At the head of the table a young man in khaki safari shorts and T-shirt sat coiled over a photocopied document. While he read in a strong resonant voice the wardroom listened in silence:

"'At four of the morning, the anchor cable parted and we threw over a cannon which was hauled up in the anchor station at the bows. But the ship dragged and at daybreak, with the water up to the beams and the bow under, we dragged until the stern came upon a rocky head where it remained seated upon it.' And the admiral goes on to say, 'I saw that any further efforts would be useless other than to save the silver, the artillery and the people.'"

He reached for another document. "Then there's the testimony of the captain of the infantry. He says, 'Because the sea was so large it imprisoned the ship where it remained with heads close all around, it appearing impossible to have entered into.'"

He looked up. "All right, according to these statements we may expect to find the wrecksite fairly far into the reef, not just on the fringe." Several listeners nodded, others remained staring into coffee cups and dessert plates.

He reached for a detailed chart, studying it for a moment, then with the edge of his hand chopped its surface with hatchet finality. "She's got to be on or damn close to this bearing line. She's *got* to be there. I *know* she is!"

This last statement bristled not only with resolution but also a deep sense of past frustration. Then, too, it seemed a challenge hurled defiantly before some unseen power that refused to yield up a great secret. For Burt D. Webber, Jr., the man who spoke, it was all these things. And if this night his voice seemed more strident, his manner tense, it was because the following morning this thirty-five-year-old professional treasure hunter would slide beneath the surface of 70-degree waters to search for the legendary wreck of *La Nuestra Señora de la Concepción*, one of the richest treasure galleons ever to sail the Spanish Main. It would be the biggest gamble of his life. In the days ahead he would encounter either triumph and treasure worth untold millions, or a crushing failure that would end his career and destroy his hopes.

If any member of Webber's hand-picked expedition team had not fully understood the magnitude of the stakes involved, he did now. Webber had already tried to find the wreck of the *Concepción*—and failed. This time out the Pennsylvania-based father of four was putting all his chips on the line. He had spent most of his savings and worked eighteen-hour days for months, struggling past delays, all the while battling critics who labeled him a nice guy but one who in seventeen years of looking had never found significant treasure. The "seventeen-years-of-failure" tag particularly rankled Webber, but he never strayed from either his dream or his meticulous and methodical approach to treasure hunting. "I don't care if the *Concepción* is next to that coral head right over there," he'd said earlier in the week. "We're gonna take our time and get everyone thoroughly familiar with the gear and the procedures. The old girl will not yield herself to any man who doesn't really prepare for her."

In recent weeks such terms of affection for a shipwreck, suggesting a form of elaborate courtship, crept easily into conversation whenever the ship's company discussed the galleon, which was often. Webber's obsession with the *Concepción* and the incredible story of its demise was contagious. Nor did he discourage its spread. For several nights running now he had read aloud from dozens of photocopied documents culled from the maritime archives of two continents, reciting a litany of facts and statistics. Perhaps he was arming himself with reassuring evidence, turning to it as a balm to ease the fear and self-doubt. Yet one sensed also that a brilliant leader was programming loyal troops, drumming into them information that would prepare them to assimilate while fifty feet under water the subtlest clues that would lead to the discovery of the greatest sunken treasure in modern times.

Complementing the crucial Old World documents was an array of the most technologically advanced search equipment ever employed under water, including a state-of-the-art device known as a cesium magnetometer encased in a housing Webber himself had designed. Tomorrow it would be used in earnest for the first time ever, but for now it lay in a special storage compartment while its battery pack was being charged in one corner of the wardroom. In fact, while Webber and his team studied data more than three centuries old, they were literally surrounded by tons of sophisticated dive equipment, machinery, electronics, salvage tools, and communications gear. The assembled men and matériel had the look and feel of a mountaineering team on the eve of an assault on Mt. Everest.

Indeed, the *Concepción* was the Mt. Everest of the treasure-hunting world. Numerous expeditions had been mounted to search for this fabled galleon. Fortunes had been spent in vain by a host of famous explorers—England's Sir Malcolm Campbell and Jacques Cousteau to name only two. Hardship, physical exhaustion, and death had stalked their paths. So complete had been past failures that treasure hunters had dubbed the ship the *De-cepción*.

And now it was Burt Webber's turn. He had the research and he had the technology, yet he knew only too well that no treasure hunt is ever a sure thing, least of all this one, not after what he'd endured. In the *Concepción* he had chosen not only one of the richest treasure galleons ever lost, but also one whose tragic demise was one of the worst maritime disasters to befall any country in the seventeenth century. It was the *Concepción*, too, that from her sandy grave had affected the destinies of men and ships, most notably the fortunes of an American colonial, William Phips, who in 1687 found the *Concepción* and salvaged part of her immense cargo. His discovery was the sensation of all Europe. In many ways the story of the *Concepción* was matched in scope and drama by the tales of Phips and those after him who sought her treasure. Certainly Webber's own life had become inextricably intertwined in the *Concepción*'s legacy and her as yet unfinished history. Only events in the days ahead would determine whether he would write the final chapter or merely add another intriguing footnote.

The moon had risen by the time most of the ship's company had turned in. Webber made a last check of the battery packs before walking out to the deck aft. He paused a moment by the stern rail and gazed at silvery clouds, then went below to his stateroom. Hours later in the predawn darkness of the wardroom a tiny microswitch in a battery charger clicked. A red indicator light marked "Charging" went out, replaced by an adjacent green light that glowed the word "Ready."

1

The CONCEPCIÓN: Six Weeks to a Seven-Fathom Grave

Man has always had a penchant for marking the past, particularly dramatic and fateful events that have in some way influenced the shape of the present. For Burt Webber, who on that November night in 1978 gazed out over the placid moonlit waters of the Silver Shoals, there were no landmarks or plaques or artifacts to evoke the memory of the great drama that had taken place there more than three centuries earlier. Yet at that moment probably no man alive had a greater understanding and feeling for the history that lay beneath the shallow waters around him. It was that history, and the promise of its legacy, that had led him here. And now he was about to become a part of it, for in the days to follow he would attempt to bring to a close an ages-old saga involving kings and admirals, sea captains and slaves, sailors and cutthroats, people whose names and exploits, whose acts of courage and cowardice were as familiar to him as the men whom he had brought with him to the shoals.

That saga, and the story of a nation and a ship that affected their destinies, is a fitting and necessary prelude to the events that were about to take place in the life of Burt Webber.

Rivers of Gold and Silver—and Blood

When in 1492 a jubilant Christopher Columbus first set foot on the hot sands of tiny San Salvador Island 375 miles southeast of Florida, he believed not only he had found a new and shorter route to Marco Polo's China and India but a gateway to great treasures in gold, silver, silks, and gems. The explorer's assessment of where he had landed may be one of history's most colossal miscalculations but, in the years to follow, his belief in the vast wealth that was there for the taking in those distant lands would be vindicated time and again in a harvest of riches that would stagger the imagination.

During the first two decades, Spain's colonization of the Caribbean produced a scanty, disappointing yield, notably pearls from the Lesser Antilles and some gold and silver mined from the islands of Cuba, Hispaniola, and Puerto Rico. But in the early 1500's the conquistadors arrived and Spain's conquest and plunder of the New World began in earnest. Cortez invaded Mexico in 1519, defeated an Aztec nation and extracted $20 million in silver and gems. Farther south in Peru the Inca civilization met a similar fate as Pizarro plundered the accumulated wealth in gold and silver worth nearly $25 million. It was a grim harvest, for everywhere the brutal pillage of the conquistadors and many less well-known expeditions was accompanied by wholesale destruction, torture, rape, and sometimes the outright slaughter of whole tribes. Estimates of the amount of gold and silver looted from the New World during the years 1520–1560 (the heyday of the conquistadors) run as high as $200 million. From the very beginning the river of gold and silver that flowed eastward to Spain was heavily tainted with blood.

To help maintain its monopoly of the burgeoning traffic to and from the New World, Spain's King Ferdinand and Queen Isabella in 1503 ordered the establishment of a supervising agency, *La Casa para la Contratación y Negociación de las Indias*, "the House of Trade." The *Casa* was almost a government unto itself for it controlled all commercial shipping, provided for the security of fleets, audited all cargoes to and from the New World, and exercised absolute authority over every ship's itinerary, cargo allowance, even daily shipboard routine. The *Casa* additionally held responsibility for ensuring that the King received a tax of 20 percent of all the wealth from the New World. This was termed the King's quintal or the Royal Fifth.

In its infancy *La Casa para la Contratación* was for the most part staffed by able civil servants and administrators with maritime experience, the latter of whom supervised the meticulous collating of data on ocean currents, weather, soundings, and navigational observations which formed the basis of charts and sailing instructions. But with the explosive growth of traffic to the New World, accompanied by chaotic commercial activity and frenzied speculation, the *Casa* soon expanded into a vast top-heavy bureaucracy staffed with armies of officials, most of whom were political appointees whose ignorance of the New World was matched only by their enthusiasm for any dishonest scheme that would line their pockets.

Bureaucratic corruption was not the only threat to the mounting flow of New World treasures. Other opportunists in the form of Barbary Coast pirates and later, French and English raiders, prowled the seas off the coasts of Spain, taking their share of booty at gun- and knife-point. Pirates also began roaming Caribbean waters, preying upon the slow, unwieldy Spanish freighters. To counter these assaults *La Casa para la Contratación* established in 1522 a system of fleets, or armadas, which would sail to and from the Indies at regular intervals. By the 1550's, with most of the New World charted, the fleet system had evolved into two major armadas.

The *Neuva España* (New Spain) armada (known as "the flota") departed Spain in the spring each year, sailed south down the African coast to the Canary Islands where it reprovisioned, then headed west with the tradewinds. Two or three months later, upon reaching the windward islands of the Lesser Antilles, the flota proceeded westward, stopping at San Juan, Puerto Rico, and Santo Domingo on Hispaniola, thence along the south shore of Cuba, across to the Yucatán peninsula, and north along the Mexican coast to Veracruz, that country's principal shipping port. (Brought to this rather dreary gulf port for transport to Spain were not only Mexico's silver but also porcelain, silks, spices, and other Asian rarities that came by way of the Philippines (Spain's principal possession in the far East) aboard the Manila galleons to Acapulco, thence by burro train across Mexico to the Veracruz docks. With its ships loaded with New World treasures, the New Spain flota followed the clockwise currents of the Gulf of Mexico around to Florida's west coast, then across to Havana, the center of Spain's New World political power and commercial activity as well as its wealthiest and most cultured outpost.

The second of Spain's great fleets, the *Tierra Firma* armada (called the Galleons) generally left Spain in the summer, and like the New

Spain fleet, crossed to the Lesser Antilles by way of the Canaries. Once in the West Indies, however, the galleons turned south to skirt the northern coast of South America en route to Cartagena, Colombia, dispatching ships to various smaller ports to off-load European goods and pick up cargo. Once the fleet reached Cartagena several of its larger cargo vessels, called *naos,* were dispatched to the port of Portobello on the east coast of the Isthmus of Panama. To this port came huge amounts of treasure carried by the south seas fleet from Peru to Panama where it was transported by burro trains and ferried by river barges eastward to the waiting galleons. With the arrival of the treasure (and a weeks-long trade fair at Portobello noted for its debauchery) the galleons returned to Cartagena and rejoined their sister ships for the voyage northward to Cuba. If the elements had not disrupted the timetable, both the New Spain fleet and the *Tierra Firma* galleons would link up in Havana and a few weeks later sail together for Spain. Barring major catastrophes, the fleets could complete the round trip in seven to nine months.

As risky as the journey to the Indies was, the homeward voyage from Havana was considerably more dangerous, for the fleet was required to sail northward to higher latitudes to encounter the prevailing westerly winds that would take them due east—and the way was perilous. Though variations occurred, the route the fleets most often followed took them ninety miles north from Havana to within sight of the Florida Keys, then eastward around the tip of Florida (aided by the swift Gulf Stream) and north through the forty-mile-wide passage between Florida and the reef-fringed Bahama islands. Continuing north to the vicinity of Cape Hatteras and the Carolinas, the fleet would turn east and, with luck, pass north of Bermuda and into blue water.

The initial portion of the voyage from the Florida Keys through the Straits of Florida was the most crucial inasmuch as the unwieldy square-rigged galleons were unable to sail more than a few degrees into the wind, which itself was as unpredictable as the weather. Tropical storms and hurricanes, while occurring most frequently from July through September, could strike at any time with little warning, unleashing high winds and seas which could push the helpless ships onto the keys or Florida's east coast beaches or onto the many islands of the Bahamas, causing terrible destruction and loss of life. On several occasions—notably in 1622, 1715, and 1733—entire fleets had been all but wiped out by such tempests, taking many hundreds to their deaths and scattering tens of millions of dollars in treasure onto the ocean floor. And if these dangers weren't enough, there were always pirates lying in ambush to pounce upon any ships unfortunate enough to be separated from the fleet by weather or breakdown. Occasionally, the toll in losses was spectacular. In 1628, for example, the Dutch adventurer Pieter Heyn literally hijacked the entire treasure fleet barely a day out of Havana Harbor, becoming in the process a national folk hero in the tiny Spanish-ruled Netherlands.

Having once reached the safety of deep water east of Bermuda, the cumbersome galleons faced other dangers. The winds could fail, leaving them becalmed in the Sargasso Sea for days, sometimes weeks at a time, a delay which played havoc with food and fresh water supplies. Nor was it possible for the ships' pilots to determine their position with any real accuracy. By measuring the noon height of the sun above the horizon navigators could compute latitude roughly within fifty miles; however, longitude determination required the use of a timepiece far more accurate than the primitive and unreliable clocks of the day.

In spite of the terrible price paid in ships and men (not to mention treasure), and despite the gamut of dangers that constantly played havoc with her fleets, Spain still managed to bring back to her shores prodigious amounts of New World plunder. By 1600, an average of eighty ships annually made the eastward crossing, carrying a yearly cargo total worth $35 million. A hundred years later the total had doubled. The great percentage of this booty was the product of massive slave labor, for no sooner had the conquistadors pillaged the amassed wealth of their subjects than whole populations were made to work the rich silver mines of Peru, Bolivia, and Mexico—or to pan for gold in rivers and streams.

There to oversee this brutal exploitation was an army of New World settlers, many of whom were soldiers of fortune, case-hardened ex-convicts, failed aristocrats, and unsavory rejects from the mother country. Life here was primitive, often cut short by malaria, yellow fever, and smallpox, yet it held promise for the strong, the shrewd, and the lucky.

As Spain consolidated her hold she began minting her silver and gold in the New World, first in Mexico City (starting in 1535), and later in Lima, Peru, and Potosi, Bolivia. In appearance the coins from these mints were primitive; however, Spain's refining techniques were first rate and the weight of every coin was rigidly controlled. The mints were capable of producing coins with a silver fineness of 99.9 percent; however, the resulting product would have been too soft and malleable to endure long circulation. Through the addition of metals such as copper, zinc, and tin, the silver coin's fineness was reduced to 93 percent but had the advantage of far greater longevity.

Silver bars and coins were set in denominations of eight, four, two, one, and one half reales, a reale being one eighth of an ounce. The coining process involved pouring a long thin bead of silver on a flat surface, then after it cooled, hammering it into a flat strip. From this strip or bar, two-inch-long pieces were cut off and weighed, then small bits chiseled off the corners until the weight of each piece corresponded with its denomination. Finally, the piece, or coin blank, was sandwiched between two dies and struck by the coin-maker with a heavy mallet. Because the die designs were slightly larger than the coin blanks, and the edges of the blanks themselves had been hammered, the resulting impression was never a complete one. Europeans called these coins "cobs," from the Spanish *cabo de barra*, "cut from the bar." The most popular of these coins was the eight-reale piece, weighing one Spanish ounce, or *onza*. This convenient one-ounce silver ingot was widely used and respected for trading throughout the world and became universally known as "a piece of eight."

Aboard the Golden Galleons

Strangely, as important as the armadas were to bringing back enormous quantities of minted silver, they were forever being given short shrift from the Crown. What funds there were usually went to His Majesty's Navy fleet to defend Spanish shores. (Despite its vaunted superiority, the Navy suffered a terrible defeat in 1588 when England's superior ships-of-the-line sank 132 galleons of Spain's Invincible Armada in an epic encounter.) This gross imbalance of maritime muscle seems all the more strange, for Europe's entire currency standard was tied to the value of the peso while Spain's economy—being based on silver and gold, not paper—literally floated or sank right along with her treasure ships.

Yet, in the absence of creative designers and a progressive shipbuilding industry, Spain's lumbering galleons remained the backbone of the transport fleet—poorly constructed, overworked, badly maintained, and frequently riddled with wood-boring teredo worms of the Caribbean. To their credit the great galleons had one major advantage that ensured their longevity on the Spanish Main: they were rugged enough to withstand abuse and could carry an immense amount of passengers and cargo. And artillery. Some of the largest ships in this class carried as many as ninety bronze cannons arrayed on three gun-decks. The great majority of galleons, however, carried few if any cannons, their decks being used instead for cargo. These freighters were more correctly called *naos* rather than galleons although both vessels were identical except for armament. In practice the *naos* sailed in convoy across the Atlantic escorted by either two or four galleons, the latter of which were not allowed to carry cargo other than treasure belonging to the King and privileged private parties.

A typical galleon of the seventeenth century was 125–140 feet in length with a cargo capacity of 600–800 tons. Its beam was broad, anywhere from thirty to forty-five feet across, while the tallest of its three masts often exceeded a height of 120 feet. Perhaps the most characteristic features were the two multi-level structures, or castles, extending up from the weather deck. The forecastle was usually two levels and built around the forward mast while the sterncastle was an elaborate three- or four-tiered affair sweeping upward aft of the mainmast at a rakish angle. On some of the largest galleons of this period the highest level (poop deck) of the sterncastle was forty-five feet above the waterline. The sterncastle housed several small cabins for the captain, pilots, and important passengers whose wealth and/or position merited private quarters.

Such a top-heavy vessel required considerable ballasting in the form of tons of boulders, rocks, and stones laid along the keel during construction. For this purpose the Spanish most often used smooth egg-shaped granite river boulders ranging from six inches to three feet across. The resulting draft was anywhere from ten to eighteen feet depending on the ship's beam.

Though the other maritime powers of Europe regarded the galleons as unwieldy and outlandish (the French called them *bailles*, "tubs," while Spanish sailors dubbed them *pájaros puercos*, "flying pigs") few vessels of like displacement could carry as many passengers, soldiers, and crew—anywhere from 450 up to 700 for an Atlantic crossing. To be sure, for those aboard, with the exception of the ship's captain and a few senior officers and personages, the voyage was a harrowing one. During the grueling two-and-one-half to three-month crossing from the New World to Spain the great majority of the ship's company lived topside, taking refuge belowdecks only in rain and heavy weather. Passengers with a disease were usually taken below and placed in dark, cramped, unventilated spaces (there were no portholes) to suffer their days breathing fetid, stifling air.

As a rule, few of the ship's crew were Spanish. Most were of mixed European descent and recruited from the ranks of roustabout sailors, thugs, beggars, and petty thieves who congregated around the major seaports. Among their principal duties while under way was the manning of hand pumps which had to be operated constantly to clear the bilges of water from chronic leaks.

For the most part the food was rotten or barely edible, particularly later in the voyage. Water was scarce and severely rationed. Personal hygiene was as nonexistent as crabs and lice were prevalent. Disease in the form of yellow fever, flu, and dysentery was rampant—and death was commonplace. Anyone completing the voyage with merely a case of scurvy was considered fortunate. Personal privacy was almost unheard of and on most galleons the only toilet available was a crude bench with a hole in the seat located near the bow. If one were driven by bad weather to spend time belowdecks, one was forced to breathe foul air that reeked with the stench of urine and excrement (this because some passengers were too ill to carry themselves to the toilet). Because of the fire hazard, candles and lanterns were forbidden below, leaving one to fend for himself in the darkness against the probings of ubiquitous rats.

Given such deplorable conditions, shipboard morale was sustained primarily by the hope of surviving the ordeal. Not surprisingly, mass was said daily while holy days and feasts of the most inconsequential saints were celebrated with great fervor. What small diversions were available consisted mainly of employing the ship's livestock for gambling, such as cock fights and pig races.

During the early years of Spain's New World conquest few women accompanied the fleets. But in the seventeenth century their numbers increased as the colonial outposts expanded. Female passengers in small numbers were assigned passage aboard the *naos* and, in accordance with strict directives from the House of Trade, were carefully segregated from the rest of the ship's company. Among the first to ignore these orders were the senior officers and passengers of noble rank. To be sure those women of high station, particularly wives and daughters of senior colonial officials, remained unmolested; but among the female travelers were regularly to be found an earthier breed of prostitutes, lascivious wives, and frontier ladies looking for struck-it-rich husbands in the New World. As a matter of practice, weather permitting, women were regularly swapped between ships, a custom which not infrequently gave rise to tales of cognac binges and late-night poop deck orgies.

The *Casa*'s rules pertaining to women were not the only guidelines ignored. The corruption that riddled the *Casa*'s bureaucracy ashore was equally extensive afloat. While merchants were required to pay a tax on all valuables brought aboard, they regularly bribed the ship's captain to omit certain cargo from the ship's manifest. In this manner large amounts of contraband in the form of gold finger bars, silver splashes, and chests of coins and gems were smuggled across the Atlantic. One way or another just about everyone had a stake in some form of contraband, particularly administrators and officers who were political appointees. These individuals had paid the Crown high prices to obtain their positions and if they survived a few years in the New World, would return to Spain rich men.

The galleons, which the *Casa* decreed were to transport Crown treasure (being sufficiently armed to protect it), regularly carried contraband far in excess of their declared inventory. Research has suggested that fully one third of all the treasure plundered from the New World was contraband. Author-historian John S. Potter, Jr., an authority on Spain's treasure fleets, determined that during the period of 1500 to 1820, a total of 17,000 return voyages from the New World brought to Spanish shores an aggregate treasure in gold, silver, and precious stones worth today in excess of $20 billion.

No less extraordinary is that only 5 percent of that total was lost or pirated. For sinkings alone, treasure with a meltdown value conservatively estimated at $600 million was involuntarily consigned to the ocean floor to await new ownership. Considering the steady rise in the price of precious metals and the even greater collector's value, the total potential value is easily twice that amount.

Because Spain depended so heavily on her New World plunder to maintain her economy, any shipwreck or piracy resulting in the loss of treasure was a serious blow. Some loss of life was of course expected when such events occurred and the annals of the Spanish Main record numerous disasters that took hundreds of lives and millions in treasure. Among these, however, only a bare handful of maritime incidents compare in scope and drama with the savage loss of the fighting galleon *Nuestra Señora de la Limpia y Pura Concepción* (Our Lady of the Good and Pure Conception) in the fall of 1641.

The Crippling of the Almiranta

She was a majestic high-sided vessel of 650 tons capacity, a forty-four-foot beam, and an overall length of 140 feet. Built in Havana in 1620, she boasted thirty-six bronze cannons, an ample number to qualify her for escort duty. Indeed, in the two decades since she had slid down the ways of the royal shipyards, the *Concepción* had made many Atlantic crossings with both the *Tierra Firma* and *Nueva España* fleets. In 1641 her owner, Captain Eugenio Delgado, no doubt looked forward to many more profitable voyages. Yet this year circumstances were conspiring to lead his ship to a most cruel demise.

The *Concepción* had not had her hull cleaned and caulked in more than eighteen months and as the numerous leaks in her bilges indicated, she was way overdue. But there was little Delgado could do. So few ships were available that in 1640 there was no New Spain flota to bring badly needed Crown silver from the mints of Mexico and Peru. Now a far greater amount of silver awaited transport.

Several months earlier, the Crown had designated the *Concepción* the *Capitana,* or "lead ship," of the fleet headed for Mexico, this because she carried aboard the fleet commander (captain general) as well as the newly appointed viceroy of New Spain. While in Veracruz, however, the fleet commander had died, most likely of yellow fever. His place was taken by Juan de Campos aboard the galleon *San Pedro y San Pablo*, which became the new *Capitana*. Admiral de Campos in turn made the *Concepción* the Almiranta, the next-senior vessel. In this capacity the ship was responsible for guarding the rear of the fleet and directing the battle in the event of attack.

As one of the two escort galleons, the *Concepción* took on in Veracruz a substantial amount of minted silver belonging to the Crown as well as a consignment of gold and jewels belonging to the archbishop of Mexico (who himself embarked as a passenger). Additional cargo consisted of Chinese porcelain and silks brought to Acapulco by Manila galleons, then carried overland to Veracruz. She then sailed in convoy for Havana, arriving on August 27, 1641. She remained about two weeks provisioning and taking on more treasure in the form of silver belonging to merchants and other private parties returning to Spain. A great deal of this cargo was put aboard surreptitiously and represented large fortunes amassed by colonial traders and administrators who had bribed the ship's officers to omit the booty from the *Concepción*'s manifest. The payoff was routine, but since there had been no fleet the previous year the amount of contraband stowed aboard was much greater than usual and had to be stacked to shoulder height in the passageways.

In addition, more gold and silver came aboard as part of the personal belongings of other important passengers. Actually, everyone from the senior officers and notables down to the lowest seaman and soldier endeavored to secrete aboard what little he could, be it only a coin pouch or a gold finger bar, trusting it would escape the sharp eyes of the *Casa's* spies and inventory clerks. For the least squeamish of crewmen a preferred hiding place was among the ballast piles deep in the hold, access to which was gained through small hatches; these same hatch openings, however, were used extensively as toilets, the result being the ballast holds were rather unsavory—putrid, rat infested, and thick with excrement.

The commanding officer of the *Concepción* was thirty-seven-year-old Admiral Don Juan de Villavicenzio, a nobleman and an experienced sailor who had gained his rank by merit, not by political appointment. Having crossed the Atlantic many times, he knew well the dangers that faced his ship and its 496 passengers, not the least being the *Concepción's* overloaded condition and numerous hull leaks. Villavicenzio had on several occasions vigorously argued for a delay in departure to make repairs and perhaps even await the arrival of the *Tierra Firma* flota that was due any day. Captain-General de Campos, an arrogant, vain, and self-serving commander who boasted he knew more about business than the ways of the sea, overruled Villavicenzio, claiming the New Spain flota of twenty-one ships could not risk bad weather by delaying longer. In reality, de Campos, who was eager for the glory of commanding a fleet carrying desperately needed money to His Majesty, wished to avoid linking up with the *Tierra Firma* galleons because he would then have to relinquish his *Capitana* position to the senior commander of the latter fleet.

Thus, on the morning of September 13, 1641, the combined flota sailed past the ramparts of El Morro Castle which guarded the entrance to the port of Havana. From the fort's parapets the guns boomed a salute to the stately parade of merchant vessels and the archbishop of Havana lifted his heavily bejeweled hands to wave an elaborate benediction as Captain-General Don de Campos' *Capitana* lumbered by under full sail. Within a few hours the fleet was over the horizon bound for the Florida Keys ninety miles north where it would slip into the Gulf Stream leading to the Straits of Florida.

Shortly after nightfall of that first day, however, the *Concepción* sprang a new and large leak. While a crew manned a pump, Admiral Villavicenzio fired a cannon to alert the *Capitana* and the other ships, following which the entire flota came about and returned to Havana, entering the following morning. Wharf crews hastily off-loaded much of the *Concepción's* cargo until she floated high enough to expose the leak on the stern above the turn of the bilge—the caulking was gone from one of the planks. Shipyard carpenters made hasty repairs, the treasure was restowed, and on September 20 the New Spain flota once again departed Havana for Spain. The seven-day delay, however, would prove costly.

Less than twenty-four hours out of port the air suddenly became still and muggy. Heavy weather was brewing. The pilots grew anxious, for the flota had by now reached the powerful 2–3-knot Gulf Stream which was carrying it eastward toward the weather system. Late on the twenty-ninth the fleet was in the forty-mile-wide channel between Florida and the Bahamas when a hurricane suddenly struck with terrific force. For the next forty-eight hours the fleet ran before the tempest, helplessly pushed northward through mountainous seas. Aboard the *Concepción* a mortal struggle began. New leaks appeared in the hull and the water in the hold rose to five feet. Exhausted teams worked around the clock manning hand pumps which frequently jammed with dirt and globs of wet gunpowder. Other crewmen used bottles and buckets to bail the bilges. Meanwhile, frantic crews clawed their way through the darkness topside across heaving decks awash with water to throw all deck cargo overboard and jettison eight bronze cannons. The mainmast was cut, taking with it into the sea massive amounts of rigging. The *Concepción* appeared doomed.

On the morning of the third day the hurricane abated to gale force, having sunk nine vessels, run aground several others, and left the rest hopelessly scattered. With the exception of the fleet's *Capitana*, the *San Pedro y San Pablo*, which continued on toward Spain, the once-proud New Spain flota was no more. Though dismasted and leaking badly, the *Concepción* was miraculously still afloat, its four pumps managing to at least stay even with the water level in the bilges. The sun finally appeared, allowing the pilots to determine the ship's latitude, from which they concluded they were somewhere north of the Bahamas (on a latitude spread marked today by Jacksonville, Florida, and Savannah, Georgia). But how far east the ship now was, they had no way of knowing. At first, Admiral Villavicenzio elected to head for Grand Bahama Island and run the *Concepción* aground to save its vast treasure for future salvage. But no sooner had the crew erected a jury mast from a spare yardarm than the wind swung around to the bow, preventing any headway.

Yet, as badly damaged as she was, the *Concepción* was not utterly helpless, having a jury-rigged sail and a still-functioning rudder. If her bilge leaks had grown no worse she might even have attempted an Atlantic crossing. However, with less than 100 pounds of dry gunpowder on hand, she would have been defenseless in the event of an attack by pirates. Accordingly, Villavicenzio conferred with chief pilot

Bartolomé Guillen and his assistant (along with several wealthy merchants with much cargo aboard). The group elected to head east, then southeasterly toward San Juan, Puerto Rico, for repairs.

For more than three weeks the *Concepción* limped slowly along, very much at the mercy of the winds and currents. Water and food were in scarce supply; disease began to take its toll among weaker passengers. Hardly a day passed that the priests did not administer last rites to some poor soul whose body was destined for the sharks that more or less regularly appeared alongside. To make matters worse, the ship was becalmed for a week, its water-starved passengers unable to do anything more than huddle under makeshift awnings and pray for rain and wind. With no land in sight and no way of estimating the ship's longitude, the resulting uncertainty fueled a growing dispute.

The pilot, Bartolomé Guillen, and his assistant, Mathias Destevan Arte, believing the ship was far enough to the east to be roughly north of Puerto Rico, were prepared to turn south for San Juan. The admiral, backed by his first mate, Granillo, and other experienced hands, argued that there was no way the ship could be so far to the east. Rather, they were very likely 300 miles west of Puerto Rico in a region north of Hispaniola. If the ship were to turn south it would run a high risk of hitting a deadly forty-mile-long reef bank which Spanish navigators had wisely named the *Abrojos* ("Watch your eyes!"). When the *Concepción's* owner, Delgado, and the chief boatswain's mate added that even the pilots' latitude was in error, the pilots suggested the pair had been drinking too much. Such high-handedness was possible, for, in accordance with the House of Trade regulations, decisions of the pilots overruled those of the admiral. Villavicenzio and his advisors were furious but in fact neither party to the dispute had any clear idea where they were.

When the pilots remained adamant, Villavicenzio ordered a silver bowl produced on the poop deck and before the assembled passengers ceremoniously washed his hands of the responsibility. He then ordered a course change to the south. It was October 23. For the next few days the *Concepción* maintained her southerly heading under indifferent winds.

Death on the Reef

At 8:30 P.M. on the warm clear night of Wednesday, October 30, almost a month to the day following a hurricane ambush, the galleon struck a coral-reef head and lurched sickeningly to one side, then scraped past it and continued some yards before running up on two others, its rudder unseated from its gudgeon and jammed hard to port. Though the noise of the collision was tremendous, there were no holes in the hull and the damage appeared light. Torches were quickly lighted as fearful eyes peered over the side at the ghastly forest of coral below. The reef was not a continuous bank but rather a random series of columns that grew up from the sandy floor fifty feet below to within inches of the water's surface. For the rest of the night the ship rode on a single anchor while ocean swells ground her hull against the heads. The murmur of prayers and the click of rosary beads were drowned in the horrible echo of a hull rasping against rock.

At first light the following morning, a crew manned the ship's *launcha, or* "longboat," and searched the bottom between the surrounding coral heads for a way out. For the rest of the morning all hands strained to warp the ship out into deeper water. To this end grapnels, cannons, and pieces of artillery were tied to cables and rowed out in the longboat and dumped overboard, following which deck crews would winch the *Concepción* slowly forward and then repeat the process. By mid-afternoon, after backbreaking efforts against an opposing tidal current, the ship was clear of all the heads but one. As the captain of the Infantry aboard (Don Diego de Aldana) later testified:

> . . . the ship was outside in nine brazas [one braza equals roughly six feet] and with twelve and fourteen brazas toward the northeast and north-northeast and in this state endeavoring to leave at about four P.M. With freedom close at hand from this great peril the wind sprang up with squalls of such force that the ship was unable to maintain its position and it had to return back onto its anchors and to remain there without touching any of the coral heads. And with this the storm raged through the night.

With all but two of her anchors lost, the galleon crew fashioned others by lashing together two bronze cannons and throwing them overboard tied to anchor cable attached to the stern. From these small threads hung the life of the *Concepción*.

At 2 A.M. on the second night it happened: the stern anchor cable parted with a hideous crack. As the *Concepción* slowly began drifting back into the reef heads, another makeshift bronze-cannon anchor was hastily tossed over the side. If it snagged on anything at all, there was hope the ship could be saved. Long prayerful seconds passed, then minutes, and still the anchor dragged. Too late—the anchor cable snapped and the *Concepción* struck first one head, then another, lurching drunkenly in slow motion farther into the reef heads. With each gaping hole gouged in her hull tons of ballast rocks spilled out, scattering on and around the coral heads, as though they were the lifeblood of some fantastic creature reeling in a gruesome death agony across this lethal seascape.

At dawn, with the weather growing increasingly ugly, the *Concepción* had come to rest deep in the reef complex, surrounded by three coral heads forming a rough triangle that seemed almost impossible to have entered. The stern section appeared to be jammed between two sunken heads. Admiral Villavicenzio later deposed:

> The stern was in five and a half fathoms, the gangway in six and a half, and the bow in seven or eight fathoms. I saw that any further efforts would be useless, other than to save the silver, artillery and the people. . . . I sought to place what silver I could up on the decks but this appeared to all as a dangerous inconvenience for the risk of the enemy and that it would be more secure left in the bottom of the hold which with its weight along with the ballast would help keep it there, although the galleon was badly holed and broken up.

For the rest of that day and into the next all hands worked to fashion life rafts from the ship's decking, spars, and passageways. In the scramble for wood, no thought was given to treasure. Gaspar Maldonaldo, a merchant's son, later stated that:

> . . . the silver which lay between decks [from the helmport to the artillery deck] was salvaged. This consisted of boxes, many bars, lenguados [silver finger bars], money bags, pouches, worked silver and many discs of gold. All were thrown into the corridors of the rocks and from the mountain made by the silver, afterward we were able to go down onto the rocks and walk around on it.

In the midst of this momentous struggle, the pilots Guillen and Destevan Arte still insisted that the ship had grounded on the shallows fifteen miles east of Anagada, a small island several miles east of Puerto Rico. The admiral and others were equally convinced they were lost on the *Abrojos* north of Hispaniola and that safety lay to the south, not west. The rankling continued on into the third night at which point a full-scale tropical storm struck.

It was a terrible night of confusion, desperate fighting, and dying that was triggered when the bow of the *Concepción* suddenly settled deeper, causing flooding of all the spaces below. Panic reigned as passengers and crew scrambled over the side to reach the presumed safety of the rafts. When Admiral Villavicenzio rushed from his quarters, sword in hand, he faced a complete breakdown of authority and could only watch helplessly as passengers threw themselves over the side clambering over each other like drowning rats. Because few, if any, passengers or crew, for that matter, knew how to swim, many drowned.

Accounts differ but first mate Francisco Granillo later deposed that at first the admiral had elected to stay with his ship, whereupon he, Granillo, believing his superior's life was in extreme danger, summarily grabbed him by the breeches and threw him off the poop deck into the sea. Villavicenzio, unable even to tread water, was about to go under for the last time when he was grabbed by a young passenger and moments later pulled unconscious aboard the longboat, which was tethered to several makeshift rafts. The craft was soon boarded by Granillo, the captain of the infantry, several ship's officers, and a score of others. With the *chalupa* now dangerously full, its occupants turned to fight with knives and swords those people who tried to climb aboard, killing many. Reports later delivered to the *Casa* stated that "Among the victims were several religious personages and people of much account." Added to the roar of the storm and the lashing of the waves were the shouts of fighting and the screams of the dying. At length the longboat and its thirty-three occupants managed to push away from the rafts at which point the wind and tidal current carried them into deep water. There was little to do but hoist the sail and hope for fair winds.

A few days later Villavicenzio's judgment was vindicated when the longboat touched the shores of Hispaniola seventy miles to the south. He and his exhausted band still faced several more days before finding fresh water, and they would endure a grueling march across the island to Santo Domingo; yet they would survive the ordeal. But for those who remained behind clinging to the hull of the *Concepción*, some 450 in all, fate would deal an uneven hand.

Eight, and possibly ten, rafts were constructed. The pilots, who thought they were near Puerto Rico, misdirected one raft with eighty survivors—it sailed westward and was never seen again. At least two other rafts departed under jury-rigged sails and disappeared forever. Yet another craft was so overloaded with passengers that waist-high water continuously swept over its decking, making the occupants easy pickings for huge sharks that simply swam up to them and pulled them off one by one. Of the sixty-four on board, twenty-eight were either taken by sharks or, driven to madness by thirst and fear, threw themselves overboard to their deaths.

Seven days after the grounding, two substantially made rafts carrying a total of 120 survivors left the raft. On board were the two pilots whose judgment had occasioned the disaster. Now, for unexplained reasons, they elected to head south, not west. Days later, near the port of Puerto Plata, the rafts were intercepted by an English corsair. The pirates howled with laughter when the pilots claimed they were off Puerto Rico. Whereupon the raft's occupants were taken aboard, robbed of everything, then deposited ashore.

For everyone who eventually made it to Hispaniola, survival was still problematic. Gaspar Maldonaldo, the merchant's son, later testified: "For thirty-three days we lived on wild and very sour lemons and at times palmettoes. The land was very mountainous. Nine men died of hunger. We met a Negro who took us to where there were some people that carried us to Santiago which is forty leagues from Santo Domingo." Fearing their lives would be in jeopardy when the *Casa's* officers in Santo Domingo learned of their errors, pilots Guillen and Destevan Arte took refuge in a monastery.

For the estimated 150 survivors who had stayed behind with the *Concepción* (there being no more wood for rafts), the only sustenance was the promises of their departed shipmates that rescue boats would be sent with all speed. As the days passed and no sails appeared on the horizon they began to die of starvation, thirst, and exposure. Each day more bodies sank into the depths between the coral heads.

Weeks later along the Hispaniola coast a lone Mexican Indian slave, half starved and dehydrated, was found clinging to a long plank just off Puerto Plata. His name was Andres de la Cruz. He told rescuers that many days previously he and two other crewmen from the *Concepción* had taken the plank and floated away from the wrecksite, hoping currents would carry them to safety. During their incredible journey southward, one man disappeared in the night. The other, de la Cruz claimed, was insane with thirst and swam away to fetch a small keg that floated nearby, hoping it contained water. Halfway to his objective he screamed as a shark suddenly jerked him like a rag doll beneath blood-red water.

Andres de la Cruz, the last survivor from the wreck of *La Nuestra Señora de la Concepción*, had prayed for deliverance. And to him it was granted.

Aftermath—the Birth of a Legend

In dealing Spain perhaps her greatest maritime loss of the seventeenth century, fate saved the last card for the *Concepción's* sister ship, the *Capitana,* the *San Pedro y San Pablo.* After surviving the hurricane and crossing the Atlantic, the great galleon ran aground and wrecked on the great sandbars of Sanlucar at the mouth of the Guadalquivir River en route to Seville. The ship broke up badly but divers were able to salvage most of the Crown's treasure. Notwithstanding the recovery, Captain-General de Campos, whose passion for glory had cost so many lives, had a great deal of explaining to do.

Of the *Concepción's* approximately 500 passengers and crew, only 190 survived the ordeal. They brought back with them tales of a mountain of silver bars and coins that had been hastily stacked atop a giant reef head to await recovery later, of chests of treasure thrown into the water at the base of a head near the wreck—all this within a day's sail from the north shore of Hispaniola. As rumors spread throughout the New World, officials in Santo Domingo held hearings. A small parade of witnesses testified. Predictably, most were self-serving, notably Admiral Villavicenzio who assured his listeners that from the very outset he had warned his pilots to stay well clear of the *Abrojos.* (Both pilots, incidentally, managed to escape trial or conviction, either by fleeing the island or melting into the population. The latter course would have been easy enough, for the King's authority was held in contempt by the island's rural citizenry.)

Elsewhere, the *Concepción's* silvermaster, Pedro de Media Malo, solemnly stated with a straight face that the *Concepción* had carried only 500,000 pesos of His Majesty's silver and 550,000 pesos belonging to authorized private parties. He had good reason to stick to a lily-white accounting for he fully expected the *Concepción* to be found and salvaged. Moreover, he had no way of knowing that of the two copies remaining of the *Concepción's* manifest, one would be lost with the wrecking of the *Capitana* on the Sanlucar sandbars while the other copy would end up on a small dispatch vessel that was destined to be seized by pirates off the Barbary Coast.

Disputing the silvermaster's report, chief boatswain's mate Franciso Granillo, who bore no responsibility in the matter, claimed, "There is much of His Majesty's and much more belonging to private persons that came out of registry [unregistered] because there was not sufficient time to obtain permission and the owners desired more to risk it than register it. The amount which is known to be aboard not counting that of His Majesty is more than four million."

All witnesses did agree, however, that His Majesty's silver remained locked in the storerooms belowdecks under water while some silver stowed in the belowdecks corridors had been thrown overboard in the process of dismantling woodwork to make rafts.

Wreck Site of
Nuestra Señora de la Concepción 1641

SCALE - ¼" = 10'

1.- ADMIRAL'S CABIN
2.- CAPTAIN'S CABIN
3.- CARGO
4.- POWDER MAGAZINE
5.- SHIP'S STORES ✦
BALLAST STORES ✦
6.- SHOT STORAGE
7.- CARGO - INDIGO,
SILVER BARS ✦
BALLAST STONES ✦
✦ TREASURE STORED
HERE

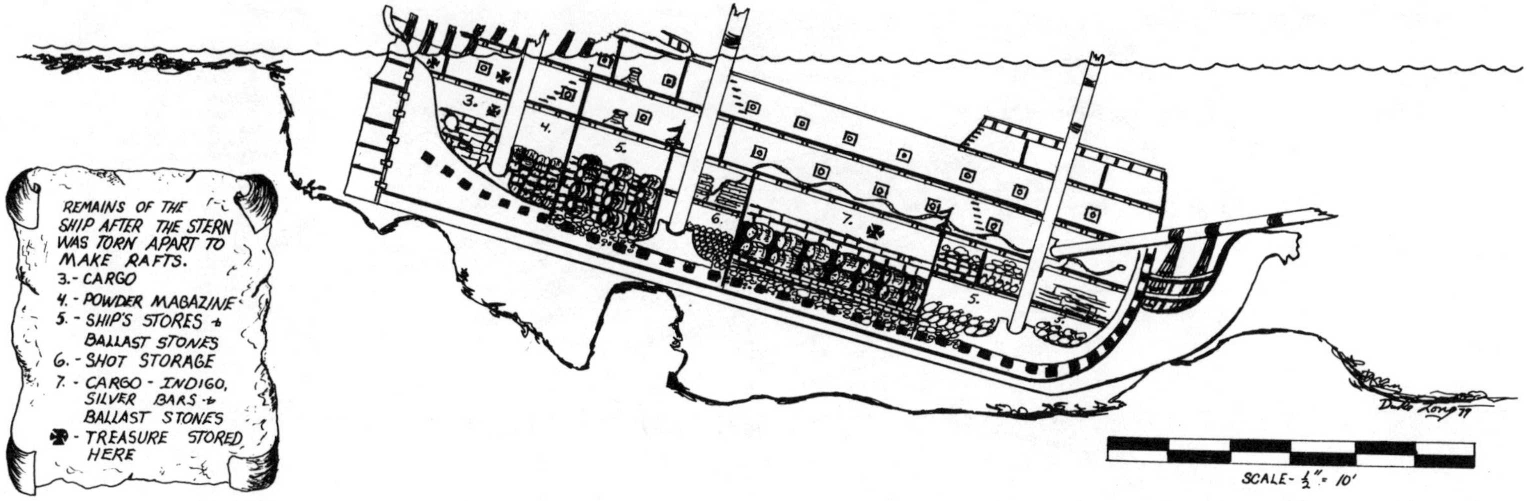
REMAINS OF THE SHIP AFTER THE STERN WAS TORN APART TO MAKE RAFTS.
3. - CARGO
4. - POWDER MAGAZINE
5. - SHIP'S STORES & BALLAST STONES
6. - SHOT STORAGE
7. - CARGO - INDIGO, SILVER BARS & BALLAST STONES
- TREASURE STORED HERE
3.
4.
5.
6.
7.
5.
SCALE - 1/2" = 10'
Duke Long 79

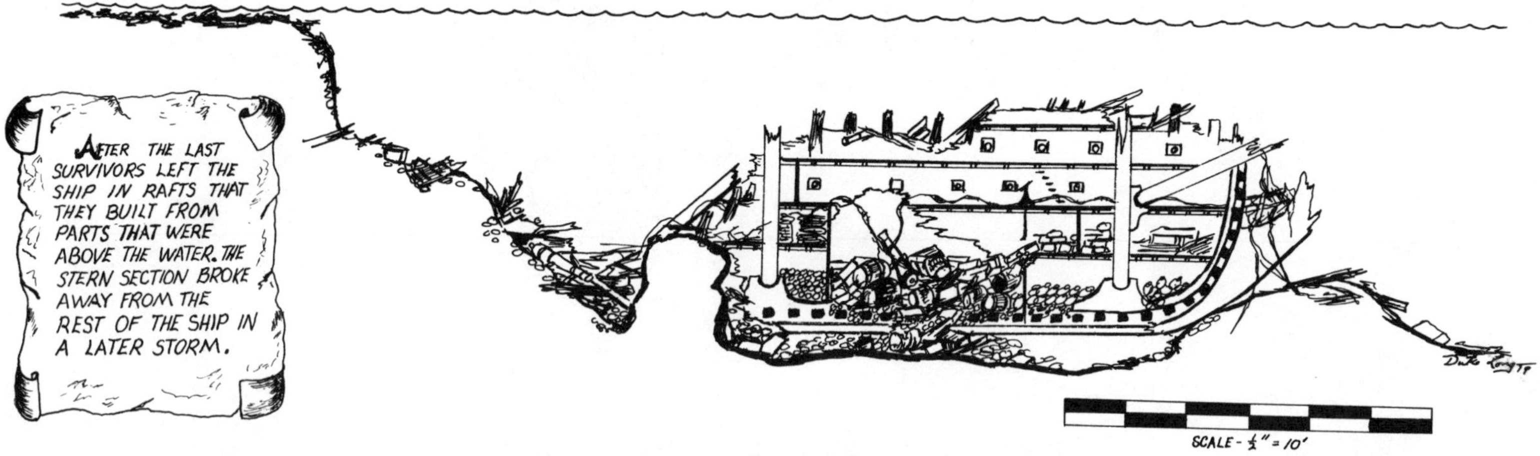
AFTER THE LAST SURVIVORS LEFT THE SHIP IN RAFTS THAT THEY BUILT FROM PARTS THAT WERE ABOVE THE WATER. THE STERN SECTION BROKE AWAY FROM THE REST OF THE SHIP IN A LATER STORM.
SCALE - 1/2" = 10'

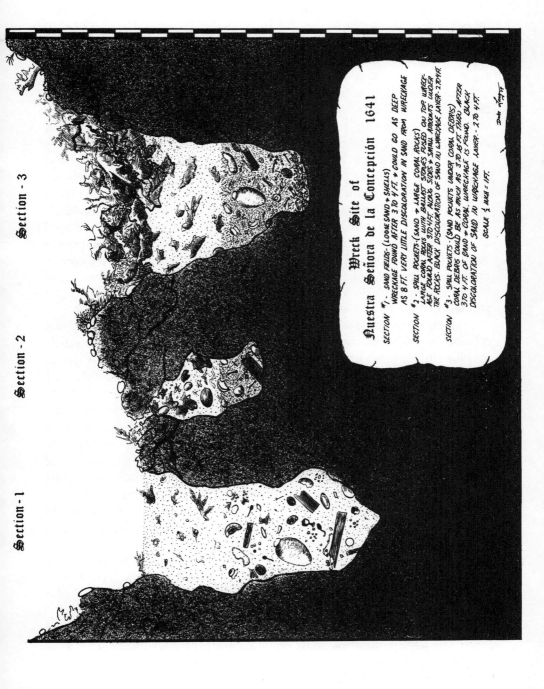

Wreck Site of
Nuestra Señora de la Concepción 1641

SECTION #1 - SAND FIELDS - (LOOSE SAND + SHELLS)
WRECKAGE FOUND AFTER 3 TO 4 FT. + COULD GO AS DEEP
AS 8 FT. VERY LITTLE DISCOLORATION IN SAND FROM WRECKAGE

SECTION #2 - SPILL POCKETS - (SAND + LARGE CORAL ROCKS)
LARGE CORAL ROCKS WITH BALLAST STONES FUSED ON TOP. WRECK-
AGE FOUND AFTER 3 TO 4 FT. ALONG SIDES + SMALL AMOUNTS UNDER
THE ROCKS. BLACK DISCOLORATION OF SAND IN WRECKAGE LAYER - 2 TO 4 FT.

SECTION #3 - SPILL POCKETS - (SAND POCKETS UNDER CORAL DEBRIS)
CORAL DEBRIS COULD BE AS MUCH AS 3 TO 6 FT. THEN AFTER
3 TO 4 FT. OF SAND + CORAL, WRECKAGE IS FOUND. BLACK
DISCOLORATION OF SAND IN WRECKAGE LAYER - 2 TO 4 FT.

SCALE ½ INCH = 1 FT.

Precisely how much treasure was on board the *Concepción* is a question that probably never will be settled. Historian Peter Earle, in his book *The Wreck of the Almiranta,* observes that the silvermaster's report of 550,000 belonging to private parties is a ridiculously low figure since such cargo was normally several times the size of the Crown's treasure. Another authority, Robert Marx, who during the sixties researched the *Concepción* in the Seville archives, maintains he found a summary of the ship's manifest indicating an additional two million pesos in silver was taken aboard just prior to her departure. If that is correct, the total cargo would have approached six million pesos. Subsequent efforts by other scholars to locate the document, however, have been unsuccessful. Marx (who still retains his notes copied from the summary) believes it was either misfiled or purloined—more likely the latter. Conceivably, the summary document may have referred to the combined treasure aboard both the *capitana* and the *Almiranta* but then, given the stories of money chests stacked high in the *Concepción's* passageways, she may well have carried it all. In the absence of hard evidence, Earle suggests the cargo of the *Concepción* was most probably close to four million pesos, an amount weighing 140 tons.

At the conclusion of the hearings Admiral Villavicenzio was officially exonerated and he immediately turned to the task of mounting an effort to return to the *Abrojos* and salvage the treasure. One would think the full resources of the Hispaniola government would be made available to this end, but in fact Villavicenzio encountered every imaginable obstacle. Though the governor was officially committed to a salvage attempt, there was little money to spare in the colonial treasury to underwrite such an effort. There were weeks, then months, of delays. The admiral, after building several small vessels capable of doing salvage work, sailed to Puerto Plata on the north shore, only to be plagued by English corsairs, bad weather, a grumbling crew, and bureaucratic indifference. Even his esteemed first mate Granillo eventually sneaked aboard a galleon bound for Havana. Villavicenzio, despite his mariner's skill, loyalty to his King, and determination, never did return to the scene of disaster. History does not say whether or not he returned to fleet duty as captain of an escort galleon but he had earned the distinction of being the first of a long line of seekers who would fail to find the legendary lady.

With so great a treasure lying on a reef, the *Concepción* was not forgotten as the months and years passed. In the 1650's and '60's numerous private parties petitioned the King to mount search and salvage expeditions to the *Abrojos*. The Crown was content to let others shoulder the expense and the risk, and indeed, quite a few well-equipped vessels from Spain did reach the reef. But they arrived to find no trace of the galleon, either stacked bars on reefs or any portion of the vessel's stern, only a long line of breakers cresting white over a submerged bank of coral heads that seemed to rise from nowhere.

Each failure seemed to add to the galleon's notoriety. The New World buzzed with stories of the fabulous wealth that lay in shallow water waiting discovery by a bold and lucky adventurer. The silver scattered on and around the *Concepción*'s coral grave began to dull with an oxide patina, but her gold would never lose its pristine gleam—or its power to inflame the imaginations of those who would dream of unlocking the mystery and priceless trove of one of the greatest and most celebrated of Spain's golden galleons.

2

The Sensational Discovery of William Phips

Salvage in the Spanish Lake

From the very earliest days of Spain's conquest of the New World the salvaging of cargo from ships that had grounded, wrecked, or sunk was an official priority second only to the business of transporting the plunder across the Atlantic. But as Admiral Villavicenzio's failed attempt to salvage the *Concepción* illustrates, red tape and politics frequently prevented salvage vessels from promptly reaching the site of a wrecked treasure galleon. Speed was essential, not only because of competition from pirates and privateers but also because even moderately bad weather and/or currents could break up an already damaged vessel, adding greatly to the difficulty of salvaging her or, worse still, cause her to vanish without a trace. An instance of the latter eventuality occurred in 1622 when the treasure galleon *Nuestra Señora de Atocha* wrecked in a storm near the tip of the Florida Keys. Spanish salvage boats were on the scene within nine days, only to search in vain for the ship's mizzenmast which survivors had reported still above the water-line.

Salvage efforts, even those launched from major Spanish ports, depended on what vessels were available and how much money could be raised, the latter being determined by how much treasure could be recovered. Usually, these operations were undertaken by private salvors who contracted with the Crown for a share of the treasure recovered. Accountants from the House of Trade were assigned to these ships during all salvage operations and kept meticulous records. The technology of the day was primitive—usually involving the use of chain grapnels, rakes, and various hoists—but the Spanish were fortunate to have the use of native pearl divers who had originated on the island of Margarita just off the Venezuelan coast. When first discovered they had amazed their Spanish captors with their ability to free dive to the oyster beds up to depths of 100 feet or more (holding onto rocks to carry them to the bottom) and remaining underwater for as long as four and five minutes. So wonderful were their abilities that the Spanish promptly conscripted the natives for salvage work, a task to which they adapted quickly. Not so wonderful was the smallpox that followed the Spanish to Margarita, virtually wiping out that island's tribe, following which West Indian, and later African, slaves proved equally adaptable as free divers.

Among the first to also see the usefulness of native divers were English and Dutch privateers, French adventurers, and other free-lance pirate/salvors who in the early seventeenth century began to poach on "the Spanish Lake." Fair amounts of treasure were brought up from galleon wrecks in the Bahamas, around Bermuda, and in the West Indies, much of it in the form of silver pieces of eight. Spain's monopoly weakened further still when the French took over the Lesser Antilles islands of Guadeloupe, Martinique, and Dominica. Elsewhere, in 1655, those notorious claim jumpers, the English, captured Jamaica after which its Port Royal became a mecca for Caribbean pirates such as the ruthless and thoroughly debauched Henry Morgan.

From the point of view of English kings treasure hunting was an entirely realistic source of revenue, and, accordingly, Crown assistance in the form of equipment, expertise and/or letters of authority was not infrequently provided private parties in return for a percentage of the treasure recovered. More often than not such ventures were failures or at best yielded very modest returns, but on rare occasions the trove was substantial. In the seventeenth century there was no more spectacular example of this than the sensational recovery of treasure from a sunken Spanish galleon by a daring young American from the Massachusetts Colony named William Phips. In 1687 Phips found and partially salvaged a galleon he believed was named *The Golden Lion*. Not until some time after this remarkable feat did the vessel's true identity become known—*La Nuestra Señora de la Concepción*. Nor would Phips ever know how major a role the story of his search would play in a drama involving the same ship nearly three centuries later.

It is odd that the history of prerevolutionary America does not accord William Phips a larger role. Granted, he was not a great statesman, thinker, or shaper of a nation's destiny, but he may well have been America's first rags-to-riches success, its first Horatio Alger, a model of the self-made man that became a cherished ideal of a fledgling democracy. He was certainly among its most colorful characters—clever, ambitious, vain, tough, swashbuckling, courageous, and in every way an intensely interesting New England sea captain from the Puritan era. As his biographer Cotton Mather also noted, Phips was extraordinarily lucky.

The Rise of an Upstart Dreamer

Of Phips' early life little is known other than that he was the twenty-first of twenty-six children fathered by James Phips, a master blacksmith and gunsmith who, together with his wife, Mary, had left Wales in the 1620's to journey to New England to start a new life. How many of their prodigious number of offspring also made the voyage is uncertain. The family settled in a rugged part of Maine, in the village of Pemaquid at the mouth of the Kennebec River, a place where years later Boston shipbuilders would come to buy the best timber for their ships. William was born in 1651 and grew up in a world of shipwrights and fishermen, his spirits unfettered by the dour Puritan atmosphere of the Massachusetts Bay Colony. Though poor and unschooled, he had a quick and imaginative mind and a knack for learning fast that in his teens earned him an apprenticeship as a ship's carpenter.

By his early twenties Phips had moved to Boston to pursue his craft in shipbuilding and repair, during which time he taught himself how to read, write, design hull configurations, and do much of his own mathematical calculations. By the time the young carpenter had built by himself his own cutter, the *Star of Boston,* he was well known in the Boston shipbuilding world. A handsome man with a rough-hewn charm and a way with words (both couth and profane), Phips had also won the hand of Mary Spencer Hull, the daughter of a ship's captain and, unusual for the times, four years Phips' senior. Cynics suggested the modest dowry that Mary Hull brought to the marriage had motivated Phips' proposal; however, by all accounts the couple were devoted to each other. Soon thereafter Phips, who had set his sights on captaining his own trading vessel, purchased a decrepit schooner, completely overhauled it, and went into business carrying lumber and trade goods along the New England coast.

Though practical and industrious, Phips was no less a bold dreamer. When carousing the waterfront pubs of Boston (which was regularly) he was forever listening to the stories of shipwrecked galleons told by sailors returned from the Caribbean and the South Atlantic. The lure of sunken treasure became a preoccupation which Phips eventually incorporated into his vocation. He was in his early thirties when he first skippered a ship south to the warm waters of the Bahamas to trade and search for a galleon wreck near New Providence Island. He was modestly successful on both counts for he managed, with the help of Bahamian divers, to locate and "fish" an old wreck that produced a small trove of silver. With the money from this treasure and from the sale of the *Star of Boston*, he paid his way to England where he set about promoting a more ambitious scheme.

Armed with audacity, salesmanship, and a good treasure story, Phips finagled his way into Whitehall for an audience with no less a personage than King Charles II. That amiable sovereign, who was considered rather more French than English, had a penchant for expensive amusements that involved a dash of adventure, and without overdue consideration, agreed to lend Phips an eighteen-gun frigate, the *Rose of Algier*, for a trip to the Bahamas to search for another Spanish treasure galleon. Apart from the romance of the thing, His Majesty was perennially short of money to maintain his life-style. A deal was struck providing the Crown with one fourth of any treasure recovered and, in early September 1683, Phips set sail from England. Aboard ship was an agent of the Crown, John Knepp, assigned to prevent embezzlement and report on Phips' conduct. Knepp's zeal for his duties nearly cost him his life, for the crew of the *Rose* was, in the words of historian Cyrus Karracker, "one of the foulest and most treacherous lot of blackguards that was ever assembled on a ship." Phips had signed on his crew, agreeing to share with them any treasure found if they would pay their own way. While the bargain seemed just, it made shipboard discipline all but impossible.

The *Rose* was barely a week at sea when it was discovered that the ship had only half the provisions required for a crossing. Phips headed for Ireland, landed at Limerick, and immediately ran afoul of customs agents who protested some of his crew was ashore selling hats. Evidently such items had been taken aboard to be sold on arrival in Boston. Next a local farmer reported men from the *Rose* had poached several sheep and taken them aboard. These complaints were less than diplomatically answered (the second mate had threatened to throw the protesting parties overboard) and Phips barely managed to get under way before the town assaulted his ship with torches and pitchforks. During the remainder of the Atlantic crossing a shocked John Knepp found Captain Phips indifferent to his charges of repeated thefts of brandy and cheese (Knepp's) and of wild, all-night drinking sessions.

Following the *Rose*'s arrival in Boston in late October, Knepp stayed up late nights writing purple-prose reports to the Commissioners of the Navy relating even darker shenanigans. For starters, the crew of the *Rose* showed a contemptuous disregard for specific directives forbidding the *Rose* to demand that passing ships strike their colors (as was done for British man-of-war ships). The crew forced this courtesy by firing shots across the bows of impolite vessels, then charging their owners the cost of the shot. The practice reached absurd heights when the *Rose*'s chief mate fired a gun at a tiny fourteen-foot dinghy, then demanded six shillings and eight pence for the shot. When hauled into court for the practice, Phips blustered that he had acted with full Crown authority but repeatedly failed to produce the orders, maintaining they had somehow been locked in his wife's trunk. To this the governor replied sarcastically, reminding Phips that Boston was quite aware of his lowly origins and there was hardly any need for him to conduct himself so loftily. Thereupon Phips threw a noisy tantrum without effect after which the governor regretted that the interests of the Crown required him to grant Phips and his insolent crew their freedom.

When the *Rose* finally left for the Bahamas in January 1684, John Knepp remained sequestered ashore, having learned that the crew despised his spying and tattle-tale ways and had planned to abandon him on a deserted island. For its part, Puritan Boston also breathed more easily, for Phips and crew had been involved in several drunken pub fights and had been charged with inciting at least one full-blown street riot. Undaunted and a day out of Boston, the *Rose* anchored off Pemberton Island where its crew foraged about stealing pigs and sheep, destroying property, and ravishing a farmer's wife.

Phips arrived on the Bahama Banks in mid-March, took several native divers on board and proceeded to the site of the galleon wreck. He apparently knew the wreck had been fished by other smaller salvors but believed enough remained "to make the voyage" or come out with a profit. But then trouble arose. While on the wrecksite, his divers came down with smallpox, causing a week's delay. When they recovered enough to resume salvage, comparatively little silver was brought up. Other wrecksites were fished with little success. Phips' crew grew restless, then angry, then mutinous. One evening they confronted their captain and demanded that he turn pirate with them. He replied by wading into the mob, knocking men down, and cracking heads in a blood-and-thunder rage. Confused and off guard, the crewmen backed away in submission and Phips, having singlehandedly quelled the mutiny, stomped aft to his quarters.

In the aftermath, frustrations ran high and it was only a matter of time before a now surly crew planned a better-orchestrated attempt to seize the ship. Opportunity came some weeks later when the *Rose* was anchored near the beach of a remote island in the Spanish Isles. While the ship's hull was being scraped and repaired, a tent had been set up ashore and the ship's guns arrayed around it as a precaution against a possible Spanish attack. One afternoon all but a few of the crew who were loyal to Phips sneaked off into the woods to plot a takeover, in the process putting under guard the ship's carpenter whom they suspected of potentially betraying them. On hearing enough of the plan, the carpenter chimed in with his full support, then feigned terrible stomach cramps. The ploy gained him momentary freedom to rush to the *Rose* for a dram of medicine, during which time he hastily told Phips of the plot. Phips ordered the carpenter to return to the mutineers and say nothing, then gathered eight or ten loyal followers and quickly brought aboard the ship's cannons which, oddly, had been left unguarded.

When a short time later the mutineers stormed en masse out of the woods for the attack they were astounded to find themselves looking down the muzzles of the ship's guns, each loaded with enough deadly grapeshot to cut the assemblage to pieces. "We've been betrayed!" they cried, to which a furious Phips yelled back, "Stand off, ye wretches, at your peril!" and ordered the guns readied for firing. At this juncture "ye wretches" fell to their knees and cried out for mercy, exclaiming they never had anything against Phips personally, save his refusal to turn pirate, and begged his forgiveness for having ever had the cheek to request it. After enduring as much of this pathetic drivel as he could stomach, Phips eventually relented and allowed the mutineers to return on board after confiscating their guns and knives. He promptly weighed anchor and sailed directly for Jamaica instructing his trusted lieutenants to maintain an armed guard and watchful eye on the dissidents. On arrival in Jamaica, Phips turned the whole batch of cutthroats off for another crew, thus bringing to an end one of the most unsavory, albeit colorful, associations of his career.

Though his salvage efforts in the Bahamas had been disappointing, Phips was in no way discouraged by the realities of treasure hunting. Several days out of Jamaica on his way back to England with a new crew, he stopped briefly in Puerto Plata. There it is believed he was introduced to an ancient Spaniard who told him the story of a great galleon that had wrecked not far north of Puerto Plata. Some accounts claim the old Spaniard was a survivor but, were this so, he would certainly have told Phips the *Concepción*'s name. However, he did reveal enough information to convince his listener that the wreck could be located. It lay in the shallow waters of what the English called the Ambrosia Bank (a word most probably derived from a transliteration of the Spanish word *Abrojos*). But the name was apt, for if ambrosia be the food of the gods, the promise of Ambrosia Bank was food enough to fire Phips' dream of recovering vast wealth.

On leaving Puerto Plata, Phips sailed northeast for the *Abrojos* and spent several days scouting a portion of the reef, advising his crew only that he was searching for a relatively unimportant wreck which may possibly yield some small treasure. His search proved fruitless but Phips concluded an adjacent area also matched the Spaniard's description. Though excited by the possibility, he knew, too, that the *Rose* was under-equipped for the task and too lightly armed to defend herself should any hostile sails appear on the horizon. Phips elected to return to England to seek the proper backing. It was the summer of 1685 and this thirty-four-year-old adventurer was now hell-bent to promote an expedition worthy of the destiny that had already begun to smile on him.

The Search for the Hispaniola Treasure

On returning to England, Phips was surprised to learn that King Charles had died and had been succeeded by his brother James II, a thoroughly intolerant, cold-hearted, narrow-minded prude who had unleashed across the land a spate of hangings, torture, and public punishments. It is some measure of Phips' audacity that notwithstanding the new King's ominous character, the colonial upstart managed to obtain an audience during which he asked not for a frigate but a fully outfitted man-of-war. The King refused the request without specifying why, but he may not have had any ships available for nonmilitary duties. Moreover, the failure of *Rose's* expedition and the reports to the Commissioners of the Navy on Phips' spotty conduct must have been factors. And finally, James II may have been aware that his predecessor had three years previously granted a commission to a Royal Navy officer, Captain Edward Stanley, to discover and salvage precisely the same ship that Phips intended to find.

Phips had also learned about Stanley's exploration of the Ambrosia Bank before his meeting with King James, but he carefully avoided mentioning it since the search had been fruitless, a fact that would have argued strongly against Phips' own chances of success. But Captain Stanley's account of his voyages to the bank appeared to offer Phips helpful clues.

Like Phips, Edward Stanley had been fascinated with the stories of a nation's ransom in silver and gold lying stacked on a reef north of Hispaniola. During a three-year tour of the West Indies he made several forays to the reefs north of Puerto Plata, spurred on in part by the testimony of an English sailor named Thomas Smith who claimed to have actually seen the wreck. Smith said he had been aboard a New England-bound ship that by accident came close upon a reef head on which were piled mounds of silver "sows" and "pigs" (these being different shapes of bulk silver) and some gold bars, while close by lay the ship's hull wedged between two coral heads. Smith testified that while the ship's master and owner argued heatedly about how to salvage the treasure a fierce gale arose and forced the disputants to depart the reef before marking its precise location. For all his efforts, however, Stanley encountered bad weather, sickness, and a near sinking, but no wreck. His quest for the fabled Hispaniola treasure, like those before, ended in frustration and failure.

Ironically, during the summer of 1686 as Stanley was sailing home to England, William Phips was rushing around London overseeing preparations for his own assault on the Ambrosia Bank. Following King James' refusal of aid, Phips had turned to Henry Christopher Monk, the second Duke of Albemarle—a spirited, shrewd, and wealthy nobleman overly fond of sherry. After listening at length to Phips' story of the Hispaniola wreck and his plans for locating it, the Duke was much impressed and agreed to help recruit other investors with the wealth and influence to underwrite an expedition.

As a first step the Duke obtained a warrant from the Crown authorizing the right to "all flotsam, jetsam, lagan, bullion, plate, gold, silver, coin, bars or pigs of silver, ingots of gold, merchandises, and other goods shipwrecked and lost before July 16, 1689, on the north side of Hispaniola, about the Bahamas, or the Gulf of Florida"—from which the Crown would, of course, receive 10 percent. The warrant was in essence a license to "fish" anywhere in the Indies but such stalwarts as Lord Portsmouth and Lord Sunderland scoffed at the wild schemes of this young colonial Phips and suggested his benefactor may have gone a little daft to help underwrite such a venture.

Undaunted, the Duke of Albemarle formed an investor group to finance the operation and immediately bought one quarter of the share offering for about £1,000. The remaining stockholders, each of whom subscribed to a one-eighth share, included Lord Falkland, Sir James Hayes, Francis Nicholson, Navy Commissioner Sir John Narbrough, Isaac Foxcroft, and a wealthy merchant named John Smith. The backers agreed to share the profits in proportion to their investment while setting aside a sixteenth share for Phips.

Of the approximately £4,000 funding money a total of £3,212 was used for salvage tools and to purchase two ships. The first, the *Bridgewater,* weighing 200 tons and carrying twenty-two guns, was to be the primary salvage vessel. The partners in the venture renamed her the *James and Mary* in honor of England's King and Queen. The second ship, the *Henry of London,* was a fifty-ton frigate mounted with ten guns and commanded by Francis Rogers, who had been Phips' second mate on the *Rose*. In addition, £500 in merchandise was stowed aboard the *James and Mary* which could be traded with the Spanish to recoup some of the losses should the expedition fail completely.

On September 12, 1686, hardly two months after a dejected Edward Stanley had returned to England, the *James and Mary* and the *Henry of London* sailed for the West Indies. Two months later, November 10, the two ships anchored in Carlisle Bay, Barbados, where they remained ten days reprovisioning. From Barbados, Phips followed the lee side of the Windward Islands up to the Mona Passage between Puerto Rico and Hispaniola, then north to Cape Cabron on the northeastern point of Hispaniola. On this leg Phips lost sight of the *Henry* and opted to put into Samana Bay where he delayed a week to wait out bad weather and stock the ship's stores with hog meat bought from French hunters. When he weighed anchor for the Ambrosia Bank, foul weather and strong currents off the cape again interfered. Phips continued west to Puerto Plata, arrived December 14, anchored in three fathoms, and announced his arrival by a three-gun salute to the port.

As a pretended British trader visiting a Spanish port, however inconsequential an outpost it may be, Phips was careful to be punctilious on all matters of protocol. In truth, Puerto Plata was nearly a deserted settlement during the winter months and had not been the scene of much activity since Villavicenzio had used it as a staging area for his abortive salvage expedition forty-five years earlier. Nonetheless, lookouts had noted the ship's arrival and after two weeks, messengers from the governor of Santiago, some thirty miles inland, arrived with instructions to find out Phips' intentions. The American made a great fuss over the delegation, sending them back with a roll of serge and a case of brandy, and assuring them he was only a friendly Englishman who had come for wood and water. The phrase "wood and water" was a diplomatic way of offering to trade, a practice Spanish possessions were strictly forbidden to do with foreigners. Phips anticipated the Spanish would ignore the dictum if transactions were done with discretion and such activity would provide a good cover while he waited for the end of the stormy season.

The ploy worked and before another week had passed canoes and scows began rowing to the ship loaded with dried hides, mahogany wood, casks of smoked pork, and hogsheads of brown sugar. They returned with cutlery, leather harnesses, medicines, shoes, yardage cloth, and, under cover of darkness, some small arms and ammunition.

On December 19, Phips breathed a sigh of relief as the long lost Francis Rogers sailed in with the *Henry*. For the rest of the month strong northerly winds bore down on Puerto Plata interrupted by short spells of fair weather. During one such lull Phips dispatched the *Henry* for the Turks Islands ninety-five miles north in search of badly needed salt but the ship returned eight days later empty-handed. For the next week the two ships remained anchored in the calm blue waters of the bay in the shadow of 3,000-foot Mount Isabella while Phips, so close to his life's dream, continued to trade at a leisurely pace.

Finally, on January 13 of the new year, Phips quietly dispatched the *Henry* with Rogers, second mate William Covell, and three divers, directing them to proceed to the Ambrosia Bank and, armed with secret directions, to search for the wreck if they "could get a slatch of faire weather." Rogers steered easterly toward Cape Cabron, then on January 17 turned north. The following morning he arrived at the easternmost end of the Ambrosia Bank and began a systematic search of the coral heads in ten fathoms of water.

During the *Henry*'s absence Phips, with what must have been consummate self-control, continued his trifling trade, giving himself away only once when he hurriedly got under way one morning to chase what he mistakenly thought was the sail of the *Henry*. Then, on February 7, the *Henry* appeared outside the entrance to Puerto Plata but was prevented by heavy seas from entering until the next morning. Phips was forced to endure an agonizing wait of nearly twenty hours while the *Henry*, anchored less than a mile away, held the knowledge of triumph or failure. When Rogers and his men at last rowed the *Henry's* dinghy alongside the *James and Mary* those on deck could tell by their crestfallen faces that the news was not good.

A somber William Phips quickly escorted them to his cabin, and, sitting at his table, listened to their account. They had encountered only three good days of weather while on the Ambrosia Bank, Rogers reported, and had searched every reef head as carefully as humanly possible. Then one evening a fierce wind came up and they were forced to stand amidst several coral heads, very much fearing for their safety. Rogers continued in this vein while second mate Covell and the divers sitting across from Phips looked on dejectedly.

When the captain of the *Henry* had finished his bleak narrative an anguished Phips threw up his arms and announced that he would prepare the *James and Mary* to weigh anchor the following morning for Jamaica. At that instant his foot struck something hard on the deck under the table. He cried out in some pain looking down at a heavy object that had evidently been slipped under the table while he was talking.

"What in God's name . . . ? What is this!" The object was brought onto the table and Phips gaped in astonishment as he stared at a brick-size sow of pure silver. "Whence comes this?" He looked up at Rogers and his associates, their faces suddenly beaming with joy.

"We found her, Captain!" Rogers cried out. "We found the wreck!"

Relieved at last of the strain of wearing tragic masks, the *Henry's* rejoicing pranksters quickly told their commander how and where they had found the treasure.

"Praise God!" an exultant Phips cried. "We are made!"

The Harvesting of Half Moon Reef

How was it that Phips—or more correctly Francis Rogers and his crew—had been able to find the wreck of the *Concepción* where Captain Edward Stanley and so many others with great courage and persistence had failed? In retrospect it would seem Phips had the advantage of refined information and luck. Though he never explained in detail how he narrowed down the search area, Phips must have known (through mutual friends of Stanley) that the wreck was to be found somewhere on the north reef of the Ambrosia Bank, very likely in the same sector that Stanley had partially searched before bad weather and a near collision had aborted his final probe. It was here that Phips directed Rogers.

This smaller search area still encompassed a formidable number of reef heads. In its entirety the Ambrosia Bank consisted of a forty-two-mile-long shoal aligned along a northwest-southeast axis. English sailors recognized two main reefs ("riffs" in contemporary spelling) lying roughly eighteen miles apart. The "south riff" was about six miles long and a mile wide while the "north riff" was roughly twenty-two miles long and likewise a mile across. The coral heads comprising the reefs grew up in tall columns from depths of ten fathoms or less and varied in diameter anywhere from four to six feet to the size and shape of a golf-course putting green. At low tide the tallest heads barely crested the surface while most others came to within three to ten feet beneath. Because the waves hitting the heads caused the water to foam and hiss as though boiling, the English dubbed the deadly formations "boylers." Thousands of them were to be found on the north reef alone.

To bring the *Henry* close to the reef past the jagged sentinels along its periphery, Rogers had stationed a lookout at the top of the mast to report approaching heads. When lack of wind made the ship's rudder useless, the launch was deployed to tow the ship. Even with these precautions the *Henry* grazed a few heads before coming to anchor at the south end of the north reef. On the first day of searching, Rogers sent the *Henry*'s boat and canoe to reconnoiter a six-mile stretch along the north side of the reef, "not for much as passing one boyler without a diligent inspection," Rogers later reported.

Finding nothing, the *Henry* weighed anchor early the next morning and moved along the south side of the reef about six miles until opposite the end point of the previous day's search on the other side, coming to anchor about noon. Again the boat and canoe were sent to scout the heads. Shortly after 1 P.M., one of the divers in the canoe with Covell spotted what appeared to be several cannons lying on the bottom. He dove down and a minute later burst the surface to confirm the find. Seeing the excitement, Rogers rowed over and sent down a diver who returned with a heavy encrusted silver sow. In an instant all the divers were at work and amidst whooping and yelling retrieved a silver bar and silver "champeen." The finds were quickly taken to the

Henry and buoys and markers brought back to mark the wreck's location. Before nightfall, the divers had managed to bring up a total of two sows, fifty-one pieces of eight, and some broken silver plate.

It was Thursday, January 20, 1687. Forty-five years after her loss, the *Nuestra Señora de la Concepción* had been found.

In his account of this momentous event, Phips' biographer, Cotton Mather, told how one of the divers had first spotted not a cannon but a particularly colorful sea feather growing from a coral head. Desiring it as a souvenir, he dove down to retrieve it, only to find close by several cannons that he could not have spotted from the boat. This version of the discovery, depending, it would seem, on the delicate instrumentality of a chance sea feather, has the touch of the miraculous that undoubtedly appealed to the Boston divine.

Rogers would later describe the wreck to his commander as being so broken up—with its bow and stern sections either missing or covered with coral overgrowth—that "had it not been for her guns she would scarce ever have been found." For William Phips the dream of wealth and fame was just beginning to unfold, yet this thirty-six-year-old former ship's carpenter, for all his courage, perseverance, and leadership, was never more a child of destiny than he was at that hour. Word of the *Henry's* good fortune spread quickly among the crews but not a hint of the momentous find reached the Spanish. Everyone, from the chief mates down to the cabin boys, knew that if word leaked out it would not be long before heavily armed galleons might well be dispatched to the bank—and all would be lost, including the crews' bonus. During the next week all hands worked to prepare and provision the ships for a long stay at sea. On the night of February 16 the expedition slipped out of Puerto Plata without ceremony and set course for the Ambrosia Bank. Five days later they arrived in the area and Phips began carefully threading the *James and Mary* among the outlying heads to a safe anchorage. His log entry reads as follows:

> 22nd February—Yesterday we steered away still NE and Ye wind at SE. After about an hour we see Ye Eastmost part of Ye reef, then we bore away along Ye reef NW keeping a good distance off. We found all along good soundings from 14 fathoms and 13½. At ½ hour after three, having run three leagues (towards Ye middle of Ye Reef) we came to anchor. Ye wreck bearing off us NE½E, distant about 4 & 5 miles. Ye reef making like a half moon. By Mr. Covell's persuasions we hoisted out our pinance [the ship's boat]. Mr. Covell, Mr. Strong and two of Ye divers went in her to Ye

wreck and just as daylight began to shut in they came on board bringing with them out of Ye wreck 189 whole dollars and 51 half dollars. [A piece of eight was reckoned as "a dollar" in English parlance.] This night Ye wind blew fresh but making a snugg ship by lowering down our yards and topmasts, by God's assistance we rode very secure.

The first day's "fishing" had been a mere trickle. With four boats and four divers working the wreck, that trickle quickly turned into a torrent. On February 26 Phips' log noted:

. . . Yesterday about 2 PM our longboat came on board with a brass gun which they had taken out of Ye wreck. Ye nature of Ye gun was a 12 pounder and about 4 PM our pinance came on board having taken out of Ye wreck 3 sows, a small dowboy, 11,009 dollars, 1,700 half dollars and a small quantity of broken wrought plate. This morning being fair weather our boats went to work on Ye wreck again. About noon our longboat came on board with another brass gun, bigger than Ye former one.

Two days after this find, by sheer coincidence, a sloop and a shallop appeared on the horizon and a short time later came to anchor near the *James and Mary*. Phips immediately recognized the masters of the two vessels, William Davis of Bermuda and Abraham Atherley of Jamaica, both of whom he knew from his trading days out of Boston and the Bahamas. Both men had been in Jamaica when the *Rose* had called on Port Royal a year earlier. Atherley had sailed with Phips to Hispaniola and had even been with him during the latter's cursory reconnaissance of the Ambrosia Bank. Surprised to learn that the new arrivals had come from Barbados to the bank to search for the galleon, Phips quickly took them in on the project, promising them half shares in return for the use of their gear and divers. The bargain was struck and the salvage continued with unabated zeal.

During the days that followed, the treasure yield was awesome. On March 2 the total was "one brass gun, 4,900 dollars, 2,600 half dollars and some broken plate." March 4 produced "2,399 lbs wt. of coins which we supposed were of silver which we put into 32 bags." Even though bad weather on March 5 allowed the divers "to make no great hand of their work," they brought on board "13 bags of coins weighing 1,139 lbs, one dowboy and a quarterweight of dowboy gold." On good days of calm weather, March 14 for example, the bounty was extraordinary: "41 sows, 4 bars and dowboys and other bullion in all quantity 2,542 lbs, and in coin 622 lbs weight"—more than one and a half tons.

And so it went day after day, a seemingly endless flow of unimaginable wealth. With the exception of illness and fatigue suffered by the divers who worked sometimes seven hours a day in the water, diving to depths of fifty feet, the work proceeded without incident. Phips, however, was entirely aware that no one aboard could long contemplate the fortune in bullion that lay about him without being severely tempted to conspire to mutiny. To forestall the notion, he repeatedly assured a bountiful share for every crewman and set his oath to the promise. Were it not for this kind of forceful and charismatic leadership and his reputation as a man of his word, events could well have taken a turn for the worse.

On March 29, William Davis' sloop sailed for Jamaica to replace a rudder lost during a collision with a coral head, taking with her for shipment to England some of the hides purchased in Puerto Plata. Davis had agreed to return as soon as possible to the bank but after three weeks had passed Phips feared that the sloop may have been seized by a French privateer that had been spotted off Puerto Plata. Though Davis had carried no treasure with him, Phips had no doubt that the French pirates would quickly resort to ruthless torture to learn of the fortune aboard the *James and Mary,* following which they would immediately set about to surprise and capture the ship.

The decision to abandon the wreck must have been agonizing for Phips. He knew he had probably brought up no more than a quarter of the galleon's vast cargo and that he could easily have accommodated aboard at least twice the tonnage salvaged to date. But in addition to his suspicions about the French privateer, the weather was turning increasingly bad and they were running short of food and provisions. Accordingly, Phips decided to sail for Cotton Key in the Turks Islands some ninety miles to the northwest, leaving behind his boatswain's mate and four divers aboard Atherley's shallop with instructions to continue working the wreck while awaiting the sloop's return. If after a week she still had not arrived, the shallop was to sail for Cotton Key.

On the morning of April 19, the *James and Mary* hoisted her yards and topmasts, weighed anchor, and "flooded from Ye reef first to the Westerly for about a glass [an hourglass, about thirty minutes] then WSW about a glass, then WSoutherly til noon keeping a man at topmasthead continuously to look out . . ." Some hours later while they were skirting the northeast fringe of the Handkerchief Bank the sea floor began to shoal abruptly and the *James and Mary* suddenly found herself with less than thirty feet of water beneath her keel. Phips shouted orders and the ship quickly swerved to a southerly heading into the safety of deeper water. Had the *James and Mary* been under a less conscientious commander (who may well have dispensed with soundings), she would soon have foundered on the bank and very likely wrecked. The remainder of the voyage to Cotton Key was uneventful and a few days later Atherley and the shallop joined the expedition. He reported no signs of the sloop but presented to Phips yet another three tons of silver. Anxious to avoid bad weather and confrontations with pirates in Bahamian waters, Phips obtained a supply of sea salt that accumulated along the rocky edges of the tide pools on Cotton Key and, on May 2, sailed for England in company with the *Henry*.

Return to Triumph

The crossing was a safe and swift one but for William Phips the voyage of a month and four days seemed torturously slow as he anticipated the events that were sure to occur upon his arrival. By the time the *James and Mary* glided into the Thames River on June 6, her captain was fairly bursting with excitement. Barely moments after she tied up, word reached the Duke of Albemarle, Sir James Hayes, and the other adventurers. They rushed down to the dock, pausing just long enough to order delivered to the ship copious quantities of ale and spirits, and clambered aboard to rejoice with William Phips in their spectacular good fortune. No sooner had messengers reached the Admiralty with the news and orders issued to place a strong guard on the ship, than all hands aboard were quite drunk. The Duke of Albemarle, not one to stand on ceremony in his hour of great joy, obliged every man and boy in the ship's company to drink to his health. The next several hours were entirely occupied by endless toasts, backslapping, hilarity, and the arrival of more libation.

An astonished Sir Samuel Pepys, the celebrated Secretary of the Admiralty, took every precaution to ensure against any embezzlement of the treasure. Before he would even allow officials of the Exchequer to board the *James and Mary* he had to personally satisfy himself of their honesty. And when the high court of the Admiralty ordered the treasure removed from the ship, Pepys simply forbade the order's execution. Finally, on June 9, senior officials of the Mint came aboard with orders to weigh and count the treasure. The warden, the comptroller, the mintmaster, and an assistant took several days to accomplish the task, after which a tenth of the total, belonging to the King according to the contract, was conveyed to the Mint in the Tower of London.

The Mint officials certified that the treasure consisted of: 450,000 pieces of eight weighing 37,538 pounds; 459 silver bars of various types (sows, dowboys, champeens, etc.) weighing 27,556 pounds; 374 pounds of miscellaneous silver plate (this being a form of bullion, not a reference to worked silver artifacts); and 25.7 pounds of gold objects such as finger bars, splashes, and worked jewelry. The total weight of the treasure was a whopping 32 tons, easily one of the largest treasure hauls in the annals of England's long maritime history—and possibly Europe's as well.

The value in pesos assigned to the treasure was about 760,000. If that figure was converted to American dollars using an average current ratio of $4.50 per peso (of silver bullion as distinct from a peso of coin) the total value today would be equivalent to an astounding $30,780,000! One can well understand the vigilance of Samuel Pepys and the unalloyed joy of Phips and his backers. In terms of English currency at that time, the treasure was valued at £210,000, exclusive of jewels and other items of comparatively little value. After King James' share of £20,700 was carted off to the Royal Treasury the subscribers set about their own division.

The Duke of Albemarle, whose share was by far the largest, realized more than £50,000. Phips was now wealthy, boasting a handsome return in excess of £12,000, while the other investors received an amount in proportion to their shares. They calculated that for every £100 invested they had each made a remarkable profit of between £8,000 and £10,000. Unquestionably, the most chagrined individual in all England in those days was one Sir Richard Haddock— he had made the mistake of selling his £100 share in the venture before Phips had returned. For their part each member of the crew received handsome bonuses anywhere between £60 and £120 depending on rank, while the officers and chief mates were each given £1,000.

If later stories are correct, a small part of the treasure somehow escaped inclusion in the official inventory, for a few months later Phips was seen wearing a magnificent hatband of braided gold while back in Boston Mrs. Mary Phips was now the owner of a beautiful gold chain. Nevertheless, the Duke of Albemarle presented to Mrs. Phips an exquisite chalice of gold worth £1,000.

The good Duke, incidentally, was much enamored of gold, even going so far as to personally supervise the melting down of his share of the precious stuff—as well as much of his silver—in the garden of his country estate. Friends at court were overheard to remark that most assuredly "His Grace would spend the rest of his days near his furnaces."

3

Spain's Twentieth-Century Legacy–and a Kid Named Webber

Return to the Reef

As word of the Ambrosia Bank bonanza spread throughout London and beyond, William Phips became the hero of all England and the sensation of Europe. King James II, in high good humor over the gift of £20,000 he'd just received, promptly knighted Phips "in recognition of good and loyal services." Though exulting in popular acclaim, Sir William and his partners were nonetheless anxious to outfit another expedition as soon as possible to return to the wreck before pirates or free-lance salvors found it. Ready to lead a flotilla of five ships was Sir John Narbrough, who was not only an investor on the first expedition but also a high commissioner of the Admiralty and much esteemed hero of the Algerian naval conflict years earlier. Aboard his ship the *Foresight* Narbrough would be commander-in-chief but in practice Sir William would be in charge.

The expedition weighed anchor for the Indies on the last day of August, 1687. The crossing was a long one and it wasn't before December that the flotilla reached the bank. Though Sir John and Sir William had received reports that a few small vessels were "fishing ye wrecke," they were staggered by the spectacle that greeted them. Everywhere for half a mile around the wrecksite were sloops and shallops and brigantines—thirty-two in number—most from the British-owned plantations of Jamaica, the Bahamas, and particularly Bermuda. Over the wreck itself were dozens of canoes and dinghies trailing rakes while everywhere about them scores of divers worked busily. Taking possession of the reef the new arrivals quickly discovered that the wreck had been all but stripped of easily accessible treasure.

Indeed, as accounts of the day would later reveal, during the seven months that Phips had been absent from the reef, wave upon wave of adventurers had descended upon the wrecksite. Fierce fights broke out, accompanied by rammings and sinkings. Divers were shot by crew members on rival boats. Gunplay, hijackings, and the clash of swords were commonplace as on-the-spot partnerships were made and broken. Chaos and anarchy reigned upon the watery battlefield.

The Ambrosia Bank turned out to be anything but ambrosial for Phips. His divers brought up only scattered pieces of bullion, plate, and silver coins while the coral shield which he believed had grown over the main plate room of the stern section resisted all attempts at penetration. Phips even tried gunpowder in a "fire chest" placed on the coral; however, the fuse tube he devised of cane ends sealed with wax and tar failed repeatedly to remain waterproof. Adding to the difficulties, a nameless West Indian virus swept through the expedition, claiming the lives of a fair number of officers and crew.

Finally, after four and a half months on the reef—and a mere 3,300 pounds of silver to show for it—an exhausted and demoralized William Phips abandoned further attempts to reach the plate room even though he was convinced it contained considerably more treasure than had already been recovered. For his part Sir John Narbrough elected to stay behind for one last try, but several days after Phips' departure in early May 1688, he himself came down with a fever. Nine days later the venerable commander died. He was forty-seven.

No one will ever know the actual amount of silver taken up from the *Concepción* before and after Phips' second visit. Historians have estimated that the several hundred boats and ships that visited the wreck fished up at least as much treasure as Phips did, roughly 800,000 pesos worth. Thus, of the estimated four to six million pesos of treasure aboard the *Concepción,* only 1.6 to 2 million had been removed.

Phips' Final Years

On his return to Boston, Sir William Phips turned from treasure hunting to build for himself and Mary a handsome two-story brick house with a columned portico, then plunged into his duties as High Sheriff of the New England colonies, an appointment he received from King James. He achieved mixed success in his new career ashore. In May 1689, he organized and led a small army north to capture Port Royal, Nova Scotia, and Acadia from the French, returning to Boston a hero. To capitalize on his victory, Phips immediately sailed for England to curry favor with the new King (William of Orange), receiving in return an appointment as governor of Massachusetts and the newly acquired provinces.

Back home again, Phips assumed the role with characteristic energy and on the whole did a creditable job despite his irksome propensity to run the government in the same manner as he would a ship. He lived in the style of a governor-general of greater means and apparently made no effort to invest a portion of his fortune to insure a lifetime income. In the fall of 1693 Phips organized yet another attack on France's American possessions, this time in Quebec—and blundered badly. The assault ran into early-winter snowstorms. The failure proved costly to Phips as his enemies in government took advantage of his sagging popularity to condemn his administration. To forestall moves to have him ousted, Phips again sailed to England to argue his case in the court of King William.

The voyage turned out to be his last. Within days of his arrival in London he came down with a serious fever, evidently influenza, and on February 18, 1694, died at the age of forty-four.

In time Phips' recovery of the Hispaniola treasure galleon gradually receded from the stage of public events. Numerous personal accounts of the expeditions to the Ambrosia Bank existed, and as the years passed, these diaries, together with journals, logbooks, and letters, found their way into private libraries, collections, and dusty archives. No effort was ever made to preserve the bulk of these documents for posterity, least of all for their potential usefulness as an aid to someday returning to the galleon. The *Concepción* and its exact location faded into obscurity.

In 1706 *The English Pilot,* an authoritative sailing guide published in London, listed the reef formerly known as the Ambrosia Bank as the Plate Wrack. A century later, English sailing charts changed the name to the Silver Bank in recognition of its legendary treasure. Still later, by the mid-twentieth century, the legend endured even as cartographers, in the interest of correct phraseology, listed that largely uncharted region as the Silver Shoals.

In retrospect Phips' treasure trove, besides becoming one of the great legends of the age, had an enduring impact on the British business community. Many years after Sir William had been laid to rest, consortiums were still launching expeditions to find and salvage wrecks on both sides of the Atlantic as well as the Caribbean. These ventures, all designed to duplicate Phips' success, were popular with investors, but with each sortie that returned empty-handed, the enthusiasm gradually waned. Indeed, there is no record of any expedition subsequent to Phips' that ever recovered anything of consequence. In time the names of once-fashionable treasure-hunting enterprises disappeared from the listings of the British stock exchange.

To be sure, the rate of ship losses in the New World remained quite high but by the mid-seventeenth century, Spain had not only discontinued her great galleon armadas—which were gradually replaced by faster frigates—but the flow of silver across the Atlantic also declined. By century's end, the days of lumbering galleons packed to the gunwales with silver had passed forever. For the most part so, too, did the heyday of pirates and buccaneers who had played such havoc on the Spanish Lake. Taking their place was a slightly more respectable breed of English salvors (known as wreckers) who lived mainly in the Bahamas and constantly prowled the east coast of Florida looking for wrecks and floating cargo. There were disasters enough to reward them for their efforts.

The wreckers were a tough and scrappy lot who were not above raiding and looting Spanish outposts when given a chance. But by the 1820's many descendants of the Bahamian salvors had migrated to Florida to ply their trade out of Key West. Though regarded by many as little more than pirates, they had actually become quite honorable as Christian sentiments gained the ascendancy in the New World. In fact the Key West wreckers saved many lives and acquitted themselves honorably with considerable courage and resourcefulness.

A famous story about the wreckers has circulated around Key West for generations. During the 1830's a well-known wrecker who was also a preacher by avocation was delivering a sermon from the pulpit of his seaside church one stormy morning. In the middle of his oratory he spied through the open doors a ship not far offshore heading for a reef. Because the congregation's back was to the spectacle no one else saw the vessel, nor did the preacher himself flinch in the slightest as he observed the hapless ship lurch hard to one side as it grounded on the reef. Instead he stepped down from the pulpit and slowly made his way to the church doors, his sonorous voice never losing its tone or pace. He timed his sermon perfectly to end just as he reached the door at which point he gave forth with a lusty "Amen! Wreck ashore!" and bolted out to his sloop. Historians record the preacher not only reached the grounded ship first to legally claim her cargo as his but also helped save many a life and limb that day.

A Paper Sea

More than a century would pass before researchers would discover that the east coast of Florida and the Keys constitute the richest, most concentrated and easily accessible treasure region in the world. During the first 300 years of New World colonization so many ships had wrecked along a 350-mile stretch from Cape Canaveral south to Key West that there was an average of one offshore wreck for every mile. A goodly number of these shallow-water hulks were galleons. Many contained millions of dollars in gold and silver coins waiting to be discovered just beneath the sand and turtle grass that had since covered their remains.

While Spain had bequeathed to the twentieth century a fleet of sunken ships scattered throughout her once-vast dominion, they were all but forgotten with the passing of her glory. True, there were singular disasters that became part of enduring local legends among New World citizenry, but once a wrecked ship had been salvaged as much as possible, the remainder of its treasures was consigned forever to the deep. The knowledge of its location often died with those who witnessed the event. Spain, too, let the memory of her galleons pass into history—but not without first recording them. The voluminous accounts of her activities in the New World in fact constitute one of her most significant and intriguing twentieth-century legacies.

From the very moment of its birth in 1503, the House of Trade, like all bureaucracies aspiring to greatness, generated an enormous amount of paperwork. These documents, together with countless others dealing with every aspect of Spain's colonization of the New World, were eventually forwarded to a large storehouse in Simancas, Spain, where they languished through the reign of numerous sovereigns. Finally, in 1784, the Crown ordered the establishment in Seville of the *Archivo General de las Indias,* "the General Archives of the Indies." From Simancas and elsewhere were transported to the AGI wagonloads of bundles of yellowing documents dealing with every aspect of the Spanish colonies. Each bundle, or *legajo,* contained inventories, reports, orders, ship's manifests, legal agreements, charters, commissions, and letters to and from the King and other government officials and citizens, all thrown together with no thought to their order other than their proximity to a given year or colonial locale. The AGI was given quarters in the old House of Trade building the storerooms of which were stacked to the ceiling with *legajos.*

Because Spanish bureaucrats insisted on the recording of practically every transaction and event that took place within their New World jurisdiction, it is very likely that there exists in the AGI some form of testimony or report on every ship loss that ever occurred, whether filed by survivors or salvage officers, or both. The problem is that most of the files to this day have not been completely read and indexed. In fact some of the *legajos* were never moved to Seville. Author/explorer Robert Marx, who has done extensive research in the AGI, discovered nearly 1,000 bundles that had been left behind in Simancas, many with incorrect subject titles. In describing the AGI in his book *Shipwrecks in Florida Waters,* Marx noted that "If a team of 100 researchers spent their whole lives searching through the more than 250,000 large legajos in the Archives of the Indies, I doubt that they could locate all the important documents. . . . The majority of the legajos are not catalogued, and about twenty percent of those shipped from Simancas in 1784 have never been opened."

This situation is ironic. For every Spanish ship and treasure lost somewhere in the New World, it is likely that a full record of the events that occurred, along with the ship's location and the amount of treasure she carried, was consigned somewhere in a sea of paper in the Archives of the Indies. Indeed, events would someday dramatically confirm that likelihood.

Hard-Hat Pioneers

While the Spanish plunder of the New World had fostered a rich tradition of wreck salvaging and treasure hunting there remained elsewhere in the world no lack of ship sinkings to tantalize many a bold dreamer.

Throughout the nineteenth century, expanding ship commerce

between Europe, Asia, and Africa resulted in numerous losses at sea of many millions of dollars in precious bullion. Where conventional marine salvors failed to raise a ship's cargo—or flatly pronounced it unsalvageable—sea scavengers from every walk of life stepped in to tackle the challenges, devising ingenious salvage equipment in a tenacious effort to grasp the prize.

There to lend an impetus to their efforts was the industrial revolution which was in full swing by the late nineteenth century. No sooner was any innovation introduced—for example: rubber air hoses, powerful incandescent lamps, and mechanical grabs—than some enterprising dreamer would attempt its application to man's age-old quest to conquer the depths of the sea. From the beginning, the biggest barrier to their success was water pressure, the kind that can squeeze to death any human being not completely protected by some form of body shield. By the turn of the century many kinds of diving bells and suits had been unsuccessfully tried, but by the 1920's engineers had developed the essential components of the so-called hard-hat diving suit which at last enabled man to move under water while connected by air hoses and communication lines to a surface platform on which was located an air compressor. The diver himself was heavily ballasted with lead weights and had to be lowered to the sea floor before attempting to move around, a laborious task. Moreover, he had to be careful not to snag any of his hoses or lines even as these same lines were easily affected by currents which could in turn drag him off his feet. In all, hard-hat diving was workable but cumbersome and expensive—and dangerous if done under less than ideal conditions.

Still, by the 1930's there now existed for the first time three ingredients which could unlock a potential goldmine for treasure hunters, particularly in Florida: the Spanish galleon wrecks themselves, the locational documentation in the Seville archives, and the diving technology to salvage the wrecks. But the key to success would depend on which documents and which wrecks.

In 1938 a twenty-eight-year-old commercial diver from Homestead, Florida, was the first to garner an inkling of the possibilities. Art McKee, who at the time was chief diver on a Navy underwater pipeline, frequently spent his weekends diving the offshore reefs with his hard-hat rig looking for brass and iron from old wrecks. On the site of a ballast mound and cannons which lay in twenty-eight feet of water some three miles off Plantation Key, he retrieved a bucketful of encrusted artifacts, including a handful of heavily sulphided silver pieces of eight—and a 1721 gold coin. Excited by the find, he began a library search for information on the Spanish ships of that period. After drawing a blank, he wrote to Spain and after many months received from the Archives of the Indies in Seville a bundle of photocopied documents. From these McKee determined he had found the *Capitana* of the 1733 fleet devastated by a hurricane in the straits. Unfortunately, the documents revealed the ship had been salvaged by the Spanish soon after it sank. But McKee was now hooked on treasure diving. In the months that followed he and several friends carefully picked the wreck apart, moving nearly 300 tons of ballast rock and eventually finding enough artifacts to open a museum on Plantation Key. In the decades since then his quest for the gold and silver of the galleons would take him on expeditions everywhere in the gulf and the Caribbean. Though a truly big strike would elude him, Art McKee would later be recognized as the father of Florida treasure hunters.

The Debut of Scuba and Burt Webber

In 1943 a technological breakthrough was made that had a profound impact on marine exploration and treasure hunting. Two Frenchmen, Jacques Yves Cousteau and an engineer named Émile Gagnan, together developed a device that allowed a diver to breathe compressed air under water. Originally called a *scaphandre autonome* (self-contained diving unit) the invention became universally known as scuba (self-contained underwater breathing apparatus). The device was a simple two-stage regulator that attached to a tank of compressed air on the diver's back. When a diver inhaled through a mouthpiece the regulator automatically delivered air at exactly the same pressure as that of the water around him at that depth, while exhaled air was vented to the surrounding water through a one-way exhaust valve. For the first time ever, man was free to roam beneath the waters, unfettered by lifeline connections to the surface.

Before long, divers equipped with scuba had determined the maximum practical depths to which one could dive safely without long decompression times—about 200 feet. Beyond that depth the nitrogen in the compressed air became toxic, causing nitrogen narcosis or, as the French elegantly termed it, rapture of the depths. A diver affected with nitrogen narcosis feels wildly euphoric, drunk, incapable of the simplest tasks, and likely to make the mortal mistake of offering his mouthpiece regulator to a passing fish. But the range of possibilities awaiting underwater explorers within that 200-foot depth was enormous.

It would be well into the 1950's before the first scuba equipment would be available to the general public, and still later before formal instruction in the use of scuba would be offered. Certainly, few in the fledgling diving industry envisioned that a generation later more than 2½ million Americans would be active sport divers. But for the adventurous soul in the late fifties, teachers could occasionally be found in ex-military frogmen. Scuba was considered a rather hazardous activity for mature experienced men only.

Which was why one sunny Sunday in the summer of 1959 sixteen-year-old Burt Webber, Jr., a boy with a history of asthma attacks and allergic reactions to just about everything, had to argue his case with forceful persuasion. He had approached two scuba divers who were preparing to dive in a deep fresh-water quarry in Pennsylvania, asking one of them if he might borrow his gear for a short dive. The divers, both in their late twenties, were amused by the kid's request.

"Can you dive?" one of the men asked.

"Well, I've read all the books and I do a lot of skin diving," Webber answered. Before they could reply he quickly added: "I've got my own fins and mask and depth gauge. I know what I'm doing."

Something about the way Webber spoke, a kind of intense and willful earnestness, did the trick. Moments later, for the first time in his life, he was strapping on a tank, regulator, and weight belt. He was as excited and as scared as the quarry water was cold and clear.

Together with one of the divers Webber waded chest-high into the water to the edge of a grassy shelf, then pushed off toward an elevator shaft protruding from the water forty feet away. The two divers began a descent to the quarry floor rumored to be some sixty-five to seventy feet below. Almost immediately his ears began to hurt but he managed to equalize his inner-ear pressure by swallowing several times. His partner descended below him at a faster rate, leaving Webber nearly alone at twenty-five feet to clear his ears.

He was just beginning to revel in the extraordinary sensation of breathing comfortably under water, feeling the easy rhythm of the regulator and tasting the slightly metallic dry air—then it happened. The next inhalation was not air but water. In an instant Webber knew that he was deeper than he'd ever been before, using scuba for the first time, and that he had absolutely no air. Death seemed a real possibility. As he looked up at the sun shining faintly on the surface far above him, panic hit. But only for a few seconds. He'd read about emergency free ascents and with a supreme act of will forced his body to relax as he slowly kicked upward. After fifteen long seconds he broke the surface, choking and gasping for air, then pushed toward shore.

As he'd discovered under water, the metal clamp that held the mouthpiece to the flexible hoses had come off, leaving an unattached mouthpiece between his teeth. The breakdown could have easily led to his drowning, but after resting a few moments, Webber replaced the clamp and made a second dive, this time getting down to forty feet before difficulty with equalizing ear pressure halted his descent.

That Webber didn't drown that day may be attributed to his remarkable presence of mind and strong survival instincts. But what is extraordinary is that Webber, after a close shave with death, would remain out of water only long enough to repair the regulator and catch his breath before attempting a second dive. Certainly, no one would have questioned his judgment had he abandoned any idea of diving again that day—or any other. The last thing anyone expected was his return to the water. But Burt Webber was not always likely to do the expected. He was a young man in a hurry, an apprentice with a sense of mission even though that mission was yet to be defined. And he was thorough. Not only had he devoured every book on scuba diving he could lay his hands on but he had also very likely memorized most of the decompression tables and could have field-stripped a regulator while blindfolded.

Such involvement in his interests was typical and went hand in glove with a passion for understanding technical details, for tinkering with machines, and experimenting with complicated toys. One sees these same qualities in Webber today, but his intensity is tempered with a sense of shared excitement, an enthusiasm for serious fun—despite certain risks. "When I think back on that first time ever with scuba," he recalls, "it's amazing the guy would actually have let me use his equipment. But then I was so fascinated with the whole thing, the whole idea that a man could actually be going under water and be able to breathe and explore."

Growing Up at High Speed

Burt, Jr., the youngest of three children, was born December 10, 1942, into an upper-middle class family from Schaefferstown, Pennsylvania, where his father, Burt, Sr., owned a successful Buick/Pontiac dealership. With two uncles who also owned car dealerships in nearby towns, young Webber and his clan were proudly linked to the Detroit tradition no less so than to a long lineage of German and Pennsylvania Dutch ancestors. Though he early on was diagnosed as asthmatic and suffered from a variety of allergies, Burt's childhood was not otherwise a harsh one. At age seven he donned a mask and fins and rigged up minnow nets to "salvage" rocks from the bottom of the local swimming hole. Together with other neighborhood children he explored the countryside, camped, and gained an early fondness for outdoor life. But he liked to be in charge:

"I always had to run the show, even then," he remembers.

By age twelve Webber had become proficient at making his own combat movies, using toy models and 16 mm time-lapse photography for special effects. By that time, too, he had amassed several collections including mineral rocks, coins, and vintage Japanese and German military paraphernalia. Yet there was something of a loner in him. True, he was a Boy Scout for a few years—and he got a lot out of the experience—but in time his self-generated projects began to monopolize his time. A quickness of mind characterized his approach. That was it, really—speed. And excitement. Webber needed both:

"Life was always too slow moving. I did a lot of things and I did them fast. Maybe too fast but I was always hyper-energetic, doing things that were exciting and creative."

By 1956 he was fourteen and in high school where by his own admission he compiled an undistinguished record, doing well only in subjects he liked such as history. He read adventure books constantly.

For additional excitement Webber for a while hung out with a gang of quasi-delinquent teenagers, wore black leather jackets, and on many a night contributed his share of blue smoke from squealing tires as he drag raced on back streets. He never got in trouble with the law but he found in the punk subculture the right mix of rebellion and zest, with its sinister associations and vague promises of forbidden thrills. But in the end his passing enthusiasm for dragging the main was eclipsed by the lure of scuba diving.

By 1960, with the help of an ex-Navy frogman who provided advanced instruction, Webber became a fully qualified diver. He was seventeen.

It was only a matter of time before the boy's activity attracted attention. One chilly fall day Webber and Ted Roberts, a member of his weekend dive group, searched a portion of the Millardsville Quarry for what a fellow diver had described as some kind of chest. At forty-five feet they found a cache of seven slot machines dumped in the quarry some years previously. Not stopping to remove his wet suit, Webber drove to the Millardsville Hotel:

"An old man ran the place. He knew my dad and had bought cars from him, so I told him I'd found this cache of slot machines. He called the police and then looked at me. There I was standing in a dripping wet suit, freezing cold, my lips blue and it's getting dark outside. Without saying anything he put a big shot of double whiskey in front of me. I'll never forget that. It was like some kind of initiation into manhood."

That night the police showed up, along with reporters and photographers from several dailies. The next day's papers carried photos of a wet-suited Webber posing with his find, evidently put there years ago by a nervous illegal casino operator. The coin boxes of the machines were empty but Webber was allowed to keep the coins still in the payoff tubes, about $10 worth. As he said later, "It was my first big break in the world of recovery." Little did he know that eighteen long years would pass before he would get his second.

Before another year had passed, Webber had done a fair bit of both cave diving and ocean diving (the latter off the New Jersey coast) and belonged to a local Civil Defense dive rescue team. He also had a high school diploma and a steady girl friend in Sandy Belleman, an attractive girl whom he'd met in school. In contrast to Webber, Sandy began life in a broken home and had spent a great part of her childhood in the Bethany Children's Home. She went along with Burt on all his dive trips. The couple dated each other exclusively and would later marry in 1964.

Dive School—and a Dream

Though his parents were disappointed their son didn't wish to follow his older brother and sister into college, they had seen the handwriting on the wall—Burt's poor high school grades reflected his lack of interest in academia. Instead he had his heart set on a career in the Navy where he planned to enlist, then volunteer for the submarine service or become an underwater demolitions technician. The plan seemed feasible until he learned his history of respiratory problems prevented him from enlisting (or being drafted). Undaunted, he applied for a civilian dive school, the first of its kind on the eastern seaboard, and by downplaying his asthma, was accepted.

The Divers Training Academy in South Miami, Florida, was ideally suited for a gung-ho student of Webber's temperament. Founded and staffed by tough ex-military professionals well versed in underwater work the school was conducted with a no-nonsense military discipline and procedure. In October 1959, Webber and more than twenty other students, many of them ex-Navy divers, began a rigorous four-month program.

At eighteen and in great shape, Webber thrived under the routine as some of his classmates, many in their late thirties and out of condition, dropped out. The training continued as students learned how to conduct nighttime commando-style beach raids while developing expertise in the use of demolitions and rebreathers (a scuba variation that leaves no tell-tale bubbles). Webber loved it.

Clearly a good deal of the academy's program had much to do with decidedly uncivilian activities. The reason: Cuba. In the fall of 1960 all of Florida was a hotbed of counterrevolutionary fervor. While a future missile crisis simmered, CIA-backed training camps were going full tilt throughout Dade County; Miami was a city of refugees, and the air was filled with rumors of conspiracy and invasion, all of which added a sense of urgency and adventure to the training. Just how urgent Webber learned when he and four classmates one weekend drove down to do a bit of diving in the keys, his first time ever in those waters. On a remote portion of Duck Key, the group decided to cross under water a lovely bay that extended to a remote promontory on which stood the old West Indies Hotel, temporarily closed because of hurricane damage. On completing the twenty-minute crossing, everyone complained of splitting headaches, evidently caused by paint fumes that had been in the air around the compressor when they had charged their tanks at the academy. Webber remembers what happened next.

"We took our tanks off but we still wore our black wet suits and knives and weight belts. Then we started to look around the hotel, hoping to get a lift back to the highway. We were passing one of those thatched-roof cabañas by the hotel when suddenly we encountered a guy with a machine gun shouting at us in Spanish to put our hands on our heads. We were marched to a sentry gate and after some very tense moments were brought before an English-speaking captain who listened very carefully. He finally believed us but told us the guard had been ordered to shoot first and ask questions later. Because that order had been disobeyed we were alive."

Webber later learned they had stumbled into a CIA-run Cuban refugee commando training camp that not even the local population knew existed.

As events would unfold in Webber's career this would not be the last time that the Cuban revolution and its aftermath would cast a shadow across his path. But the remainder of his academy training was largely uneventful, focusing now on commercial hard-hat diving techniques. And there were good times like weekend trips to Key West to dive the offshore reefs, consume enormous quantities of beer and fresh lobster, and talk of high-salaried futures.

But while others spoke of building piers in Jamaica and working on oil platforms or undersea pipelines, Burt kept bringing up the subject of sunken Spanish galleons and his dream of tracking them down and salvaging them using modern technology. His classmates were skeptical but they didn't scoff. Something about him suggested he would somehow find the means to pursue his vision.

In the spring of 1961 Webber took his final exams, finishing second highest in his class. On graduation, as a first class commercial diver, his instructors presented him with a silver pin in the shape of a hard-hat diving helmet. No one was prouder that day. Nor did anyone face a future more full of uncertainty and frustration. Burt Webber, Jr., the young man who dreamed of galleons, was about to face the severest test of reality. And it would be a long one.

4

The Making of a
Treasure Hunter

Testing Caribbean Waters

Burt Webber completed his commercial diver's training at a pivotal moment in the annals of treasure hunting, for new information and technology were about to trigger a Florida gold rush. During the late fifties more and more ballast mounds of galleon wrecks belonging to the 1733 Spanish plate fleet had been found along the keys as scuba-equipped weekend treasure divers, sparked by Art McKee's earlier success, combed the offshore reefs, often following up tips supplied by local fishermen. These wrecksites were yielding a goodly amount of artifacts and an encouraging trickle of coins.

Most Florida wreck divers had no inkling of the names or histories of the shipwrecks they worked and their explorations were unsystematic and conducted by visual means only. But some 200 miles north, Kip Wagner, a building contractor in Sebastian Inlet (on Florida's east coast), used solid research to follow up a hunch. Convinced that pieces of eight found on the beach must have originated from a lucrative offshore wreck, Wagner wrote to the Archives of the Indies in Seville and received encouragement. In May of 1961, hardly three months after Webber had graduated from dive school, Wagner and a group of weekend dive partners found hundreds of silver coins from the wreck of one of the ten galleons of the 1715 plate fleet destroyed by a hurricane.

The discovery led Wagner's group, the Real Eight Corporation, to go partners with west-coast diver/explorer Mel Fisher, a man whose name years later was destined to be linked with that of the galleon *Nuestra Señora de Atocha*. When he met Wagner in early 1963, however, Fisher had just returned from the Silver Shoals where he had spent several exhausting weeks searching in vain for *La Nuestra Señora de la Concepción*. It had been his second and last attempt. Fisher's partnership with Wagner's group would result in a treasure yield from ships of the 1715 fleet that would eventually top $5 million.

Contributing to the developing treasure ferment was the publication of several resource and adventure books that fired the imaginations of thousands who dreamed of finding an underwater Eldorado. In 1959 Marion Link, the wife of Edward Link, inventor of the Link aircraft trainer, published *Sea Diver*, an account of the couple's treasure searches aboard their research vessel *Sea Diver* in the Keys, the Bahamas, and particularly the Silver Shoals for the *Concepción* (no luck) during the years 1953–59. Elsewhere, one could spend hours perusing F.L. Coffman's *1,001 Lost, Buried or Sunken Treasures* (maps included). Finally, in 1961 the first edition of John S. Potter, Jr.'s *The Treasure Diver's Guide* appeared. This scholarly, definitive, and exciting compendium lists thousands of tantalizing wrecks the world over and its publication has been responsible for launching hundreds of expeditions—and indirectly figuring in the breakup of not a few marriages. So many have succumbed to the book's siren call that the treasure hunting community often refers to Potter's book as "The Homewrecker's Guide."

Webber devoured these books and followed closely every report of new finds in Florida's waters. Moreover, he now felt ready to break into the profession of treasure hunting. Typically, he would not only do so with a remarkable singlemindedness, but would also pack enough adventure into the next ten years to fill several lifetimes.

Just prior to graduation Webber drove to Plantation Key to the Museum of Sunken Treasure and managed to talk his way into a job interview with the now world-famous Art McKee. "Meeting Art McKee," Webber later recalled, "was like meeting a reincarnation of Long John Silver—the same weather-beaten features, the smiling face, the danger in the eyes." McKee was impressed with Webber's fervor and dive school credits, adding he was in fact outfitting an expedition to the Caribbean. But since he already had a full complement of divers, he could agree only to call Webber if a position opened up. Weeks later, following Webber's return home to Pennsylvania, McKee called with good news—a spot was open—but the contract terms were unusual: Webber would receive 5 percent of any treasure found but he would not be paid a salary and would be expected to contribute his share of expedition expenses, which amounted to $1,000. The terms seemed less than fair to Webber but he would later learn that not a few treasure hunters used such tactics to raise money for expeditions, knowing that there were always investors willing to pay their own way in return for the thrill of participating.

Webber wasted no time persuading his aunt and father to invest $500 each and in short order he was back in Florida, this time on the Miami River to help outfit the *El Amigo*, a 136-foot ex-Navy minesweeper owned by a short, chunky bulldog of a captain rumored to be a rough customer.

Even before the eighteen-man expedition, code-named Operation Caribbean, got under way it was clear that McKee and the captain were not on friendly terms. And on that note the newly christened *El Amigo* left Miami in April 1961, bound for Grand Cayman. The expedition's objective: to find and salvage the *Genovese*, a fifty-four-gun Spanish frigate sunk in 1730 on the Banner's Reef section of the San Pedro Bank some seventy miles southwest of Jamaica. The *Genovese* had allegedly carried 3 million pesos in gold and silver, only two thirds of which were salvaged.

Webber sensed the voyage would be far from routine when at sunrise on the second day he awoke to find the *El Amigo* just off the beaches of Cuba, rather than in the middle of the Yucatán Channel fifteen miles westward. The captain's navigational error soon led to a visit by three Cuban gunboats filled with trigger happy interrogators. After an elaborate display of flags and papers showing the ship was of British registry, the expedition was allowed to proceed.

The encounter was only a precursor of more serious problems yet to come but it mattered little to Webber. He was on his first treasure hunt in the Caribbean, seeing for the first time the spotless beaches of Grand Cayman, learning wreck exploration procedure, and all the while listening to McKee's tales of galleons and gold that he would spin after the evening meal when everyone relaxed on the afterdeck beneath the stars. The wrecksite McKee chose on Banner's Reef produced a rich array of artifacts but no gold and no evidence it was the *Genovese*. Nevertheless, Webber worked with gusto: operating an air lift and using a Desco face mask/ regulator connected by an air hose to a compressor which enabled him to remain under water indefinitely. One day Webber went down at 6 A.M. and remained in twenty-six feet of water working continuously until 6 P.M. —a solid twelve-hour stretch under water. "I wasn't trying to impress anyone," he recalls. "But that's how intriguing it was to me. I couldn't learn fast enough from McKee. He's a master of working a site. He can detect things under water and work a wreck very skillfully."

Webber's routine of long days under water was interrupted only twice, the first occurring when a boatload of club-wielding riffraff from Port Royal, Jamaica, came out to the site intending to rob the gringo treasure hunters of their rumored stash of found gold. They were dissuaded from the attempt when the *El Amigo*'s crew brandished a small arsenal of rifles, shotguns, and magnum pistols. Days later Webber was sidelined with a severe fever contracted in part because of overexertion. One night as he lay in his bunk, sweating and miserable beneath blankets, the captain entered and gruffly ordered him to drink the contents of a large mug. When the patient demurred, the captain shoved a fist before his eyes and growled, "Kid, you drink this or you get this." Webber obeyed, and downed a large hot toddy of steaming Jamaican rum, cane sugar, and lime juice whereupon he slept soundly for almost thirty hours and awoke nearly recovered.

Six weeks out of Miami the expedition turned seriously sour when the captain apparently suspected (without grounds) that the wreck really *was* the *Genovese* and that McKee knew where the gold was but was plotting to leave it unsalvaged and return later with another ship. Back in Grand Cayman during a reprovisioning visit, the two men argued furiously. McKee stormed off the ship leaving the *El Amigo* and company to return to Miami. Thus, Operation Caribbean ended in fiasco but despite failure and hard times Webber had loved every minute of it. By this time, too, he had followed the lead of several other expedition members and now wore a black beret (with his silver diver's pin proudly affixed), a practice which became his personal hallmark, a sign that he was a professional treasure hunter—and proud of it.

Barnstorming the Bahamas

Back in Pennsylvania, Webber stayed in touch with two people he'd met on the *El Amigo*: Gordon Patton, a wealthy businessman and investor, and Fred Dickson, a Yale graduate in his mid-twenties who spoke fluent Spanish and had worked in department store management before getting into diving. Patton announced his intention to return to Banner's Reef the following spring with his converted trawler *Pisces* and invited Webber and Dickson to be on the team. In the interim he agreed to let a crew take the boat to the Bahamas to search for galleon wrecks. Webber jumped at the chance and in January 1962 joined Dickson and several other young adventurers for a short foray to the old Bahama Passage.

They found and worked only one wreck which turned out to be a nineteenth-century vessel but the trip was memorable. Webber had several close calls with barracuda that mistook his shiny dive watch (and hand) for dinner, then later encountered in a deserted cay a tough-looking group of Cuban "fishermen" who were suspicious of Webber's black beret (which he always wore) and his status as a seeker of sunken treasure (not to mention the .32 caliber automatic he carried in a shoulder holster beneath a light jacket). The Cubans, too, were armed, for both parties knew these waters seethed with counterrevolutionary intrigue. But after tense moments everyone relaxed and the fishermen offered the *Pisces'* crew cups of freshly brewed Cuban coffee and *centrofinos*, cigarettes made of black tobacco, strong but good.

Several weeks after returning to Florida, Webber, together with Dickson and three others, again crossed the straits aboard the *Pisces*, this time headed for the Mucaras Reef in the Bahamas. The trip turned out to be a hellish five weeks for Webber, marked by bickering and dissension, but not before the group found the ballast pile and cannons of a galleon wreck (guarded by large hammerhead sharks). When Webber talked of using explosives to blow away coral overburden, Dickson, who was in command, adamantly refused. Amidst squabbling and disarray, work on the wreck was abandoned. En route to Nassau the *Pisces* was caught in a horrendous storm, battered by twenty-foot seas, ran aground twice, and nearly sank from hull leaks, all of which Webber was convinced could have been avoided by prudent seamanship and navigation. On arrival in Nassau, he, together with two others, left the expedition and booked a freighter back to Florida.

In the aftermath, Gordon Patton retained Dickson as the *Pisces'* skipper despite the poor marks given him by three of the five crewmen. When Patton later called Pennsylvania about the upcoming Banner's Reef trip, Webber, on learning that Dickson would be navigator, refused to sign on, reiterating his feelings about his former amigo.

That spring, while en route to the forty-mile-wide Windward Passage, the *Pisces* ran aground and sank on a reef off the coast of Cuba, having missed the passage by an astounding thirty miles. All hands survived but were promptly arrested and subjected to days of gunpoint interrogation. The ordeal ended happily as Cuba turned gracious host by ensconcing everyone in a plush Havana hotel before putting them on a homeward-bound plane. Back in Pennsylvania, Webber himself garnered press attention in a local story headlined AMERICAN GLAD HE DIDN'T MAKE TRIP.

Hardly had Webber lost his Caribbean suntan before he managed to raise $6,000 from two friends of his father to charter a boat for his own expedition to Banner's Reef. For a salvage vessel he chose an old Chesapeake Bay oyster trawler tied up on the Miami River. Her captain was Leo Barker, a tall, gaunt, seventy-three-year-old ex-Navy diver whose adventure stories fascinated Webber and a young associate. Barker agreed to charter his boat, the *M/V Norma,* for the trip but offered to cut Webber in on something even better right in Florida waters. Whereupon he swore his listeners to secrecy and told them of a discovery he'd made years earlier while doing a lighthouse survey down through the Florida Keys: a ballast pile and cannons of a galleon he was convinced was the fabled *Nuestra Señora de Atocha,* sunk in 1622 off the lower Matecumbe Keys with more than $60 million in silver aboard. To back his claim he embroidered his story with exquisite and credible detail. In exchange for data on the galleon's exact location Barker asked for a fourth of the treasure.

Webber was sold and in a few weeks' time other investors were brought in, together with a cash fund that topped $10,000. By July 1962, the *Norma* and company were off on Operation Alligator Reef. Using the compass bearings Barker supplied, Webber set up a survey grid across which boat-towed divers conducted a meticulous visual search. But after several weeks of fruitless underwater search—and the gradual appearance of contradictions in Barker's story—Webber and several investors began to realize the whole scheme was an elaborate concoction, a mishmash of fact and fancy from the mind of an obsessed old man. After an eventful but frustrating three months, the expedition headed back to Miami and the old man returned to his books. Webber remembers the end: "Barker died in poverty some years later. His ship sank on the Miami River. Till his dying day he honestly thought he was just a foot away from that big treasure find. God rest his poor soul."

Back to Banner's Reef—the Hard Way

Clearly a pattern was developing: Webber would remain at home in Pennsylvania only long enough to convince investors to back an effort to return to the hunting grounds. Remarkably, as young as he was, Webber never had serious difficulty rounding up backers. Thus, in the spring of 1963, following a work stint at his father's dealership, twenty-year-old Webber had raised $5,000 to once again return to Banner's Reef. He vowed not to be sidetracked.

After scouting Miami on his own Webber met an easy-going, cigar-smoking Cuban tugboat owner in his mid-thirties, fellow by the name of Sergio Brull, who agreed to take men and equipment to Grand Cayman Island if Webber would pay for badly needed repairs to his sixty-five-foot harbor tug *Joan*. Since he intended chartering a turtle schooner for the Banner's Reef run, Webber agreed.

Two weeks later the *Joan* was off for Grand Cayman. What Brull didn't tell Webber was that he was in some way connected to the Alpha 66 group, which had made many raids on the Cuban coast to smuggle out exiles, and that if the *Joan* were ever caught, Brull, Webber, and associates would all be shot with no questions asked. Political risks aside, the voyage to Grand Cayman which usually takes five days turned out to be a month of peril and hardship at sea. The drinking water was stale and green and food stores were rapidly depleted. Recalls Webber: "We were soon down to eating fried oatmeal. We stood six-hour helm watches and slept on the deck. Everyone was filthy, greasy, covered with soot from diesel exhaust. It was inconceivable. But then, we were young adventurers."

After weeks of bad water, poor food, storms, and close calls, the *Joan* and her exhausted crew limped into Georgetown, Grand Cayman. The sight of Brull and a fellow Cuban crew member, Norman Contreras, caused a few raised eyebrows among nervous locals, for that very morning, by sheer coincidence, a Cuban national passenger jet from Havana had landed without authorization in Georgetown. This had heightened fears the Cubans were plotting to use Grand Cayman to smuggle agents in and out of South America. Hours later the plane and passengers were allowed to leave but now suspicion had shifted to Webber and his Cuban associates who appeared to have arrived as part of some well-timed rendezvous with the plane from Havana. A mob of locals, most of them drunk, some wielding pistols, stormed the dock, accused Webber of being a Cuban agent and were literally preparing to hang him when Norman Contreras, cigar clenched in his teeth, appeared from the wheelhouse holding an M–1 with a banana clip, and ordered Webber released or he would open fire. The mob did so just as the constable arrived, sirens wailing, to restore order.

It was many hours before the tangle of coincidence and suspicion was unraveled and Webber and his friends were cleared. Sergio Brull quickly departed, leaving Webber broke and homeless on Cayman.

He stayed there for the summer, camped in a tent next to a beach, and lived hand to mouth doing maintenance work for a hotel. Reprieve came in August when his old mentor Art McKee showed up with a boatload of gung-ho diver/investors all ready to search for the *Genovese*. Webber jumped at McKee's invitation to join the effort but as events came to pass, McKee's well-intentioned hunt on Banner's Reef got sidetracked: "Art had a deal set up to salvage some cannons for the Reef Club Hotel in Jamaica. It was worth pursuing, but in the meantime there was dissension in the ranks—guys were leaving left and right, stealing equipment and fencing it, anything. I stayed by Art's side and said, 'Look, I'm not leaving. You need me and as long as we're going back to Banner's Reef, fine, I'll stay.'"

Expedition Cannon found and raised five cannons for the Reef Club yet never looked for the *Genovese*. But before returning home, Webber was approached by one of the investors on the trip. George McDonald, a tall, lanky twenty-two-year-old, was much impressed with Webber's credentials and ideas for a well-equipped professional treasure hunting entity. He was seriously considering launching such an enterprise, he told Webber, adding that funding would be no problem because he'd recently been left quite a bit of money. Webber returned to Pennsylvania thoroughly fired up.

"I was really excited about this, especially when I learned George was telling the truth. The marine oceanographic firm that sold us an ex-minesweeper ran a credit check on McDonald and learned he was worth about forty-five million."

By the end of 1963 Webber was on a salary of $100 a week, plus expenses (and a good percentage) and was operations director of a newly founded company, M.A.R.C. Ltd. (Marine Archeological Research Corporation), based in Jamaica. Next he supervised the extensive outfitting of the ex-minesweeper, an elegant 136-foot craft rechristened the *Revenge*. "When the *Revenge* was outfitted it was second to none. I installed new generators, $13,000 worth of compressed air systems, an eight-ton hydraulic crane on roller tracks, a recompression chamber, the latest hydraulic tools, even a two-man submersible submarine. Not even Cousteau's *Calypso* had such fine equipment."

The whole setup seemed almost too good to be true. As Webber later realized, it was:

"As beautifully equipped as the *Revenge* was, she was really just a shell. We had no hard research to back up our target wrecks and we had no electronic detection gear to support our survey work. Here I was twenty-one and George was twenty-two and we were going to sail the Caribbean and we'd read John Potter's *Treasure Diver's Guide* and it would all become reality. That was the concept."

Other problems began to surface: The crewmen of the *Revenge* (who were given only shore leave money and a percentage, but no weekly salary) resented McDonald and considered him less than competent. Webber himself had run-ins with his employer: "He had ideas I didn't like. For example, he'd want to place davits way up high on the overhead to launch the boats and I'd say, 'Look, George, this is my profession, you don't know anything about this.' And he'd say, 'Well I'm spending the money and we'll do it my way.'"

By the time the *Revenge* left for Jamaica and Banner's Reef in the summer of 1964, Webber's relationship with McDonald had deteriorated. But at long last he was back working the same wreck on which he'd dived in 1961. After three days and the help of blasting to break open more ballast rocks and potential treasure (none turned up), Webber concluded the wreck was not the *Genovese* and abandoned the site. For the next few weeks the *Revenge* conducted a visual search using divers towed behind underwater sleds. Webber found several seventeenth- and eighteenth-century wrecks of limited potential along with hundreds of large sharks who followed at an uncomfortably close distance whenever he was being towed under water. But still no treasure. Several weeks into the expedition, the *Revenge*'s gyro compass and radar went haywire, following which Webber elected to return to Miami for repairs.

On the way back the *Revenge* hit the cliffs of Cuba's Cabo Corrientes head on, without ever touching bottom, springing the deck planks as far back as ninety feet. Amazingly, the vessel remained intact and, after backing off, managed to escape without being intercepted by Cuban patrol boats. She limped back to Miami where a subsequent Coast Guard inquiry traced the cause of the accident to the ship's magnetic compass which had never been adjusted to compensate for the localized magnetic deviation of the *Revenge*'s hull.

The Search for the Atocha

Wrecked along with the *Revenge* was Webber's friendship with McDonald. Calling it quits, he returned to Pennsylvania, having failed to find treasure for the seventh time in as many attempts. Frustrated, defeated, and out of money, he once again was back in the parts department of his father's dealership, looking at catalogs and numbers—and assessing with cold hard logic the mistakes made and lessons learned:

"I realized there are important elements to a successful treasure hunt that have less to do with the treasure itself than the character of the search. You have to have good leadership and people who are socially compatible, who respect each other and are loyal to the cause. And you have to pay the people who work for you, pay them a decent wage, not string them along on a percentage and free bunk and board. And lastly, you can have the most modern tools in the world but unless you research your target wreck and learn all you can, you can spend years running around looking at nothing more than a lot of underwater scenery."

Webber dropped out of treasure hunting for a year but he never lost sight of his dream. Sharing that dream, and ready to endure the hardships its pursuit would surely entail, was his high school sweetheart Sandy Belleman, and in early 1964 the couple married. Though it may have seemed an ill-advised move for a man whose eyes would ever turn to the aquamarine waters of the Caribbean, marriage provided Webber a foundation of stability and responsibility that contributed to his developing professionalism. In the years to follow, Webber always sent his paychecks home, even when doing so often left him with little more than pocket money.

To escape the humdrum routine of his job, Webber turned for excitement to amateur mountain climbing, caving, and weekend drag racing on the local circuit, driving a factory-class stock Pontiac sponsored by his father's agency. He was also the proud father of a son named Burt III. Elsewhere he plunged into a serious study of the Spanish fleets. The more he read the more convinced he became that the answers he sought could be found only by going to the Archives of the Indies in Seville. Somehow he must find a way to get there.

A way was found in the person of Martin Hall, a solvent New Yorker, an executive of a New York bank and himself a weekend circuit race-car driver. A graduate of Harvard business school, Hall was a realist about the risks of treasure hunting, yet when a mutual friend told him of Webber's activities he was fascinated. His interest led to a series of meetings with Webber in 1965, during which the young explorer argued that with proper research in Spain he could find the locations of the wrecks of the galleons *Santa Margarita* and *Nuestra Señora de Atocha*, the latter of which had been the target of the ill-fated

Operation Alligator Reef with Captain Leo Barker. After weeks of deliberation, Hall phoned Webber one evening and said, "All right, Burt, let's start it."

Once more Burt Webber was back in business, but this time he headed not to Miami to look for a boat, but to Seville to look for pieces of paper. For a twenty-three-year-old American with no academic credentials and who spoke not a word of Spanish to attempt to gain access to the highly restricted documents of the archives would seem the height of presumption, let alone for motives less than scholarly. But Burt Webber was no ordinary petitioner and as he stood on the steps outside the ancient sixteenth-century building built in the style of a Renaissance palace, the determination within him grew:

"Looking up at that building and knowing that it housed all the secrets of the wrecks throughout the New World inspired me tremendously. And I felt the letters of introduction I carried with me would help me during my meeting with the archives' director, Dr. José de la Peña, who I was told could speak English well. He was very cordial and after we'd talked a few moments in his office he said, 'Señor Webber, one does not just walk into the archives. Those who have access are important senior scholars or students working on their theses. In past years we have had Americans come here to research shipwrecks but they have been turned away. And here you have come all the way from America. You are very bold and have shown much nerve in doing so, especially since you speak no Spanish.'"

At these words Webber's heart sank. The director went on to say that there were not even available in the archives translators who could be contracted for a fee. He paused several seconds, glancing once again at the letters of introduction that lay before him, then returned his gaze to his petitioner. There must have been something about Webber, a combination of drive and sincerity that one could feel in his voice, perhaps see in his eyes, for at the brink of turning Webber away Dr. de la Peña appeared to change his mind. There was one possible way, the director continued. If Webber were able to engage a qualified bilingual researcher who could decipher the archaic seventeenth-century handwriting, the director would allow Webber access. He suggested the American look for an assistant at the university in Seville and, as a generous afterthought, added he would write a letter of recommendation to aid in his search.

Wasting no time, Webber went to the university and within two days found a female graduate student who spoke fluent English. With family consent she began working for him compiling index cards, notes, and outlines. Days later he hired a second woman, an anthropology major trained in calligraphy and manuscript research. At last receiving Dr. de la Peña's blessing, Webber and his two assistants were admitted to the *sanctum sanctorum* of the archives—a long, narrow room with arched ceilings, marble floors, and rows of sturdy oak tables with straight-backed chairs. The high ceiling lights baely provided adequate illumination to decipher the documents, many of which were riddled with holes made by tiny *pollila* worms during the previous three and a half centuries, but researcher Webber plunged into the paper sea with the same enthusiasm with which he had entered the clear waters of Banner's Reef to explore his first wreck in 1961.

For more than two months the team worked steadily in the scholar's room, laboriously reading every scrap of paper relating to the ill-fated *Atocha* and the fleet that wrecked off the Florida Keys in 1622. Providing them with the bulky *legajos* was Señora Angeles Flores Rodriguez, a staff researcher who had already assisted Robert Marx and who would later work closely with Mel Fisher and historian Eugene Lyon as they, too, pursued the famed galleon. The Spanish had made eighteen futile attempts to locate the *Atocha* during a sixty-six-year period before finally abandoning the search, but Webber knew that if he could determine even an approximate location of the ship when she sank, he could then explore the area with a search tool which the Spanish did not have—a boat-towed magnetometer which can detect the presence of ferromagnetic metals such as ships' fittings and anchors.

Before he was finished, Webber had photocopied and catalogued more than 2,000 documents pertaining to ship construction, cargo manifests, armaments, survivors' testimony, and salvage reports. The most promising leads were provided by the account written by one Francisco Nuñez Melian who had led a lavishly equipped 1626 expedition to find and salvage the *Atocha* and other ships of the 1622 disaster. Melian found and partially salvaged the *Santa Margarita* which sank in sight of the *Atocha*. In his report to the Crown, Melian mentioned that the *Margarita* lay several miles west of *la ultima caya de matecumbes* (the last key of the Matecumbes). Checking Spanish navigation charts from the mid-eighteenth century, Webber noted that the two keys known as the Upper and Lower Matecumbes corresponded nicely with Melian's description. A search area along a ten-fathom line west of what is today Lower Matecumbe Key looked promising.

Returning to Florida in January 1966 with a trunkload of photocopied documents, Webber reported his findings to Hall who in turn cut loose with the first portion of what would eventually amount to a

$250,000 outlay to search for the elusive *Atocha*. A corporation was formed, Marine Archeological Enterprises, Inc., and a fine sixty-five-foot trawler was purchased and rechristened the *Melian,* in honor of Webber's ancient predecessor. While arrangements were made with the State of Florida to obtain an exploration lease for the target area, Webber contacted Varian Associates, a Palo Alto, California-based company that had just developed a highly sophisticated proton magnetometer. Webber, who knew nothing about magnetometry and geomagnetic survey work, leased a unit from Varian and spent days and nights studying the accompanying instruction manual. Neither he nor anyone else realized at the time that ten years later Varian engineers and other industry experts would acknowledge Webber as a world authority on applied search instrumentation. What Webber did know in 1966 was that the magnetometer was an essential tool of the modern treasure hunter and he had to learn fast.

Developed during World War II to detect submarines, magnetometers are sensitive instruments which register changes (or gradients) in the earth's magnetic field caused by iron or other ferrous material. A ship's hull or an iron cannon, for example, has its own small magnetic field which creates a tiny deviation in the earth's larger field. If the sensor head of a magnetometer is brought within range of those objects, their presence will register as an anomaly which is indicated by a needle on a continuous graph, a high-pitched sound on earphones, or by a change in the digital read-out of a console showing the earth's gravitational field in gammas. What makes the magnetometer so immensely useful for contemporary treasure hunting is its capacity for detecting objects the size of a hull nail buried beneath feet of coral, sand, and rock. The best magnetometers (mags, as they were quickly dubbed by treasure hunters) can detect an anchor or similar iron object buried under sand or coral to a distance of fifty feet.

With an exploration lease in hand, Webber began a slow methodical survey of an area off the Lower Matecumbe Key, towing the Varian mag sensor behind the *Melian* and carefully watching the console graph needle for any swing that would indicate a "hit" from a ferrous object. Whenever a hit registered, the spot was buoyed and a diver later sent down to identify the source of the anomaly. Time and again the hits turned out to be abandoned lobster traps, scrap metal, lost fittings, a whole panoply of ferrous flotsam and jetsam that had accumulated over the centuries—but no hint of the *Atocha.*

Because boat-towed "magging" required fairly calm seas, the weather pattern in the Florida Keys generally limited Webber's survey periods to the five months between May and September. But nature could still play havoc, as when hurricane Alma caught the *Melian* by surprise, driving it through heavy seas and ninety-m.p.h. winds for a harrowing twenty-eight hours before Coast Guard helicopters were able to lower portable pumps aboard to assist pumping out the vessel's flooded bilges. Though the vessel was badly damaged by the hurricane, benefactor Martin Hall had her repaired at great expense and encouraged Webber to continue searching during the 1967 season.

These long months of survey work off the upper Keys were grueling, frustrating, and time consuming, a tough test of the patience of any seeker, let alone a man of Webber's hyperactive and intense character. But the period was also an immensely important phase in the making of a treasure hunter. Webber became thoroughly practiced in the use of longitudinal transit buoy survey systems, radar transponder buoys for pinpoint triangulation in open water, and seismic sub-bottom profiling equipment (which can bounce sound waves off the hardpan rock bed beneath the layers of coral and sand, revealing evidence of ballast mounds not otherwise detectable). In an effort to calculate the depth of sand and mud that might have accumulated over a shipwreck during several centuries, Webber used special core-sampling devices and consulted with geologists to interpret the resulting data.

When analysis of core samples and calculated rates of sand build-up suggested the *Atocha*'s wreckage may be ten to twelve feet or more beneath sand and mud, Webber turned his attention to developing a way to monitor and control the depth of the mag's sensor at the optimum distance from the bottom. A solution to this problem was imperative because if the sensor were too high off the bottom it could very likely pass right over the wreck without detecting it. After months of experimentation, Webber developed a sensor housing that included room for a small transducer unit that continuously bounced an electronic pulse off the bottom, and provided a constant depth read-out on a recorder aboard the towing vessel. If, for example, the recorder showed the sensor was too high off the bottom, the helmsman simply slowed the boat's speed slightly to lower the unit to the desired depth.

Hardly had he achieved a means for precision depth control when Webber tackled another vexing problem, this being the difficulty of placing marker buoys on or near the location of an anomaly, particularly when the sensor head was at the end of 200–300 feet of cable behind the towing vessel. At the time the most common way of buoying an anomaly was to make one or more additional passes over a registered hit, each time tossing overboard a lobster pot buoy (usually a white

foam ball tied to a cinderblock brick). However, because the buoy
marked only the position of the towing vessel when the hit was
registered, the actual location of the anomaly had to be determined by
calculating the distance and bearing of the sensor head at the moment
the buoy was dropped, after which a diver with a compass was required
to swim the computed distance back along the bearing line. On
reaching the spot he would either find the object visually or (as was
more likely) survey the area with a hand-held underwater metal
detector to pinpoint his target beneath the sand. Clearly, the entire
procedure to find readings was primitive, imprecise, and above all
enormously time consuming. Indeed, it was not unusual to spend the
better part of a working day tracking down and identifying a single
reading. The Florida treasure hunting community appeared resigned to
the system's shortcomings—but not Webber. Once more he plunged
into the world of technology in search of a solution.

He found it by inventing an ingenious gadget called a survey-buoy
electronic release system. The device consisted of a fiberglass housing
in which was recessed a lead slug attached to a line and a buoy. This
unit was trailed on the surface directly over the underwater magnetometer sensor head. The buoy could be released by a solenoid trip
system activated from the towing boat. Thus, when the needle of the
magnetometer console moved, indicating a hit, the operator simply
pushed a release button and, bingo, a buoy was released, pinpointing
the location to within five to ten feet of the anomaly.

The system worked beautifully and saved Webber and his team
many hundreds of hours search time. Among those most impressed
were the engineers at Varian Associates. But when asked if there was
interest in marketing the device as an accessory for deep-water survey
work, Varian advised Webber that he was already so far ahead of
anybody else in his business that potential customers wouldn't be
interested, let alone understand its application.

Varian's response may have seemed odd, but in fact the number of
clients who leased or purchased the company's instruments to look for
sunken ships could be counted on one hand. Moreover, Webber was
hardly inclined to advertise his innovations to other treasure hunters,
particularly since one of his most experienced and successful rivals, Mel
Fisher, was also looking for the *Atocha* off the Upper and Lower
Matecumbe Keys. Like Webber, Fisher had turned to the archives in
Seville, working with Florida historian and friend Eugene Lyon who
regularly visited Seville, supplying him with evidence which continued
to point to the Matecumbe Keys as the *Atocha*'s burial place. Fisher,

too, was spending weeks and months on end magging first one area, then another, and occasionally suspending operations while he scurried about to raise money to continue.

In June 1967, after eighteen long months, Martin Hall called a halt to the hunt until such time as he had additional funds to underwrite a continued search. Once again Burt Webber, Jr., was defeated and once again he returned home to Pennsylvania. In September, Sandy gave birth to the couple's second child, Eric, while her husband became service manager for his father's Buick and Pontiac agency. For the next two years Burt would work and wait, continuing to sift through a small mountain of *Atocha* documents and making regular trips to the map division of the Library of Congress to compile charts and descriptions of the Florida Keys.

Finally, in the late spring of 1969, Martin Hall called with long-awaited good news: funding was once again available to restart the search. Webber packed his bags for Florida, eager to return to the hunt. Here on the eve of the seventies, he vowed once again that only fate would prevent him from discovering at last the grave of the *Atocha*.

5

Into the Seventies–
the December Group

The Agony and the Atocha

When Burt Webber packed his bags for the Florida Keys in the summer of 1969, Sandy was about to give birth to their third child, Kurt. Her husband would return to Pennsylvania to be at her side for the event, but days later, after making sure all was well, the twenty-six year-old explorer would once more be headed for the Matecumbes, knowing that while he searched for silver off the Keys his reputation in the eyes of some of his neighbors back home was less than sterling:

"By now everyone in the community was convinced I was an irresponsible husband, always galavanting around the Caribbean and coming home with nothing to show for it. Sandy had to bear the brunt of it: 'There goes Webber off on another wild goose chase.' 'Webber's a nut.' 'Webber never grew up.' Well, I never *have* grown up in a sense. I'm still sixteen if you mean I still dream of great discoveries. But despite community feelings, Sandy took it all in stride—my trips, the insecurity, the financial ups and downs—because she believed in me. When I asked her about the situation she said, 'Look, you're first. I knew what you were when you came into my life. You pursue your dream, keep trying, and some day you'll make it.' Not many women tell their men that, particularly in these times, and that's a great credit to a great and wonderful woman."

As Webber pursued his dream in Florida his professional reputation in those warm waters likewise began to spread. The treasure hunting community, composed of highly competitive, secretive, and usually egocentric seekers, is slow to welcome newcomers to its ranks. But Webber made a strong impression on the most jaded veterans. Whether the subject was Jamaican pirate hideouts, hard-hat diving, *legajo* research, or high tech geophysical instrumentation, Webber was thoroughly conversant, articulate, and often dazzling. His information was firsthand and up to date, his delivery was crisp, forceful, and intense. Moreover he didn't try to hide his professional failures. True, he had yet to find anything but he had paid his dues. As one Key West treasure hunter observed: "Burt's all right—he's methodical, scientific, honest—and he's never killed anybody."

Looking back, Webber's apprenticeship had taken an unusual course. Having started on an artifact-laden shipwreck on Banner's Reef, Webber had gradually moved away from hands-on contact with treasure itself to master each step that he knew must be taken to find future prizes: from on-site diving to vessel outfitting, then to fund raising, library and archive research, and finally the intricacies of electronic survey techniques. He had moved away from treasure to get closer to it. In the process he had outdistanced an entire generation of old-time treasure hunters who remained ignorant or disdainful of the enormous advantage of electronics and primary-source research. Webber had cultivated a systems approach that he found as romantic in its own way as it was professional. As important, he believed in its effectiveness.

So did Mel Fisher, the king of the Florida treasure hunters who had helped Kip Wagner crack the secrets of the 1715 treasure galleons and who himself had devoted several years of seasonal searching for the *Atocha*. Fisher, then in his early fifties, knew that if anybody had a shot at finding the galleon, it was young Webber. The two men seldom saw each other face to face, but while one surveyed a sector off the Matecumbe Keys, the other was often just over the horizon scanning another. Both men were obsessed with finding the galleon and both maintained continued contact with the Seville archives (Webber with staff researcher Rodriguez, Fisher with historian Gene Lyon). So intense was Webber's pursuit that he thoroughly explored the same areas Fisher had surveyed on the assumption that his rival could easily have missed the *Atocha* because of lack of precision depth control of his mag sensor.

Then in the spring of 1970 Webber was surprised to learn that Fisher had shifted his operation to Key West and was searching an area some forty miles to the west, not far from the Marquesas Keys. The new locale seemed absurd since all evidence pointed to a site near the Matecumbes, and Webber continued magging well into November before poor weather and a depleted budget forced a suspension. Finally, in June 1971, a jubilant Mel Fisher announced that he had found a giant galleon anchor and an eight-foot-long gold chain—and that future discoveries would prove that both belonged to the *Atocha*. Like others in the treasure hunting fraternity Webber refused to accept the conclusion. But as the months passed and Fisher's divers unearthed silver coins, gold finger bars and artifacts, it was clear that the wrecksite was certainly yielding treasure whether or not it was the *Atocha*. In September a resolute Webber resumed his meticulous magging off the Matecumbe Keys, taking time off to rejoin Sandy as she gave birth to daughter Gretchen.

Webber's third survey assault on the *Atocha* lasted nine months, ending in May 1972, by which time Mel Fisher had amassed treasure and artifacts that now strongly suggested he had indeed found either the *Atocha* or the *Santa Margarita*. For Webber and his backer Martin Hall this was no longer a laughing matter.

Why had Fisher shifted his sights a hundred miles westward? Two reasons, it appears. Historian Gene Lyon, after much cross checking, had determined that the Spaniards of the early seventeenth century had called *all* the Florida Keys the Matecumbes (in recognition of the Indian tribe of the same name), and that consequently the *Atocha* must have sunk west of Key West, that being the last key referred to in salvage reports. Second, Lyon found a textual reference to Spanish salvage camps on the Cayo del Marques (today the Marquesas atoll thirty miles west of Key West), this being the closest point of land to the wreck of the *Santa Margarita*. Webber later learned that this latter reference had been found in the very same *legajo* which he had asked researcher Rodriguez to peruse during his visit to the archives more than a year before Lyon:

"That reference to the Marquesas was absolutely the key—and she should have spotted it. But she may have missed the document because she felt she knew all the references and didn't want to bother going through all the documents again in detail. Or she may have been bored. To this day I don't know how or why she missed it."

Of all the defeats that Burt Webber had sustained in eleven years of treasure hunting, his failure to find the *Nuestra Señora de Atocha* hit him the hardest. Over a span of seven years he had spent four months in Spain researching the 1622 fleet disaster and a total of forty-two months in the field looking for the *Atocha*. Webber was as heartbroken as if a rival suitor had stolen his betrothed on the eve of their wedding. Granted, Mel Fisher had expended an equally stupendous effort and deserved great credit for the find, but Webber was devastated:

"I really was. I had lost. All those years. I had lost Hall's money, his faith. He was a very dedicated, sincere, decent guy and we went through this a long time together. The day we finished magging that last least segment I almost had tears in my eyes. It was all wrapped up now. You could pack all the charts and graphs up in ribbons. Every sector had been precisely gridded, every square foot had been surveyed and marked on an analog recorder. There were miles of tapes with coded numbers, definitions, terms, anomalies, all correlated with daily reports. You could go back there today and use that data to pinpoint any reading in a one-hundred-square-mile area to within plus or minus ten feet. We had developed a beautiful system and I felt that for myself and as a team, if anybody deserved anything for the methodical methods and application of high technology, we certainly did. We deserved it but we didn't find anything.

"What was hardest about this was that, although I knew I was far ahead of everybody else, I felt I was the one who was laughed at most. People would say, 'Webber has good methods but he never finds anything.' Or 'Webber raises money but he never finds anything.' But Webber was learning."

The Finding of the Maravillas

Hardly had Webber returned to dockside from the last day's magging when he was greeted by Art McKee, his eyes glittering with excitement, and carrying news of a fantastic treasure. His old mentor's enthusiasm, as eternal as it was contagious, was a needed tonic for Webber. McKee said he'd been approached by an old sponge diver who had spotted a ballast pile on top of which were stacked hundreds of silver bars somewhere along the gulf coast near Georgia. The diver had offered to show McKee the location in return for a percentage but time was running out because a group from Ft. Pierce was also on the trail. Webber agreed to charter his survey gear for a fee and a few days later he and his team arrived off the Cedar Keys, not far from the Florida-Georgia border.

The three-week caper turned out to be a typical treasure hunt: "Our sponge diver friend told us he'd seen the wreck thirty-six years ago while diving with his father. The compass coordinates he provided yielded a search area of twelve to fourteen square miles, not the quarter-mile radius Art was led to believe. We spent days searching but all we found was an anchor allegedly lost by one of General George Meade's Civil War gunboats. I doubt if the guy had ever seen the wreck himself. He probably had read about it in a book as a kid and had always believed the story."

As he had done off the Matecumbe Keys, Webber employed in the Cedar Keys area the most advanced mag yet, a Varian V-85, for which he had designed an elegant slip-tube housing shaped like a V-2 rocket with a built-in transducer (for depth monitoring) and low center-of-gravity ballast chamber. The package produced better readings and could be towed deeper with less cable, a feature which allowed for better tracking. The system's capability, as well as that of its developer, was of special interest to Webber's friend Jack Haskins, an Irishman in his mid-forties who lived aboard a boat in the same marina where Webber had docked the *Melian* between survey trips.

A former technical writer and professional pilot who flew mostly corporate executive planes (and taught instrument flying on the side), Haskins had become interested in scuba diving and treasure hunting in the early sixties, so much so that he moved to the Florida Keys. While he supported himself with the help of some land investments and playing the stock market, Haskins learned about dealing in coins and artifacts, became intrigued with the search for the *Atocha* and other galleons, and finally decided to pay a visit to the archives in Seville. Like Webber two years earlier, Haskins understood not a word of Spanish but with the help of a naval attaché at the American embassy he managed to gain access to the archives. To assist him he hired Angeles Flores Rodriguez who by now was the principal staff contact for American treasure hunters. Haskins returned to Florida with rolls of microfilmed documents, had them printed on continuous-strip Xerox paper, and purchased several Spanish dictionaries. Many nights for the next several months Haskins pored over the documents, laboriously translating everything word for word, often using a magnifying glass to puzzle over the florid scrawl of the seventeenth-century scribes. Gradually, he became familiar with certain phrases and words peculiar to his subject and with the manner in which the documents were organized. He filled notebooks with archaic nautical terms and definitions, studied syntax and grammar, and slowly learned to decipher the often convoluted Spanish bureaucratic writing style.

By the late sixties Haskins had taught himself to read the documents in their original. He had also done some searching for the *Atocha* himself but when Webber offered to finance several trips to Seville to verify the documents that historian Gene Lyon had provided Mel Fisher, Haskins agreed to assist. He regarded his lengthy self-education as a labor of love but it would turn out to be possibly the most valuable investment in his life. In fact by 1972 he had already discovered information that revealed precisely where the treasure galleon *Nuestra Señora de las Maravillas* had wrecked in the Bahamas in 1656. Armed with that information Haskins decided to approach Webber.

"I took one look at the documentation," Webber recalls, "and I knew right away it was good enough to raise backing if it were properly presented. And we certainly had the right mag set-up. I believe Jack had already tried to put an organization together on his own but hadn't had much luck. So I agreed to help raise the money. Since we'd only need about twenty thousand dollars to get over there and make a survey, Art McKee said he could find help."

The story of the *Maravillas* was a classic disaster. Mortally crippled by a collision with another galleon in the Florida Strait she was blown on to the lethal reefs of the Bahamas where all but forty-five of 650 passengers and crew perished. One of the survivors, a priest, wrote later that during the perilous hours while the ship drifted, some of his fellow clergymen were charging as much as 200 pesos to hear last confessions. Once the ship hit the reef and the priests were obliged to jump overboard, their pockets were so laden with gold and silver that they promptly disappeared from sight. Spanish salvors later retrieved a fair portion of her cargo of 4 million pesos but silver and emeralds easily worth several million dollars remained to be found. Haskins' research placed the *Maravillas* close to the Matanilla Shoal, the name of which was quite likely a bastardization of the galleon's name. The historian was also convinced that the *Maravillas* was the very ship that had been worked in 1682 by none other than the illustrious William Phips.

While Art McKee was fund raising, Burt Webber received a dinner invitation one Sunday from rival treasure hunter Robert Marx, a colorful adventurer in his late thirties and a pioneer in marine archeology who had written more than a dozen books on shipwrecks and treasure hunting. With Marx was his associate Willard Bascomb. Webber sensed the pair was after something:

"Bob and I had always gotten along well despite a few past run-ins. I knew he was organizing an expedition and now here was Bascomb, who was a wealthy industrialist/oceanographer backing Marx, asking me all through dinner about magnetic systems and survey work. He even wanted to contract me to do some magging for them but wouldn't say where. Marx did not appear at all enthusiastic about involving me but obviously he thought he was on to something big."

Webber heard nothing more from Bascomb after that meeting but in the meantime he and Haskins blocked out two tight survey areas off the Matanilla Shoal while lawyer Kenneth Beall flew over to the Bahamas to line up search and salvage leases. When there appeared to be no legal obstacles Webber and Haskins' group outfitted an air-sea rescue craft in Palm Beach, Florida, then shot across to Freeport on Grand Bahama Island to await the formal go-ahead.

Webber's team waited—and waited, and still no permission was received. Finally, Webber visited the secretary of transportation, whose office was in charge of issuing contracts. In a flash Webber guessed the problem:

"I could smell Marx all the way. The official kept asking suspicious questions like, 'How well do you know Marx? Isn't he quite a professional?' and 'He writes books, doesn't he? You don't write books, do you, Mr. Webber?' I replied I had been too busy seeking treasure to take time out to write about it."

Webber returned to his boat and headed straight for Matanilla Shoal forty-three miles to the north. On arrival there was Marx's salvage boat on the very site Haskins had selected as a prime target, busily taking up treasure. The irony of the situation was mind boggling: By extraordinary coincidence, more than 300 years after the vessel sank, Bob Marx had found the *Maravillas* the very morning Webber had sailed from Freeport. Which of the two protagonists was the more surprised on that balmy September morning in 1972 is a matter of conjecture, but for Burt Webber, to have come so excruciatingly close to his first major treasure find only to be foiled by coincidence and possible bureaucratic hanky panky would seem a cruel jest of a merciless god.

With the failure of the *Maravillas* expedition and the subsequent demise of Martin Hall's Continental Exploration, Webber had no choice but to find some way other than treasure hunting to support his growing family. Returning to Pennsylvania (the Webbers now lived in Annville, not far from Harrisburg), he hired on at a brick plant and took on the toughest job on the premises—loading onto carriage racks heavy industrial bricks just out of a 400-degree furnace. The work was hot and dangerous but it paid enough to support a family of six. Webber also began working weekends as a salesman for the World Book Encyclopedia. Not surprisingly, he was terrifically effective and was soon invited to work full time. It was a tough decision:

"I believed in the product and the company and I was doing very well, but I hated the job, really. I didn't like dealing with people that way, selling them on that level. But I agreed to go full time because I needed to fill in with a steady job until my dreams came true again."

Then in the fall of 1974 Webber was told an intriguing story about Mel Fisher's activities off the Marquesas. Fisher had found a goodly amount of treasure from the *Atocha* but so far it was mostly passenger contraband that had probably fallen from the ship's stern section which apparently had broken off and drifted some distance away. The main cargo and ballast mound had not yet been found. According to a former crew member who had been with Fisher when the first evidence of the *Atocha* was discovered, mag readings which could well have indicated the *Atocha*'s main ballast mound had been ruled out as being an unrelated anomaly. He believed as a consequence Fisher was actually picking up only perimeter scatterings while the mother lode section lay several thousand yards eastward in an area which just happened to be outside the boundary line of Fisher's salvage site.

There were other details that added to the story's plausibility and by the beginning of October, Webber had convinced Martin Hall to lease the area directly adjacent to Fisher's dig on the off chance that Webber's superior magnetometry gear (he would be using a Varian proton mag with a slip-tube housing) would sniff out the jackpot deep beneath the sand. Webber quickly pulled together a crew and went to Key West to get rolling. When he walked into the Raw Bar, a popular seafood restaurant, and was spotted by Mel Fisher and his wife Deo, the couple's faces appeared to turn white. Webber could almost hear them groan, "Oh no, he's back again. What's he doing here?"

For the next two months Mel Fisher and the crews aboard his two dive boats worked each day knowing that out there on the horizon to the east Burt Webber's survey boat could find the *Atocha*'s main cargo section at any minute. One day during a lunch break Webber invited aboard Bleth McCaley, Fisher's savvy press representative and general factotum. A veteran of many dives and survey runs, McCaley was amazed at the sophistication of Webber's equipment, his use of radar transponder buoys for tracking, and the meticulously tidy organization of his boat. "My God, Burt," McCaley said. "What you've got here is just fabulous. It's way ahead of anything Mel's got, but there's only one difference—Mel's lucky and you aren't."

She was right, of course. And Webber understood the role that luck played in the machinations of every treasure hunt. Certainly if anyone in his profession was about due for his share, Webber was. But fortune seemed to have lost Webber's bingo card when, after eight weeks of magging the E-50A lease area, not a trace of the galleon had turned up. Webber's last-ditch stand for the Big A had failed.

"Burt, have you ever considered the Concepción?"

Though 1975 began with no prospects on the treasure hunting horizon, Webber was at least able to derive his income from related activities, notably a marketing and consulting agreement with Varian Associates (now based in Canada) by which the company would sell his slip-tube magnetometer housings, his depth-monitoring system, and his survey-buoy electronic release system. Elsewhere, he continued to stay in touch with historian Jack Haskins whose annual pilgrimage to the archives in Seville were now regularly producing new and tantalizing data on the locations of treasure galleons. One chilly day that fall Haskins called Webber with a suggestion that was destined to have momentous consequences. Webber remembers the conversation well:

"Jack said, 'Burt, have you ever considered the *Concepción* on Silver Shoals?' I replied that like everyone else I'd certainly read about it. Many of the treasure books I'd read as a teenager told the story of the Phips galleon. And I knew that everybody had looked for it and failed, that Phips and others after him had cleaned out the wreck. In fact as I rattled on to Jack about these things, I actually felt a little insulted that he would even mention such a speculative target to me.

"But then Jack told me he felt the wreck was significant because he'd found documents telling of tons of treasure dumped on the reef that Phips never found. After talking about the rate of coral growth and the new search technology I'd developed that could be applied, Haskins added that everyone had thought the *Maravillas* had been cleaned out, too, until Bob Marx found her and allegedly raised two million dollars worth of treasure in ten days. Plus Haskins had found good locational data to supplement the surviving charts" (which everybody knew about).

"Well, I wasn't immediately fired up by the idea, because so many people who had searched the Silver Shoals—Mel Fisher and Ed Link, to name two—had failed to find the *Concepción*. That meant it had to be an extremely weak target, perhaps buried beneath several feet of

The Antigua-based M/V Samala, *chartered for Operation Phips II, moored a quarter mile from the Silver Shoals.*

Burt Webber, Jr., leader of the expedition, coordinated most activities of the four reef boats with frequent use of walkie-talkies.

Left to right: *Mate Frank West and the* Samala*'s captain and owner, Tony Garton.*

Each day's search began with a map conference to brief the dive team on the sectors to be surveyed.

The first clues: bits of pottery and ballast stone found visually.

An intact olive jar, the first significant find, is carefully lifted
from the reef boat aboard the Samala.

The awesome beauty of the Silver Shoals, one of the world's most unique coral formations. (Photo: John Berrier)

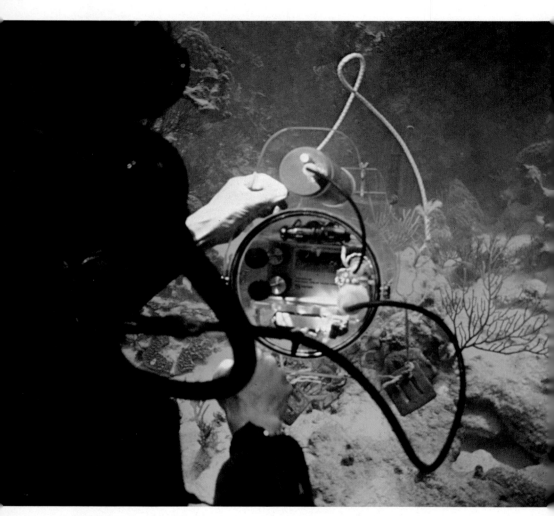

An over-the-shoulder view of the cesium magnetometer console. Note earphones connected to housing to provide an audio signal read-out. (Photo: Stan Waterman)

Webber conducts electronic survey with the mag at sixty feet, achieving for the first time total control of sensor depth. Lead weights tied to housing are to compensate for slight positive buoyancy of the unit. (Photo: Stan Waterman)

Webber, assisted by Dominican Navy Lt. J.G. Diaz, swaps several components of the two mags to isolate electronic outages during one of several tense episodes in which malfunctions threatened to delay the surveying of crucial sectors.

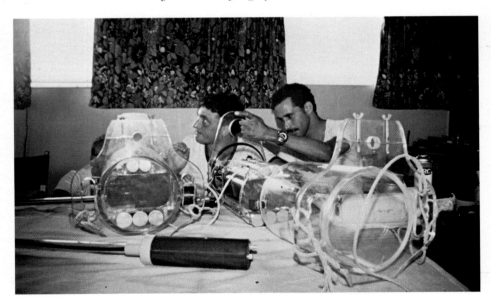

While the sensor head of the cesium, nicknamed Big Foot,
registered the surrounding force field eleven times a second,
Webber probed every head and canyon methodically.
(Photo: Stan Waterman)

The exact instant that diver Jim Nace handed Webber the first coin from the Concepción, *marking the triumphant end to a search that had lasted nearly three centuries. As the flurry of air bubbles indicates, the adrenaline had started pumping.*

Webber (holding Ming dynasty cup) and dive master Bob Coffey moments after confirming the discovery of the Concepción. The burden of seventeen years of struggle has already begun to slide from Webber's shoulders.

Diver Jim Nace with a handful of encrusted coins and a silver incense burner, the first of a trickle of treasure that would soon turn into a torrent.

The dive team on the day of victory. Left to right, *clockwise:*
Bob Coffey, Billy Fothergill, Don Summers, Duke Long (with
hat), Jim Nace, Burt Webber, and Carter Leary.

Dive master Bob Coffey uses an Aquapulse metal detector with special probe to check for evidence of silver and gold in coral outcroppings of the B9-#1 sector. (Photo: Stan Waterman)

Using an Aquapulse, historian Jack Haskins surveys one of several deep sand pockets adjacent to the main wrecksite of the Concepción.

Webber, flanked by Dominican Navy Colonel Montes-Arrache (on his right) *and Lt. J.G. Diaz, admires the two gold chains recovered from the main wrecksite.* (Photo: Stan Waterman)

The main ballast pile of the Concepción, *discovered by Jack Haskins and Duke Long. These, together with scattered pottery shards and some iron fittings, were all that remained visible of the famed galleon.*

Henry Taylor aboard Samala *with an inventory board of cleaned and polished pieces of eight in uncirculated mint condition.*

Silver plates, jars, an astrolabe, chests of coins still fused together, Ming dynasty china, porcelain, and in the background bags of silver coins—just part of the immense treasure yield of the Concepción. *(Photo: Stan Waterman)*

Members of Operation Phips II aboard the Samala *just prior to departing Miami in November 1978.* Left to right: *John Grissim, Duke Long, Jim Nace, Don Summers, Frank West, Henry Taylor, Billy Fothergill, Bob Coffey, Carter Leary, Tony Garton, Jimmy Blackburn, Kevin Lawson, Burt Webber, Jr., and Chunky Cardwell.* (Photo: Judi Mackesy)

hard coral. But then I thought about the challenge. I remember thinking, 'Burt, there are so many technological innovations you've come up with that if you were to combine them with thorough historical research and carefully controlled survey work, there is a good chance this ship can be found.' The more I studied the project, the more I became convinced it was in the 'good risk' category and would hold up under the scrutiny of potential investors. Most certainly the treasure yield would be substantial. Aside from these primary concerns, success in a venture of this nature would vindicate the worth of my systems and once and for all establish my credibility as a professional treasure hunter."

Considering the number of expeditions that had vainly sought the *Concepción* in the last half-century alone Webber could not have picked a tougher ship. In 1936 Waldo Logan and Colonel John Craig sailed from Puerto Plata aboard the sixty-two-foot schooner *Isabella*, hoping to use aerial photographs made from a plane supplied by Dominican Republic dictator Rafael Trujillo to pinpoint the *Concepción*. They failed but did take what are said to be the first 16 mm underwater movies. In the 1940's Alexander Korganoff, who helped develop the strobe light, searched the Silver Shoals but failed when his native crew (from the Dominican Republic) mutinied. He made a second attempt a short time later but found only a coral encrusted hull (not the *Concepción's*) and an old anchor. In 1955 Edward and Marion Link visited the Silver Shoals aboard the *Sea Diver* and with the help of some documentation provided by Korganoff, discovered a wreck that was later identified as a late eighteenth- or early nineteenth-century merchantman. Elsewhere during that same decade England's Sir Malcolm Campbell (who aboard his jetboat the *Bluebird* had set the world's speed record) launched a search for the *Concepción*. He failed, as did Dominican playboy Porfirio Rubirosa whose visit to the Silver Shoals was more fashionable than professional (Rubirosa later produced a handful of silver coins, claiming they were from the *Concepción*, although intimates later admitted they were merely a face-saving gesture).

In 1963 Mel Fisher arrived on Silver Shoals and discovered an iron cannon wreck he thought might be from the *Concepción*, but excavation of the site yielded artifacts from a later era. Fisher returned to the reef a second time several months later but this search, too, proved fruitless. Three years later Ted Falcon Barker made a bid to find the *Concepción* aboard the yacht *Charon* but after working the Link wrecksite and finding a second iron carronade wreck of a later vintage, abandoned the effort.

Finally, in 1968 Jacques Cousteau and crew arrived aboard the

Calypso, documentary cameras at the ready. After a brief visual search of a likely-looking portion of the shoals, divers found several iron cannons and remnants of a wreck that appeared to be of Spanish origin. With everyone suffering from gold fever, divers inspected the site and returned carrying mysterious evidence of a modern-day visit. As the cameras filmed this tense moment the crew clustered around Cousteau as he examined a diver's weight belt on which were printed the words "Mel's Aqua Shop." Though the find indicated the wreck was most surely not the *Concepción* and that the search should continue elsewhere, Cousteau spent the next two months excavating the Fisher wreck and featured the site as the questionable candidate for the *Concepción* in his documentary film *Sunken Treasure* (and spin-off book *Diving for Sunken Treasure*). Oddly, any mention of Fisher's weight belt or earlier visit was omitted from both accounts.

If there was one hopeful conclusion to be culled from this history of spectacular failures, Webber noted that in every instance the hunters appeared to have done scanty research and possessed little or no electronic search equipment. In contrast Webber now had access to the best electronics and research that was good enough to warrant a shot at the *Concepción.* The real problem facing him now was not the intrinsic viability of the project but how to find investors willing to back a not-yet-successful treasure hunter bent on finding a ship that inspired so many failed expeditions by famous people. Though his long-time friend and supporter Martin Hall was no longer investing in treasure hunts he offered to help Webber assemble a prospectus and recommended the venture to others.

By early 1976, with no takers in the offing, Webber was discouraged and losing heart. Nor was it easy providing for a household with four growing children. Sandy was working part time in the fine-jewelry department of a department store while his own earnings from Varian sales would not last much longer. To top matters off, a Chicago friend called to report a feature article in the papers there about a financier named Jerry Mandel who had raised a whopping $300,000 to finance an attempt to raise the Spanish galleon *San José* off Cartagena, Colombia. The expedition was to be led by Dennis Standefer, a thirty-one-year-old California treasure hunter who had worked a galleon wreck in the Florida Keys without substantial success but had been more involved in land and sea treasure-hunts in Central America. Curious to know more about the Cartagena project and how the fund raising was set up, Webber phoned Mandel. The call resulted in a fast lesson on how to dump tax shelter money and a request that Webber send Mandel a résumé and keep him posted on his own activities. For the next few months the two men stayed more or less in touch by letter and phone. Webber finished his draft of the Silver Shoals prospectus, then in the early summer flew to Houston, Texas, for the huge Offshore Technology Conference where Varian was to display several Webber-developed systems as part of the company's product line. It was while he was in Houston that Burt Webber's destiny began to change:

"Seeing my systems on display was a needed boost to my morale, especially since on the way down I had tried and failed to interest a potential investor in the *Concepción*. I also saw Varian's new compact, portable cesium magnetometer. Now I'd used cesium magnetics before, the large marine-towed system. I'd even designed one of the first deep-submersible aluminum housings for cesium magnetics during my search activities in the Florida Keys. But looking at this new portable unit I immediately thought about designing an underwater housing that would allow its use for pinpointing well heads and pipes with far greater sensitivity than standard metal detectors. I didn't think at the time that I would someday need precisely such a portable system to look for the *Concepción* but it was my close association with Varian and the latest developments that would someday allow me to break through a critical impasse."

For its part Varian flew Webber up to its headquarters for a visit and hired him as a consultant to help its laboratory engineers design a housing for the portable cesium. Later, while waiting for a change of planes in Chicago, Webber called Jerry Mandel to up-date him on the Silver Shoals project.

"Mandel asked me to send him the prospectus but added: 'Look, I don't want to mislead you, Burt; I'm wrapped up in the Cartagena project and the people I'm involved with don't have the necessity of sheltering any more money. But I've read your résumé and talked to you and you seem to know what you're doing. Maybe I can help. In fact I'll get a finder's fee if I do. I know of an investor group here and they have done some pretty risky investment deals. And in a week to ten days you'll have either a full yes or a full no.'"

Webber complied with Mandel's request and waited, not really sure whether the Silver Shoals project would be more likely to sink or swim in the swift-flowing waters of Chicago's investment banking world. Exactly ten days later he received a call from Chicago. It was from a man named Warren Stearns who said he was the chairman of a private investor's firm known as the December Group. He would later be known in some circles as the Wizard of Oz.

The Business of Operation Phips

Considering Warren Stearns' background, he was an odds-on favorite to get excited by Webber's well-written proposal, for behind the cold statistics and orderly assessments was a sprawling romance of ships and sea and lost treasures—precisely the elements that appeal to the little boy in all grown men. Moreover, like Webber, Warren Stearns at thirty-six was himself something of a wunderkind who liked to run his own show unfettered by the inertia of large organizations and corporate mediocrity. Illinois-born and -raised, Stearns graduated from Amherst College in 1962 and received his master's degree two years later from Harvard business school. Returning to Chicago, he worked for several years for Procter and Gamble in the area of brand management (PineSol was one of his accounts) before shifting to a large Chicago-based advertising agency. While there he got into investment banking on the side and after two years was earning more in commissions than by his regular salary—and having more fun. By the early 1970's he was working full time in investment banking and had developed a solid reputation as a shrewd counselor who earned his clients' money through a combination of hard-nosed business sense and a flair for bold projects.

In 1973, together with a securities lawyer, Jerry Neavolls, he formed the December Group Limited (named after the month of its founding) and from the beginning invested largely in wildcat schemes in the field of oil and natural gas resources. Stearns moved easily in the rarefied regions of higher finance, a world of long lunches in carpeted club rooms, where one talked of leveraged buy-outs, offshore shelters, Eurobonds, and venture capitalization. Once he himself was sold on a project, Stearns was a persuasive salesman who, like Webber, was particularly effective in a one-to-one or small-group situation.

On the phone that summer morning in 1976 Stearns told Webber he was fascinated by the project, that he had spoken to Martin Hall, and "If you're for real, this sounds like an exciting deal, and we'd like to fly you out here to discuss it further." Stearns agreed to allow Hall to come, too, at his own expense, although he was not sure why Webber had requested it. Days later the two men met the December Group principals in Stearns' offices.

"Marty and Stearns didn't hit it off well," Webber recalls. "Probably because Warren saw him as a heavy attachment to me that would endanger future plans. When they asked me where Hall fitted in I told them that we were no longer legal partners but that he had been a longtime supporter and that I insisted on giving him a substantial share of the expedition—fourteen percent in fact. The December Group didn't like it but Warren finally said, 'Well, if you're doing that you certainly have integrity and honesty since you don't have to carry him.'"

Discussions continued at lunch at the Chicago Club during which Webber met seventy-year-old Timothy Lowry, a savvy attorney who still maintained an active practice and who had considerable experience in negotiating offshore oil and gas leases with many foreign governments. He asked if any country claimed jurisdiction over the Silver Shoals. Webber replied that the United Kingdom and the U.S. State Department had said in writing that they regarded the Silver Shoals as being on the high seas and that neither country recognized the claims to the shoals made in the past by Haiti, the Turks and Caicos Islands, and the Dominican Republic. Thus, he was prepared to regard the salvage of the *Concepción* as a high seas situation. Lowry grinned and shook his head:

"Bullshit," he replied. "Sure, the U.S. will say it's high seas, and on that basis they should protect an American flag vessel in such waters. But if you have trouble with any claimants to the shoals—and you could hear from all of them if you find something—don't expect the U.S. to come to your aid. They're not going to get involved in an international confrontation over a treasure find. I know what I'm talking about because I've seen the same thing happen with the expropriation of oil rights in Arab countries. Frankly, Burt, I wouldn't invest dollar one in your project unless you had a contract with a country that would agree to back up your position." Lowry went on to say that from what he'd heard, the Dominicans were nobody to fool with, that they would be the most desirable allies to have in the situation. Webber agreed to pursue a contract with the Dominican Republic.

At the end of the day's meetings Stearns summed up for Webber his own assessment:

"A project like this hinges on three key elements: the existence and amount of the treasure, the research data to locate it, and your expertise as director of an expedition to find and salvage it. I frankly don't know one treasure galleon from another but from the letters of recommendation I've seen on Jack Haskins, he appears to be tops in the field of shipwreck research. As for your qualifications I'm going to ask you to talk to a friend of mine, Dr. Pete Foose. If he tells me you know what you're doing, you got yourself a deal."

Stearns added that if the project was launched and successful, Webber would have to agree to continue his association with the investor group to go after a specified number of other wrecks, all part of a new business called corporate treasure hunting that would embrace high technology, high finance, and high credibility—an approach not unlike that applied to wildcat oil and gas exploration projects. The concept was virtually identical to the one Webber had talked of for years and he enthusiastically agreed.

Shortly after returning home to Annville, Webber got a call from Dr. Richard M. (Pete) Foose who said he would soon be in nearby Hershey on a consulting job and suggested a meeting. The call led to a breakfast at the Hershey Motor Lodge where the two men spent several hours talking. The conversation was wide ranging, detailed, and relentlessly technical. Warren Stearns could hardly have chosen a better judge of Webber's credentials than Dr. Foose. An internationally recognized authority in the field of mineral and petroleum exploration, geological engineering, and marine geology, Foose, age sixty, was (and is) the Hitchcock professor in, and the chairman of, the Department of Geology at Amherst College. (Stearns had first met Foose on a rafting trip down the Colorado River sponsored by the Amherst Alumni Association.) A well-paid consultant for private industry on the side, Foose's credits include the discovery of some of the largest deposits of magnetite and manganese in the contiguous United States, finds that relied in part on the use of airborne magnetometry and aerial cartography. Like Webber, Foose was a Pennsylvanian, a traveler, and an experienced hunter of the earth's treasures; yet he differed in manner, tending to mask his reactions with a vaguely professorial aloofness, even arrogance. The more Webber talked of the Concepción, the more Foose felt a growing excitement. Still, he posed his questions with Mission Control tonality. Foose was the quintessential image of the scientific American.

The morning after his talk with Webber, Foose called Stearns in Chicago and reported that the Concepción was not only a feasible project but that Webber was without question a leading authority on applied search and detection magnetometry. Knowing that Foose was not one to bandy about superlatives, Stearns was impressed, then delighted when the geologist volunteered to be associated as the expedition's scientific advisor. Stearns immediately informed Webber he was starting that day to gear up for a fund drive to underwrite the expedition, appropriately named Operation Phips.

Before the hunt for the Concepción became a reality on what Stearns referred to as "the wet side," the project had to be launched and well under way on the "dry side" (i.e., the offices and boardrooms of Chicago). In the latter case there were weeks of stormy weather. For starters, fewer than half of the December Group's members were in favor of the expedition, which would be offered as a high-risk limited partnership capitalized at $195,000. Flatly opposed was the December Group's president, Jerry Neavolls, whose deserved reputation as a brilliant securities lawyer carried considerable clout. Stearns opted to seek investors outside the group to bring in the additional funding necessary to reach the total. Next were long negotiations over points and percentages. Meanwhile, provisions had to be made to go after a second galleon wreck in the event a contract with the Dominican Republic was not secured in time. Webber chose the *Santa Margarita,* the sister ship to the *Atocha,* which he believed could be found with Haskins' supporting research and his own superior mag systems. But since the *Concepción* was the jackpot goal, Webber redoubled his efforts to obtain a contract.

On State Department advice, Webber contacted Marine Colonel Stanley Houston, a military attaché to the U.S. embassy in Santo Domingo, and requested his aid in arranging a meeting with the Navy's Chief of Staff. There followed an inevitable submission of résumés, copies of State Department letters and professional references, but in a matter of weeks an appointment was arranged. Together with lawyer Timothy Lowry, Webber flew to Santo Domingo. The pair drove to the naval base and was escorted into the carpeted air-conditioned office of Rear Admiral Francisco Rivera Caminero, base commander and the Navy's Chief of Staff. As a steward poured cups of excellent Dominican coffee, the three men, plus an interpreter, sat in leather chairs around a coffee table while Webber discussed his plan.

"The meeting was very cordial," Webber recalls. "The admiral liked the whole idea. Our initial offer was for an eighty-twenty split, twenty percent for the Dominican Republic—the King's Fifth so to speak. Our reasoning was because the Silver Shoals are pretty far out offshore and it is a territorial question in the view of some countries. But we wanted to respect the Dominican claims and insure a peaceful relationship that would provide us protection in case we were challenged out on the reef. We certainly had no objections to recognizing the Dominican claim and abiding by it. That was the whole basis for our request. Well, Admiral Rivera said, 'Go ahead and send us a draft contract and we'll determine whether the terms are acceptable.'"

Within two weeks a draft contract in Spanish was mailed to the admiral. Three weeks passed, then a month, then five weeks. Webber and his associates grew uneasy. They knew that another reputable group of American treasure hunters, Caribe Salvage, led by William Strube, had been waiting for a year for a signed contract that would allow it to salvage an artifact-laden galleon wreck found by Dominican Navy divers in Samana Bay on the country's north shore. Caribe had even formed a Dominican corporation to facilitate matters and had offered the Dominican Republic a quarter share of its treasure find. Elsewhere, Webber had received a letter from Florida-based treasure hunter Norman Scott who had learned of Operation Phips: "Scott warned us not to dare going to Silver Shoals, that he was already dealing with the Dominican government and already had a contract with the Turks and Caicos. Mixing the two countries made no sense to us at all. It seemed a real scattershot bluff but irritating. Plus, my memories of the *Maravillas* discovery made me less than comfortable about any other treasure hunter's interest in *Concepción*."

Lastly was the question of whether some form of cash "fee" informally paid (in American dollars) to some government official was necessary or even expected. The tradition of *la mordida* (the bite) is an old one around the Caribbean. Though Webber was not enthusiastic about the practice, it worried him. Authoritative sources had advised that if he failed to make a discreet offer he might ruin his chances. On the other hand, if he did broach the subject, it might be construed as a breach of courtesy and undermine the Dominicans' assessment of his own integrity. Because the matter was delicate, Webber wanted an American interpreter along for the next meeting in Santo Domingo. He chose twenty-nine-year-old Stanley Smith, one of Stearns' associates in the December Group who had already been tapped to oversee the administrative side of Operation Phips.

Smith spoke fluent Spanish by virtue of having spent many summers in Spain as a youngster, at one point living in Barcelona for a year's schooling (his family is from Milwaukee, Wisconsin). His father, who in the early fifties was the export manager for Mercury Outboard Motors, had prospered along with the company and his son Stan was no stranger to Europe by the time he entered Cornell University. He continued on to receive a master's degree in finance from the University of Chicago, followed by a very-hard-to-get internship at the Federal Reserve Bank in Washington, D.C., thence back to Chicago for a stint as the personal assistant to the president of the First National Bank of Chicago. While in this latter capacity in 1974, Smith met Warren Stearns and the December Group and soon was working for them. A top-flight manager with a quick grasp of complex financial dealings, he also understood the more leisurely pace of business in Hispanic countries and could help soften Webber's occasional flights of Germanic intensity.

As the two-month mark approached, Webber received an invitation from Admiral Rivera's attorney, a Colonel Strudele, to come to Santo Domingo to review and, if desired, sign the contract. Smith, together with Webber and lawyer Tim Lowry, quickly flew down and met in the attorney's offices. He remembered the occasion well:

"I was given a copy of the contract, in Spanish, and while Burt and Tim and Colonel Strudele waited in silence I quickly went through it. The first thing that hit me was our offer of an eighty-twenty split of the treasure had been changed to fifty-fifty. Apparently, Caribe Salvage had earlier yielded to the same demand, which probably came from higher up in the government rather than the Navy, which would be supervising the contract. Thus, a precedent had been set.

"Needless to say, the discovery was very distressing. For one thing we had already mentioned the high probability of an eighty-twenty deal in our offering circular. Well, Burt and I took a walk through the old-town section to discuss the situation and we ended up in the garden courtyard of the Nicolas de Ovando Hotel right on the banks of the Ozama River. We ordered rum and Coke, relaxed, and after a call to Warren in Chicago, we decided fifty percent of something is better than eighty percent of nothing. So the next morning we went back to Strudele's office and signed the contract. Next I broached the matter of possible 'fees' which we might pay to Dominican Republic attorneys. The colonel replied, 'Oh, that's too expensive. Don't bother with them.' He politely brushed aside one or two other oblique suggestions—I certainly didn't want to appear vulgar—and it was clear that he and everybody we were dealing with was as straight as an arrow. From the very beginning our deal with the Dominicans was run in an honest, completely above-board manner. In fact, the whole process actually took only two months, which was very fast. We were very impressed."

Even before negotiations with the Dominican Republic had progressed beyond the initial meeting with Admiral Rivera, Warren Stearns and Webber had begun a series of luncheon meetings with potential investors. He was looking for fifteen units of limited partnership interest at $13,000 per unit (limit, two per customer) but would consider smaller units, allowing up to thirty investors. As with any business venture he spoke of profit potentials, start-up costs, and capital calls and where possible he flew Webber and Haskins to Chicago to help pitch the project before small groups of clients. Unquestionably, one of the most attractive features of the project was the treasure potential, even though there was no way to ascertain how much had been recovered by salvors after Phips or even how much the *Concepción* had carried in her holds when she left Havana. The lack of documentation in the latter instance stems from the loss of the two remaining copies of the

Concepción's official manifest, both of which were lost at sea in later sinkings. However, some survivors' testimony culled from the Seville archives indicated an initial 4 million pesos were taken aboard. William Phips recovered approximately 800,000 pesos. Webber and Haskins estimated that Phips' successors may have hauled up at least a similar amount, bringing the total to 1.6 or 2 million pesos. Thus, the treasure remaining to be recovered could be as much as 2.4 million pesos.

Additionally, there were research notes from Robert Marx indicating the possibility that an additional 2 million pesos had been taken aboard prior to departure, bringing the total cargo to a potential 6 million pesos.

> Accordingly, [the offering circular read] there should still remain, buried and grown over by coral within the *Almiranta* wrecksite, up to approximately 4,400,000 pesos in registered gold and silver alone ranging in current melt-down value from over $22,000,000 to a collector value approaching $156,000,000. This computation is based on a 100% recovery which, of course, is a virtual impossibility.

Of course. Yet there certainly seemed to be enough down there to satisfy everyone's greed. Outwardly, the deliberations were serious but everyone knew in his heart that this was a modern-day application of scientific methodology and professionalism to a quest as timeless in its appeal as it was romantic. The payoff would not be gas, oil, or ore but gold bars and silver pieces of eight, something one can hold in one's hand and almost feel the pulse of a great age of epic adventures.

Stearns was careful to thoroughly discuss certain risk factors inherent in the project, echoing the offering circular's caveat that only those persons who can comfortably assume the complete loss of their investment should consider participating in the venture. The emphasis was commendable; however, Stearns, like his seventeenth-century predecesor the Duke of Albemarle, was aware that stressing the risk factors often fanned the flame of enthusiasm in those who had made their money in predictable and boring ways. Or, as he once remarked, "Sometimes the best way to get a guy in on a deal is to tell him he can't get in on the deal."

By the end of August, Stearns called Webber to report the good news: A total of twenty-seven investors had collectively plunked down the required $195,000.

Operation Phips had been launched.

6

Five Months, Thirteen
Wrecks, and Heartbreak

Gearing Up

During William Phips' second visit to the Silver Shoals in 1688, an unknown cartographer aboard the HMS *Foresight* drew a chart of the shoals. The document, known as the "Hubbard Wreck Reef Chart"—perhaps because it may have been commissioned by the *Foresight's* executive officer, Lieutenant Hubbard—showed a small likeness of the *Foresight* alongside one of the reef sections. In the center of the section are several crossed ship's timbers while on the windward side are the words "ye Wrack." Later discovered in the records of the British Admiralty, the chart was in every sense a treasure map, complete with a traditional X-marks-the-spot while being sufficiently detailed in appearance to convince not a few adventurous souls that only a few days' poking around the reef stood between them and a vast fortune.

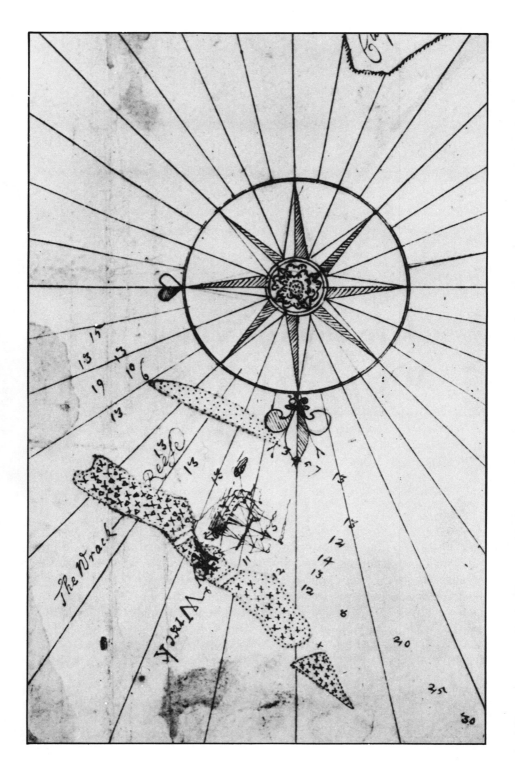

Unfortunately, the chart is also sufficiently vague as to be of no use to any explorer lacking a very clear idea of what the Silver Shoals actually look like. Burt Webber, who had studied the accounts of his unsuccessful predecessors, knew this—and he was determined not to be led into the same dilemma.

Shortly after receiving the go-ahead from fund raiser Warren Stearns, Webber began shopping around for an airborne photographic service to conduct a reconnaissance of the Silver Shoals from which a photomosaic and a detailed chart would be made. His requirements were stringent: The photographs must clearly reveal every reef head three meters or closer to the water's surface along the twenty-seven-and-one-half-mile stretch of the north section of the bank.

Webber hired Aero Service, a Philadelphia-based firm recommended by Varian. When the forecast predicted minimum cloud cover over the shoals, a survey crew flew down for a three-day reconnaissance. Webber well understood what they would find, for weeks earlier he had flown out to the reef for the first time in a private plane from Santo Domingo. From his 3,000-foot altitude Webber saw the sprawling line of hundreds of ocher-colored reef heads jutting up from the deep blue of the South Atlantic. Somewhere within that vast uncharted lethal labyrinth lay the *Concepción*. To attempt to solve its secret with ancient maps and faded words from worm-eaten parchment almost seemed an act of presumption.

Nevertheless, Webber eagerly awaited the arrival of a carefully assembled six-foot-long photomosaic, a composite of several dozen high-quality color enlargements selected from hundreds taken in various lighting conditions. The day it arrived Jack Haskins joined Webber to scan the panorama for clues that would tie in the base map with the Hubbard chart. Both men immediately spotted two recognizable reef channels in the mosaic that corresponded with the channels on either side of the "wrack" reef shown on the Hubbard chart. This was encouraging. Gazing at the mosaic, Haskins put his finger on the center of a six-mile-long reef roughly shaped like two half moons end to end.

"Phips mentioned the wreck was located 'where the reef makes onto a half moon,' so it could be right about here."

Then again, Haskins noted, the spot was way too close to the southeasternmost tip of the six-mile reef which Phips sighted before moving up along its lee side. Based on the distance the *James and Mary* covered, the wreck was most likely several miles farther to the

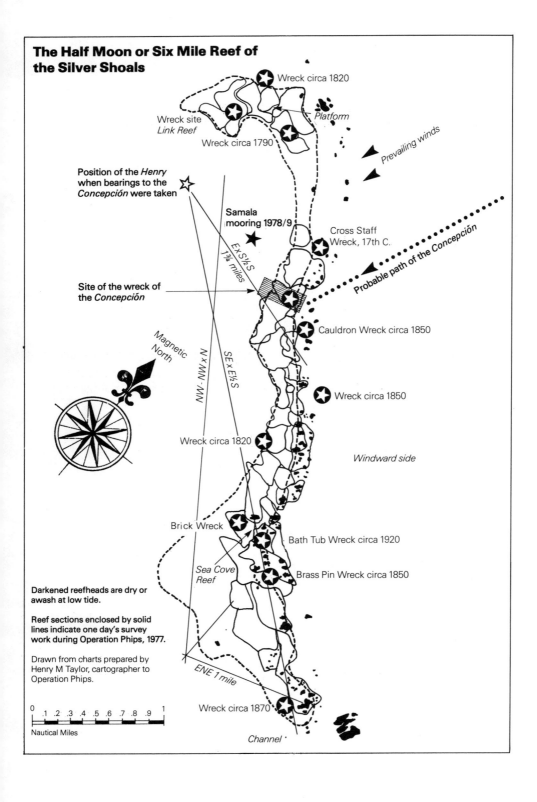

The Half Moon or Six Mile Reef of the Silver Shoals

Wreck circa 1820

Platform

Wreck site
Link Reef

Wreck circa 1790

Prevailing winds

Position of the *Henry*
when bearings to the
Concepción were taken

Samala
mooring 1978/9

Cross Staff
Wreck, 17th C.

E x S½ S
1¾ miles

Probable path of the *Concepción*

Site of the wreck of
the *Concepción*

Cauldron Wreck circa 1850

Magnetic
North

NW x NW · NW

SE x E½ S

Wreck circa 1850

Wreck circa 1820

Windward side

Brick Wreck

Bath Tub Wreck circa 1920

Sea Cove
Reef

Brass Pin Wreck circa 1850

Darkened reefheads are dry or
awash at low tide.

Reef sections enclosed by solid
lines indicate one day's survey
work during Operation Phips, 1977.

Drawn from charts prepared by
Henry M Taylor, cartographer to
Operation Phips.

ENE 1 mile

Wreck circa 1870

0 .1 .2 .3 .4 .5 .6 .7 .8 .9 1

Nautical Miles

Channel

northwest in a center reef between two channels. The two men dubbed this target the Mysterioso Reef.

Because the Hubbard chart did not appear to be drawn to scale, Haskins was anxious to plot on the mosaic the distance and bearing lines given in the logbooks of the *James and Mary*, the *Foresight*, and other ships that had visited the site. The result should be a rough triangulation that would narrow the search area. Yet there was no denying that the one logbook the historian had yet to find was probably the most crucial of all, this being the log of the *Henry of London* which had actually found the *Concepción*. It stood to reason that inasmuch as the *Henry* was scouting unknown territory, her captain would have made careful sightings and measurements, that upon finding the wreck he would have taken multiple bearings using as reference points parts of the reef that were dry or awash at low tide. What was so vexing to Haskins was that he had found portions of the log of the *Henry* quoted in other accounts of the day. Thus, it was highly unlikely that the document had been lost or destroyed. But where was it? And did it contain the missing pieces to the puzzle? Or would the less-detailed data he had helped assemble be enough to lead Webber to his target? Many questions remained but the answers to some at least seemed closer. Operation Phips now had a detailed color-map of the territory.

For his expedition vessel Webber chartered the *Big G*, a sixty-five-foot charter dive boat based in Islamorada, Florida. Her captain and owner, Gordon Hutchins, was a veteran skipper and navigator while the boat itself had enough deck space for compressors and salvage gear. Sleeping quarters were in an amidships bunk area large enough for ten crewmen, just short of being cramped but certainly adequate.

In his dive team Webber assembled a group that was not only thoroughly qualified but also trained in a variety of skills. Robert Coffey, thirty-three, the expedition's dive master, had been a high school classmate of Webber. A certified master dive instructor who had logged more than a month of diving on the wreck of the *Andrea Doria*, making fifty dives to depths of 240 feet, he'd even managed to do a spot of diving off Jacques Cousteau's *Calypso*. Out of the water Coffey had more than a decade of plant management experience for several major textile mills. He brought to the expedition a steady, easy-going temperament and an underwater knowledge that inspired confidence.

Duke Long, a twenty-five-year-old resident of Myerstown, Pennsylvania, had met Webber in the early seventies through a shared interest in diving, antiques, and exploring, and had crewed with Webber during the 1974 *Atocha* survey off the Marquesas Atoll. A slightly paunchy, balding young man with steelworker's arms who often wore a digger-style Army Ranger fatigue hat of camouflage green, Long was a self-taught scrimshaw craftsman as well as an illustrator whose pen-and-ink and water-color work showed great delicacy.

Rounding out the four-man dive team under Webber were Ken Matz, a professional diver from the Florida Keys and a veteran right-hand man of Webber who had been with him on Florida and Bahama expeditions since 1966, and John Berrier, forty-four, a retired Navy lieutenant-commander whose Miami-based business of exporting maritime machinery and parts to several Central American countries would prove useful in expediting needed supplies to the expedition while in the Dominican Republic. Berrier was also a licensed ham radio operator whose home-based single-side band short-wave transceiver would allow direct communications with the *Big G* while the vessel was on the Silver Shoals. (Berrier's wife was also licensed.)

To handle the exacting and sometimes tedious cartographic chores (which would require as much as two hours of charting each day), Webber turned to Henry Taylor, forty-eight, a retired beer distributor from Wilmington, Delaware, who had moved to the Florida Keys in the mid-sixties to become an accomplished free diver, scuba diver, and an expert in Spanish coins and artifacts. A laconic adventurer in horn-rimmed glasses, a T-shirt and Bermuda shorts, Taylor possessed an encyclopedic knowledge of the Spanish Main, an ability to work fast and thoroughly, and a well-developed appreciation of the opposite sex. He had also worked with Webber on magnetometer surveys in both Florida and the Cedar Keys.

Webber had met most of the members of the team in Florida during the seventies. Besides being first-rate professionals, they knew Webber's temperament, his drive for perfection, and how to work together during long hot days at sea. For his part Webber acknowledged the fact by paying each man $1,000 a month, plus travel expenses, plus at least half a percentage point of the cash value of any treasure found. Such salaries were more than those earned by any other treasure divers in the business, but Webber knew well that guaranteeing his men a decent livelihood in the months ahead was not only a gesture of respect but would amply be repaid in loyalty and enthusiasm. In short, they were worth every penny.

In late November 1977 Webber and his team began a three-week outfitting of the *Big G* in Islamorada. Among the more exotic items were a Varian-supplied Scimtrex MP-2 proton magnetometer with special modifications allowing a two-second cycling rate and usage with a Rustrac field recorder, a Webber-designed prototype delta-fin dry housing for the sensor and—lastly—four Heckler & Koch model 91 semi-automatic rifles and a riot pump-shotgun. The weapons were promptly locked in a small arms cabinet from which they would be removed, Webber prayed, only for occasional cleaning. But he well understood that more than eighty yachts and motor-powered vessels had disappeared in the South Atlantic and the Caribbean in the previous eighteen months, many of them under mysterious circumstances. One frequently heard stories of modern-day pirates hijacking boats at gunpoint, killing the occupants, then using the vessel to smuggle marijuana and cocaine shipments to and from South America and finally scuttling it on the high seas. If hijackers made any such attempt on the *Big G*, they would have to contend with the fire-power of one of the world's most formidable assault rifles.

"They Look Scary as Hell, Burt"

Ten days before Christmas, Webber, together with Stan Smith and Tim Lowry, flew to Santo Domingo to sign the contracts with the Dominican Republic. With preparations all but complete, the expedition team took a break for the holidays, returned to Islamorada after New Year's Day, and a few days later got under way for the six-day passage through the lower Bahamas to the north shore of Hispaniola. Joining the ship's company as a mate and handyman was twenty-four-year-old Donald Summers, a tall bespectacled athletic Missouri farm boy who had never before been on a boat and knew nothing about diving. He was, however, hard working, smart, anxious to learn, and diplomatic. A 1975 graduate of the University of Missouri (majoring in geography), Summers, who spoke Spanish passably well, had traveled extensively through Europe before returning home to Missouri. Through his older sister Susanne (who lived in Chicago) he met Warren Stearns, saw the offering circular for Operation Phips, and successfully talked his way into a berth aboard the *Big G*. His salary: a meager $500 for the duration plus bunk and board. What Summers lacked in shipboard experience he soon began acquiring. Barely two days out at sea the *Big G*'s generator went out and Summers spent long sweaty hours in the cramped engine room helping Captain Hutchins make repairs. His enthusiasm and interest quickly won him acceptance.

For Burt Webber, the return to sea aboard a well-equipped vessel hot on the trail of treasure was immensely gratifying. After more than two years of land-side activities, of endless phone calls and investor meetings, of long discussions over points and percentages, the whole *business* of the business, he was once again out on the main, unreachable by phone, and ready to do what he did best—search for sunken treasure. He knew, too, that he was heading up probably the most well-equipped, well-staffed, and well-prepared expedition in the annals of modern treasure hunting. In the weeks and months ahead he sensed his every resource would be put to the test, and he was ready.

Several days later, as the *Big G* slowly entered the small harbor of Puerto Plata, Webber gazed out on the partially restored ruins of Fort San Filipe which had existed even before the time of William Phips. Change had come slowly to Puerto Plata since then; it had grown to a large coastal town of more than 50,000 yet the geography of the tiny harbor was essentially the same. Webber was acutely aware he was treading in the steps of Sir William.

The *Big G* remained in Puerto Plata for a few days to reprovision, establish formal contact with local officials, particularly the officers aboard Navy patrol boats #206 and #106 which would be on call in case of trouble. By prior agreement, the expedition took aboard Nedi Adamas, an amiable enlisted man in the Dominican Navy who seemed rather an odd choice as a field agent. Adamas spoke no English, showed no interest in the hunt for the *Concepción*, slept all day when out on the reef, and spent most nights fishing off the *Big G*, saving most of his catch to sell in Puerto Plata. Those fish that he caught for the crew were regularly prepared by the *Big G's* "cookie," Bob Weatherbee, a hard-drinking salt who chain-smoked Pall Malls and served up three hearty meals a day. Weatherbee also had the distinction of having formerly been both a Parris Island Marine drill instructor and a professor at M.I.T.

Having touched base at Puerto Plata, the *Big G* cast off at dawn one morning and set a northeasterly course for the Silver Shoals seventy-five miles away. By noon the vessel had reached the outer fringes of the bank's lee side and begun a very cautious approach using loran, continual fathometer checks, and, most important, a horizontal scan sonar which provided an acoustic ping response that was identical to the soundtracks of World War II submarine movies. The constant pinging sound added to an already tense approach. The sky was filled with a heavy overcast, which rendered the coral heads all but impossible to see, even with Polaroid glasses. Webber stood atop the pilothouse overhead and scanned the featureless horizon with binoculars. As the *Big G* crept forward there gradually appeared in the distance to starboard a long line of breakers surging silently out of nowhere to break on the reef heads mere inches below the surface. The ominous sight was enough to send chills down the spine of any sailor. Alongside Webber, Duke Long muttered, "They look scary as hell, Burt."

The heavy cloud cover would be a serious obstacle to this initial reconnoitering of the reef for seven days. Nonetheless, Webber launched one of the two Zodiacs (inflatable boats) and visually scouted the reef in an attempt to identify several large heads that he could key to the photomosaic. The process took time but eventually he was able to plot loran bearings and principal features on a Mylar overlay that cartographer Henry Taylor was developing. While waiting for visibility to improve, Webber used a Varian V-85 deep-scan magnetometer mounted on the *Big G* to survey for possible traces of the deep water anchorage used by Phips on both his expeditions. The effort was cut short, however, by an electronic outage, but had the anchorage been identified, Webber may possibly have been able to plot a bull's-eye bearing line to the wrecksite of the *Concepción* given in the logbook of the *James and Mary*.

Day eight brought clear skies for the first time, allowing the *Big G* to maneuver cautiously to a point close to the channel northwest of Mysterioso Reef. A boat was sent to this sector to check out Chaney Reef, named after a commercial airline pilot (and friend of Jack Haskins) who during his regular overflights had noticed what appeared to be wreckage of a ship on an unusually large reef. A visual checkout of the top proved negative but a subsequent mag survey of the reef head just to the southeast of Chaney Reef produced multiple anomalies in the 40-gamma-plus range. Webber and two others immediately went over the side to investigate and soon found scattered iron hull spikes, deck fittings, iron ballast bars, and several datable artifacts such as glass bottles and pottery. Webber conferred with Haskins and Taylor and the trio estimated the ship's vintage as early nineteenth-century. Though the wreck and still others to come may have yielded interesting finds, Webber paused only long enough to assure himself the discovery was not the *Concepción*.

That same day the *Big G* moved down to an anchorage off the Mysterioso Reef. By now Webber had refined an exact positioning on the mosaic and that afternoon began searching this new sector.

The procedure worked well: A three-man survey team in reef boat no. 1 would first go to a specific portion of the reef carrying individual photos of the reef and daily survey plotting sheets extrapolated from the aerial mosaic. The sheets were covered with transparent Mylar paper and each coral head would be numbered. Buoys made of yellow plastic one-gallon jugs (also with numbers) would be placed on each coral head in sequence. This done, reef boat no. 2 would enter the sector and begin a circumference survey of each buoyed head, towing the sensor as close as possible to the base of the heads without snagging on coral outgrowths. At the end of each survey the sector surveyed would be plotted on a master survey chart.

To ensure absolute control over his survey positioning, Webber had leased a Motorola Mini-Range III positioning system which used small radar transponders that could be stationed at either end of a reef section on specially designed floats. However, the photomosaic and individual enlargements were so detailed that use of the Motorola system was never required.

For those who spent any time at all under water, however, a psychological adjustment was required to maintain an accurate sense of direction and location. The instant one slipped beneath the surface one entered a vast world of awesome and complex beauty belonging to one of the most unique and untouched reef complexes on earth. With visibility seldom less than 100 feet, one viewed columns of coral rising toward the surface from an average depth of forty-five feet, each a pedestal that formed a massive wave-resistant structure. Everywhere around and between the heads flourished coral colonies of seemingly endless variety and color: branching corals such as Elkhorn and Staghorn, delicate whorled fronds, brain coral, and giant mushroom-shaped colonies right out of *Alice in Wonderland*. Amidst this prodigious ecosystem grew hundreds of encrusting organisms, sponges, purple-hued sea fans (gorgonians), sand-producing calcareous algae, delicate plant life that yielded gracefully to the rhythm of the ocean surge. The heads themselves, comprising living corals superimposed on dead ancestral colonies, were often irregularly shaped with caverns and deep undercuts, some with tunnels large enough to accommodate a scuba diver. Between the heads were either lush canyons of fine white sand or jagged mounds of coral branches that had collapsed from their own weight from the spreading tops of the heads. In all, the distracting beauty of the reef, together with its convoluted marine topography, was a bit disorienting at first, but Webber and his team soon developed a comfortable command of their new environment, and before long would train themselves to pick out from a considerable distance any man-made artifacts that spelled the presence of ship's wreckage.

There was one problem posed by the reef's unique configuration that did not appear resolvable. So profuse were the long clusters of

Staghorn and Elkhorn coral that the magnetometer's sensor or cable was constantly in danger of snagging on the branches, particularly if the unit was more than fifteen feet beneath the surface. Webber had intended using his depth-monitoring system but from the beginning it was clear that the rugged terrain around the coral heads prevented the survey boat from controlling the sensor depth by merely changing the towing speed (which averaged 3.3 m.p.h.). Instead, the towline had to be hand held and manually shortened or lengthened by an operator using only visual judgment while the reef boat crabbed around the circumference of the heads. As a result, sensor depth greater than ten to fifteen feet was rarely attained and even then sensor head and cable snags were frequent.

The immediate concern raised by this depth limitation was that ferromagnetic anomalies such as ship's fittings from the *Concepción,* which were most likely buried beneath coral rubble at the base of the coral heads, would be too far away from the sensor head to register. Adding to the problem was the fact that the *Concepción*'s cannons (the few which may not have been salvaged) were made of nonferrous bronze and were thus undetectable by magnetic instrumentation. Further, her anchors, which were made of iron that would register at a considerable distance, had all been lost during her long struggle to survive. Thus, the galleon, a weak target for starters, was made weaker still by the surrounding coral heads. Nevertheless, Webber needed only a single anomaly, however faint, for him to send divers down to the bottom with metal detectors to scour the area. Just one hit from the *Concepción*—and he would find her at last.

Confrontations

As it developed, the next anomaly encountered on the reef was not beneath the water but on it. On the evening of January 30 after a long day's work, a crew member spotted a light some six miles to the northwest. The *Big G*'s radar confirmed the sighting, apparently a vessel at anchor. That night Webber ordered a beefed-up watch and reviewed repel-boarders procedures. Just after sunrise the following morning the vessel got under way and slowly approached the *Big G*. Through his binoculars Webber saw a rust-streaked converted pleasure boat, its decks cluttered with salvage gear. As the boat came within a few hundred yards of the *Big G* Webber spotted on its sundeck a bikini-clad female and a portly man wearing sunglasses. Whoever he was he was traveling with all the amenities. The vessel dropped anchor and lowered a small boat into which three men climbed, one of them apparently a policeman in uniform. Webber was relieved to see no one carrying firearms. He was sure now the intruder was rival treasure hunter Norman Scott for he recognized the vessel as the *Reina del Mar*, Scott's Expeditions Unlimited support vessel.

Minutes later the small boat came alongside the *Big G* and Webber allowed aboard a Caicos Island policeman and a Mr. C.W. McGuire, minister of tourism and development. McGuire, after an exchange of courtesies, presented Webber a handwritten notice informing him that the Silver Bank belonged to the United Kingdom and that he was there without its permission. Webber, bristling slightly, announced that the Turks and Caicos representative was out of order, that they were the ones infringing on Dominican Republic property. He handed his visitors a copy of the contract. It was written in Spanish. The Turks and Caicos representatives pretended to read it.

Faced with a standoff, the visitors departed the *Big G* and returned to the *Reina del Mar* which moved to an anchorage two miles away. That afternoon it was joined by a seventy-foot trawler that later turned out to be the Turks and Caicos Navy. In the meantime Webber tried desperately and without success to contact the Dominican Republic Navy by radio. The next morning as soon as the sun had risen high enough to render the heads visible, the two reef boats began surveying a new sector, leaving all but Captain Gordon Hutchins and two others aboard the *Big G*. Webber was well into magging the first few reef heads when he noticed the two intruding vessels headed toward the *Big G*.

"God, I hope Gordy doesn't get into it with them," Webber said. Just then the *Reina del Mar* altered course and proceeded on a northwesterly course in the direction of Caicos Island while the trawler turned west and proceeded right into the heart of the reef toward the survey boats! A man was on the bow calling out the heads as they approached them but the maneuver reeked of madness.

"I can't believe it!" Haskins cried. "There's a maze of heads there. The guy on the wheel is either crazy or the world's best boatsman."

"Start moving into the sun," Webber ordered, signaling the other reef boat to come over. Soon both rubber boats were traveling in tandem. Clearly the trawler intended to pick up one or both reef boats and haul the occupants off to the Caicos slammer. For several long moments the trawler followed as the glare of the sun increased, making it all but impossible to see the reef heads. Suddenly, the air was filled with frantic shouting from the trawler as the bow lookout wildly signaled the wheelhouse. The trawler's engines roared full astern and barely managed to bring her to a stop before striking a head. A minute later the trawler turned tail and left for the northwest. Webber's quick thinking had worked.

Norman Scott's failure to have Operation Phips kicked off the Silver Shoals was apparently not his only problem. The *Reina del Mar* had departed with considerable smoke discharge from her exhaust stack, indicating possible engine trouble. Some time later Webber received a report that she had evidently grounded on a reef while entering Cockburn Harbor on South Caicos Island and sunk.

Following a reprovisioning visit to Puerto Plata, the *Big G* returned to the shoals with a Dominican Navy escort vessel. Clearly the Dominican government was taking its obligations seriously. Two of the warship's officers spoke English well, an asset that helped form a friendly working relationship with Operation Phips and came in handy during a second incident involving a visitor to the reef. Late one afternoon an unidentified vessel appeared in the area and anchored near the northwest tip of the Half Moon Reef. She was a shrimp boat roughly sixty-five feet in length, and her destination seemed to be a crude cement platform about twenty-five feet square that someone had erected months or years previously atop one of the larger reef heads. This time Webber, at the request of the Navy patrol vessel, went with diver Ken Matz and Jack Haskins to the Dominican ship in one of the reef boats and took aboard the executive officer and an enlisted man armed with a sub-machine gun.

The group then headed for the mystery ship. As the party approached the vessel someone aboard abruptly hoisted aloft an American flag where none had been before.

Pulling alongside, Webber and company were greeted with some nervousness by an American in his thirties, presumably the skipper. Without waiting for an invitation the executive officer climbed aboard together with his machine-gun-toting assistant. A quick interrogation revealed that the vessel, with half a dozen American crewmen aboard, had come from San Juan, Puerto Rico, under contract to an unnamed U.S. party to enlarge and strengthen the platform with concrete and steel I-beam additions. When asked for what purpose he was to do this the vessel's captain pleaded ignorance. Left unsaid was the structure's potential usefulness as a drop-off point for sizable quantities of drugs and/or contraband. While the Dominican officer relayed the information to his ship via walkie-talkie, Ken Matz who had remained in the reef boat noticed a figure crouching behind the barely open hatchway to the wheelhouse. Matz suspected he was armed and was stationed there as an ace in the hole in the event of a showdown. He assumed—incorrectly—that his companions had also spotted the figure. A moment later the officer was advised by his ship that it was in direct contact with the Navy Base in Santo Domingo and was awaiting instructions. Another minute passed in tense silence. The walkie-talkie crackled in crisp Spanish.

"You have twenty-five minutes to leave this area," the officer told the vessel's spokesman.

"All right, we'll leave," the American replied. "But could you give us until tomorrow morning? We're all dead tired from fighting rough seas all the way from Puerto Rico."

The Dominican officer quickly conferred with his superior. A reply came back almost immediately. "You have twenty-five minutes to leave," the officer said. The shrimp boat's skipper seemed to understand that the alternative was arrest. He quickly nodded and began issuing orders to get under way.

As the reef boat returned to the *Big G*, Matz turned to Webber and the executive officer. "You did see the guy crouched in the wheelhouse, didn't you? I'm pretty sure he was armed." The shocked pair shook their heads in astonishment and realized how dangerous the encounter had been. An hour later the intruder was hull down on the western horizon.

Following this second encounter Webber and his crew settled into a steady routine without further interruption, save by an increasing number of humpback whales that annually came to the shoals for several months of breeding and calving. The sight of these noble creatures broaching the calm water, then raising their mammoth fluked tails skyward before sounding was a spectacle to rival the beauty of the reef itself. The whales, in fact, seemed more numerous than the fish in these waters. By day one may spot at most several dinner-sized groupers and perhaps a snapper or two. Not a few ended up on the *Big G*'s galley table for by design fresh fish was included in the crew's diet at least twice a week. Elsewhere, Webber was relieved by the absence of sharks. In their stead was a small number of barracuda, usually two to four feet in size, which were by nature curious and occasionally followed the divers as they explored the heads. Whenever one of the larger critters seemed too close for comfort, nervy pros like Duke Long discovered that swimming toward them with a mealtime resolve was enough to make them keep a respectful distance.

Webber completed surveying the 116 reef heads of the Mysterioso

Reef, then moved south to the Indian Key Reef area (twelve heads), then to a reef grouping of similar size where he got substantial readings—which he expected to find. Here was not only an eighteenth-century shipwreck but also a veritable junkyard of modern debris including steel-mesh debris baskets, cable, fittings, mountains of coral debris, and miscellaneous droppings from a salvage vessel. Everything pointed to this being the much publicized wreck that Jacques Cousteau had worked so thoroughly in 1968 (and which Webber had plotted on his chart). Apparently, at the end of the visit, the *Calypso's* crew had simply dumped over the side any and all items that would no longer be useful, adding to the artifacts already left by Mel Fisher's first visit five years earlier. One of the *Big G's* divers later remarked that the resulting underwater garbage pile seemed a teensy bit out of keeping with the Cousteau Society's otherwise laudable commitment to marine conservation.

Following the location of the Cousteau wreck, Webber moved his team to the north end of the Half Moon Reef, finding several scattered anchors and then, in the space of three days in late February, three wrecks, one of which appeared the one worked by Ed Link in the 1950's. The other two were new discoveries that generated early excitement, followed by disappointment after exploratory digging yielded evidence that the find was not the *Concepción* after all.

Puzzles and Poisoning

Each evening after a long day's work, Webber would fill out a daily operations report, detailing the areas surveyed and progress made. As often as not he would confer with Jack Haskins, reviewing Spanish and English documents, and check again and again with the photomosaic. While most of the crew would be asleep by 10 P.M. each night, Webber often stayed up an hour or two later going over every scrap of evidence, trying to put the pieces together.

There were times during these hot days and nights when a cold beer would have hit the spot (the Dominican brand El Presidente is a world class brew) but Webber refused to allow any alcohol on board the *Big G*. His justification was the same as for his prohibition against females—both were a potential source of problems. While the latter restriction was accepted, there had been at first a bit of grumbling in the ranks about the former rule, but it soon ceased. Webber knew the reef was a distant and dangerous territory and living and working safely in its environs required a clear head. The dive team respected him for that stand, but on the other hand the *Big G*'s cookie, Bob Weatherbee, while not openly disagreeing with the rule, was not above taking the odd nip of rum when Webber and associates were out on the reef, or late at night when everyone else had turned in. Cookie was very circumspect, however; he decided early on that the only safe hiding place for fine quality Brugal and Bermudez rum was in the engine room, which meant that lowly Don Summers would have to be included in the conspiracy. Summers, whom the crew had nicknamed Abner because his guileless farm-boy openness reminded one of the comic strip character Li'l' Abner, reluctantly complied and before each trip to the reef he would hide bottles of rum in the bowels of the *Big G*. During the ten-day stints on the reef, he would break out one bottle at a time as requested.

As Webber worked his survey team southward along the Half Moon Reef he continued to puzzle over the discrepancies between the distances given in the logbooks of the Phips expeditions and those indicated on the Hubbard chart. The latter document was a quite good rendering of the southeast bank of the shoals but when the wrecksite coordinates from the logbooks were plotted, the resulting location was nearly three miles northwest of the site shown on the chart. Jack Haskins was equally mystified, so much so that when the expedition returned to Puerto Plata he took all the documents and charts and checked into a room at the Monte Mar, a quiet beachside hotel, and spent the next three days wrestling with the problem, conferring with Webber and scientific advisor Dr. Pete Foose who had flown down for the next trip.

By the time the *Big G* departed for the shoals, Haskins, who was no closer to a solution, decided to return to Europe to do more research. In the meantime, his best assessment was that the wreck was in an area of large reef heads somewhere in the Mysterioso Reef and Indian Key sectors, both of which had already been surveyed.

Like everyone else aboard, cookie Bob Weatherbee had looked over the Hubbard chart, but one afternoon as he listened to Webber discuss the matter at the galley table, he piped up with a suggestion:

"Have you looked at the chart as though it was drawn correctly to scale and that maybe it depicts the entire north bank, not just the northern portion? They might have done that because the whole area was dangerous to sailing vessels and hadn't been well charted."

Webber reached for the chart. If cookie was right, the chart represented not just the twenty-seven-mile-long northern dry reef portion of the shoals, but the whole forty-one-mile length of the north bank. He did several quick measurements using the new scale, then looked up, grinning.

"Bob, you're right. This *does* represent the whole bank. In fact the distances and proportions are very accurate for a chart drawn in the latter part of the seventeenth century. We've been thinking too hard."

As he studied the chart further from his new perspective, Webber soon solved another mystery, this one regarding the heads in the southeasternmost portion of the bank which were marked with both X's and triangles instead of X's only. The X's marked heads that were awash while the triangles designated heads deeper under water.

These new revelations provided a needed boost to the expedition's morale. Not only did the solutions bring all the available evidence in line, but the target area had narrowed to the six-mile-long Half Moon Reef, the central portion of which Webber had recently begun to survey. After more than two long hard months, there was renewed excitement.

The weather remained fair and hot and the survey proceeded smoothly. Because of calm waters, few buoy lines became entwined on coral outcroppings and thus divers rarely had to swim down to unravel snags. March 14 in particular was a no-snags day—not in itself remarkable, but had a buoy line snagged, a diver would have entered the water. Had he done so, on that occasion he may well have spotted an unusual collection of egg-shaped ballast rocks lying on a coral pedestal forty-five feet below him. He would have seen no other evidence of a shipwreck, however. No cannons, no anchors, no fittings. In fact, when the sensor head of the proton mag slowly passed over the spot, the recorder needle never so much as flickered. Unbeknownst to the occupants of the boat above, the grave of the *Concepción* had once more escaped detection.

Three days later, however, the mag picked up large amomalies on the windward side of a reef head. The source: a fourteen-foot anchor and several cannons. Divers found hull fittings, miscellaneous rigging, and datable artifacts identifying the wreck as being of seventeenth-century English origin. But there were other artifacts such as Spanish olive jars that were clearly not English. Could the ship have been a salvage vessel that took them from the wreck of the *Concepción*, then subsequently struck a reef herself and sank? The theory seemed plausible and, if true, Webber could be close to his prey.

In the weeks to follow, the dive team would regularly return to work this wreck on days when rough weather prevented survey work. The site yielded fascinating artifacts, including pewter plates, jugs, a silver spoon and fork, and ceramic pitchers. It was here, too, that Webber discovered deep in a sand pocket a square-shaped wooden rod nearly a yard long. It was a cross staff (also called a Jacob's Staff) used by seventeenth-century English and Dutch navigators to measure the sun's angle to determine latitude. The perpendicular sliding bar that accompanies such an instrument was missing but the rod itself was in excellent condition, having along its length well-defined numerical increments, small stars, a sun, even the date—1680—and the maker's initials S.T.R. The find was both valuable and historic, and the first cross staff ever retrieved from a sunken wreck.

By March 21 Webber had discovered three more wrecks, two of them found visually as well as magnetically, all of them of nineteenth-century vintage. The team pushed onward, aided now by Don Summers who had shown a remarkable talent for free diving, being able to comfortably descend as far as sixty feet for up to two minutes at a time. When diver John Berrier had to leave the expedition because of prior U.S. commitments, Summers was given his slot. After a week of intensive and thorough training by diver master Bob Coffey, "Abner" was as comfortable in the coral canyons of the reef as he was on the north forty back home. He also got acquainted with Firethorn coral with its tiny stinging cells that cause a sharp pain at the merest touch, and with coral cuts one inevitably sustains even though wearing a long-sleeved cotton jump-suit under water. Because the divers spent so much time each day in the water their coral cuts never really healed and infection was always a possibility.

There was another, more subtle, problem that now plagued Operation Phips. Almost everyone on the Big G was unaccountably nervous and irritable. At first Webber thought the situation was the natural result of long hot days at sea in cramped conditions. But now there were other symptoms: inability to sleep, occasional bouts of blurred vision, a tendency for one's legs to fall asleep shortly after sitting down, and a bizarre condition in which one feels as if warm metal objects were as cold as dry ice while cold objects were too hot to touch. Not until weeks after the expedition had returned to the U.S. would Webber learn that the ship's company was suffering from sigatura poisoning, an illness contracted from eating the fish caught in the waters around the Silver Shoals. With every grouper served up by cookie, the men of Operation Phips were unknowingly taking in more poison which in turn increased the severity of the symptoms and required everyone to make a supreme effort to avoid lashing out at each other. To this mix were added sleepless nights, the heat, and grueling workdays—altogether it was enough aggravation to break down the patience and goodwill of all but the strongest and most dedicated of souls. But the team persevered.

The Specter of Failure

The month of April began on a note of growing frustration as Webber slowly continued eastward along the Half Moon Reef. He was now surveying areas that did not conform gracefully to historical descriptions. By month's end his labors had produced only two large stockless anchors. The *Big G* returned to Puerto Plata and Webber drove to Santo Domingo for a scheduled huddle with Warren Stearns and Stan Smith.

Over a poolside lunch in the courtyard of the Nicolas de Ovando Hotel, Webber, his face peeling from sunburn, his hands nicked with coral cuts, got down to the heart of the matter.

"Gentlemen, here's where I'm at: You know from the beginning we've had a pretty severe restriction on how deep we can tow the sensor head. We didn't know we'd run into the problem until we got out there but the upshot is the mag may be too far off the bottom to pick up a weak target like the *Concepción*. Second, all the research points to her being somewhere in the central portion of the Half Moon Reef and with the exception of some fringe sectors, we've thoroughly magged that area. Frankly, I'm not encouraged. In fact, there's a good probability that we've missed the wreck."

Stearns and Smith looked grim. In recent weeks they, too, had sensed the possibility of failure. Further, the expedition was coming to the end of the ninety-day survey period for which funds had been budgeted. Several periods of rough weather had caused unavoidable delays, but now additional funds would have to be raised to complete a thorough survey of the remainder of the Half Moon Reef. Was it worth doing? The trio agreed it was.

While everyone knew that Operation Phips may well be destined to fail, there was no lessening of resolve. Despite the hardships (not the least being the as yet undiagnosed fish poisoning) there had been no major breakdowns or injuries and everyone was holding up well with the possible exception of Weatherbee. Of late cookie had upped his rum consumption at sea, so much so that he had nearly exhausted the engine room supply before the *Big G* returned to Puerto Plata. To prevent such a disaster, Don Summers attempted, with little success, to ration the goods, even hiding a bottle in the engine room bilges where no one would likely search. A week into the trip as he slipped yet another bottle of Brugal rum to cookie, Summers solemnly warned that it was all that was left of the stash and that he hoped Weatherbee would make the bottle last the remaining four days.

Cookie promised he would but failed completely. The bottle was empty in less than two days. A day later Weatherbee had begun to act nervously, but no one noticed, for that afternoon Don Summers almost died.

It began with a sudden weather change while the two boats were on the site of the seventeenth-century "cross staff" wreck. A squall on the horizon abruptly changed course and moved toward the reef. With only minutes to secure operations, Summers free dove to the bottom forty feet below and signaled to Webber and Ken Matz to return topside. By the time the pair reached the surface, high winds and blinding rain had hit the reef. Webber ordered the boats' anchors brought up immediately—but both had become fouled in coral.

Summers, breathing fairly hard from his free dive, volunteered to unsnarl the anchors. He entered the water to pull himself down the anchor chain. In the adjacent reef boat dive master Bob Coffey repeatedly yelled, "Keep an eye on Don!" The sky turned dark and the temperature plummeted ten degrees. While all hands worked quickly, Summers returned from an aborted free dive to put on a weight belt to compensate for the buoyancy of his wet suit. Again he took several deep breaths and kicked down to forty-five feet. In the gathering darkness he saw the anchor lines were tangled. He reached out to free them—and blacked out.

On the surface the wind was nearly gale force. A minute passed. No Summers. "What's happened to him?" Duke Long shouted. Everyone peered over the side into the murk. Visibility was hardly more than fifteen feet. Then Webber, who was hanging way over the bow with a facemask trying to spot Summers, saw the faint glow of orange reflector tape on Summers' snorkel. He signaled Long who was over the side in a flash. Webber followed and the two men kicked down to grab Summers. His body was streaming languidly in the current, his left swim fin entwined in the anchor line. The two rescuers quickly dragged him to the surface.

As soon as Bob Coffey in the other reef boat saw Summers' unconscious body being lifted aboard, he dove into the water and sprinted across to Webber's boat. Helping lay Summers on his back, Coffey immediately began cardio-pulmonary resuscitation. To do so he had to literally pry the snorkel's mouthpiece out of Summers' clenched teeth. A little more than a minute later Summers began to breathe again and he regained consciousness. He coughed slightly but there was little water in his lungs. The seven anxious men hovering over him breathed a collective sigh.

With the immediate danger past, the two boat crews still faced a serious threat, finding themselves on the reef's unprotected windward side where big waves could easily hurl the boats onto razor-sharp coral heads with lethal consequences. Wasting no time Webber directed Matz to buoy the two anchor lines and cut them loose. Under way in a dangerous following sea, Webber faced the task of guiding the boats through a narrow cut between the reef heads in a blinding rain with zero visibility. Fortunately, before he had left the *Big G* that morning, Webber had used a hand compass to note the bearing of the cross staff wrecksite. He now steered a reciprocal heading to bring the boats safely through the cut and back to the *Big G* anchored nearly a mile away.

When he realized what had happened to him, Don Summers was very glad to still be alive. His blacking out under water was caused by a lack of oxygen but one he couldn't feel because there had not been a sufficient build-up of carbon dioxide. It is the presence of the latter, not the absence of the former, that triggers pain and the intense desire to breathe. Summers' strenuous work and rapid respiration between dives had blown off a much greater than normal amount of carbon dioxide while his need for oxygen had increased. Thus, he felt only moderately uncomfortable before losing consciousness. What everyone later realized was that were it not for Summers' fin tangling in the anchor line, the strong current very likely would have swept him too far away to be found. That death did not visit the reef that afternoon was in large measure the result of the heads-up work of the dive team. From another perspective, Burt Webber's judgment in recruiting only first-rate professionals had once more been vindicated.

Though Summers' vital signs indicated he was recovering, he was running a fever and Webber opted to return that evening to Puerto Plata where a doctor could thoroughly check out Summers. As it happened, the *Big G*'s horizontally scanning sonar went out during warm-up, delaying departure until daybreak. That night, as Summers lay resting in his bunk, everyone aboard at one point or another stopped by to chat and see how he was getting along, including poor Bob Weatherbee who had gone for more than a day now without a drink. Summers saw his trembling visitor was clearly in far worse shape than he was. Touched by Weatherbee's concern, Summers relented:

"Cookie, do you remember my telling you a couple of days ago that

I was giving you the last bottle, that there was no more after that? Well, I confess I wasn't telling the truth. There's one more bottle down there. I'll tell you where to find it."

Cookie's face suddenly reflected a confused mixture of joy and resentment. After getting directions to the hiding place, he leaned over Summers and rasped, "Why, you dirty sonofabitch!" and dashed off to the engine room. When fellow crew members later learned of Summers' conversation, it was thereafter referred to as Abner's deathbed confession.

Failure

On the afternoon of May 29, Webber completed his magnetic survey of the Half Moon Reef. He had discovered two more wrecks (one eighteenth century, the other nineteenth) and another twelve-foot stockless anchor—but no *Concepción*. There was nothing more to be done other than to secure operations, and return to Puerto Plata for refueling, then head back to Florida.

"Burt, I want you to know something," Stearns said during a phone call before Webber departed the Dominican Republic. "This expedition may have failed but I absolutely believe in you and your approach to treasure hunting and I promise you I will somehow see that in the future you have some kind of ongoing professional business organization to support your continued work. You have done a tremendous job."

Webber thanked him for his kind words but the compliments failed to alter his deep disappointment. All that mattered was that Operation Phips had failed, its members were exhausted, and it was time to go home for a much-deserved rest.

As the *Big G* sailed from Puerto Plata, Webber was sure he never again would lay eyes on the Silver Shoals—or would ever want to. In five months he had found thirteen shipwrecks and thirteen anchors (a number that nautical tradition has never regarded as auspicious). He had accomplished the feat safely with no significant injuries or mechanical breakdowns, had proven the effectiveness of aerial charting and a professional team approach to a complex challenge. He could be justly proud of these things, but there was no escaping the bitter taste of defeat. Burt Webber was heartbroken. He had spent nearly a quarter of a million dollars to search for the *Concepción*, had sacrificed so much of himself in the process, and he had failed.

7

Aftermath—an
Invention and a
Startling Discovery

The Formation of Seaquest International

"Any postmortem analysis implies 'unpleasant' or 'unfortunate' results," wrote Dr. Pete Foose in his "Scientific Advisor's Report" at the conclusion of Operation Phips mailed to all the investors. "For all who were involved with Operation Phips this is partly true," he continued. "But only partly. Everyone who participated recognized in advance of their involvement the element of risk and the magnitude of the problem—that of finding a very small target (the *Concepción*) in an extremely complex coral reef in a large sea . . . In my opinion, however, there has not previously been any search for sunken treasure that has involved better equipment or as sophisticated and precise a method for search as that carried out by Operation Phips. It is doubtful that any prior treasure expedition has had more highly motivated and dedicated personnel or direction."

Foose went on to mention successful highlights of the expedition: the use of an aerial photomosaic as a base map, the remarkable sensitivity of the proton magnetometer, effective survey procedures, and the strategy sessions conducted regularly to update field observations with new historical data. Commenting on the "less-than-ideal" aspects of the trip, Foose mentioned the inability to precisely control the magnetic sensor depth, the lack of a handheld underwater sensing unit to compensate for that shortcoming, and the lack of time and funds to carry out realistic shakedown exercises which may have revealed the problems beforehand. These assessments were perfectly sound, of course, and Foose tried his best to sound upbeat, but for any investor who had dropped thirteen big ones on the hunt, the report sparkled about as much as a glass of day-old Perrier water.

In his director's report, Burt Webber was rigorously objective, tackling the job of explaining failure with a forthrightness that was his trademark.

"The ultimate inability to locate the shipwreck of the *Nuestra Señora de la Concepción*, lost on the Silver Bank," he began, "falls into two categories: research and survey magnetometry, although the former appears to be exempt from doubt."

The report recapped the research before the expedition as well as the revised interpretation of the Hubbard chart, all of which "indicated the shipwreck to be within the southeasternmost dry reef in the 'half moon' area." After discussing in detail the survey procedures used on the reef (and the critical problem of sensor depth control), Webber mentioned that ongoing research during the expedition had produced documents that revealed that ballast and hull timbers from the wreck of the *Concepción* in greater quantities than indicated in other accounts had been removed by divers, the result being there would likely be little or nothing left of the ship besides her treasure, rendering her a still weaker magnetic target. "Such a degree of dismantling," Webber concluded, "combined with the difficulties of the magnetometer survey plus the inability to precisely control the sensor depth, all suggest that the *Concepción* wrecksite escaped detection by the system we used."

(Webber later tested and confirmed this conclusion in the Florida Keys using a wreck in twenty-five to thirty feet of water which, because it had no cannons or anchors, represented a weak magnetic target similar to the *Concepción*. With the sensor head towed on the surface the wreck failed to register. On subsequent passes, it was not until the sensor was lowered to ten feet off the bottom that Webber was able to detect the anomalies produced by the wreck's hull fittings.)

Speaking for the December Group Ltd., president Jerry Neavolls declared himself generally pleased that the expedition was underwritten, "and I feel confident that investors probably received a 200 percent effort from the crew and other active participants for every hard dollar invested." He added, "We remain firmly convinced that efforts of this type, properly organized and done on a continuing basis, can become a legitimate business that will be financially rewarding to all concerned."

Neavolls tactfully neglected to say that he felt the whole idea of Operation Phips was a financial pipe dream from the get-go. In fact, during the expedition, life in the Chicago offices of DGL had not been smooth sailing, particularly for young Stan Smith who was responsible for the land-side coordination:

"Towards the end of the expedition none of us could get along with each other except for Warren and me. The more Neavolls hated Operation Phips the more I loved it. Tempers flared and egos clashed. I think I was fired and rehired at least twice during that unhappy period. Finally, as Burt was returning from the Dominican Republic I said to Warren, 'I can't live with this company anymore.' He said, 'All right, go away and think about it but don't neglect the idea of doing something with Burt.'"

Smith cleaned out his desk, picked up a paycheck, and went back to his Chicago apartment, determined not to think about anything for the next few days, least of all a very bleak-looking future. A few weeks later Stearns himself cashed out of the December Group then promptly sustained a slipped disc while playing a hard game of tennis. He ended up in the hospital for ten days, flat on his back, with no medical insurance, no job prospects, and a rapidly declining bank account. (Before the year was out he would have spent a total of seventy-five days at home in bed.) When he was recovered enough to get around, Stearns called a meeting with Webber and Smith.

"It was the darkest hour for all of us," Smith remembers. "There we sat in that room, each of us thinking we were the world's biggest failures to each other and in our own eyes. It would be hard to imagine three more despondent people."

Webber talked of the previous five months but at the first hint of apology, Stearns interrupted: "Wait a minute, Burt. Nobody bought the wreck of the *Concepción*. They bought a piece of a venture. That means they bought the risk as well as the treasure. OK, so you didn't find the wreck but you did everything to the letter, you proved the concept can work as a business, you didn't lie, you didn't pass the buck or blame Haskins or anybody else. Once more, I promised you I'd help put you in the treasure hunting business on a level that it's never been done before, putting together our concepts to do it the right way."

Stearns' comments were not intended as therapy. Rather, they were a preamble to the creation of something that on that dreary afternoon neither Stearns nor Webber nor Smith could really envision clearly or tackle with enthusiasm. But there was something operative within that nucleus, an inspirational momentum collectively initiated by a trio of remarkable individuals each of whom was in his own way brilliant. As that momentum gathered strength in the months ahead, spurred on by hard work, miracles, and coincidence, the vision would gradually attain form and definition as perhaps the most sophisticated, innovative, well-funded, professionally run—and successful—treasure hunting entity in the history of free enterprise.

What came out of that meeting was the framework for Seaquest International, a Chicago-based corporation that would underwrite full-time first-rate research in the world's depositories, conduct the legal staff work necessary to acquire leases of desired search areas, raise additional funds as necessary for specific projects, find treasure, and oversee all phases of marketing same. Stearns estimated Seaquest would need enough capital to operate for an initial period of three years exclusive of any treasure discoveries. The price tag: $1,165,000.

The plan looked promising on paper but the goal seemed hopelessly out of reach for three men who were not altogether sure how they were going to come up with grocery money in three months' time. Webber remembers the struggle well:

"I can't adequately describe what Warren and Stan and I went through. Of course, Pete Foose and my lawyer Ken Beall and Seaquest attorney Tim Lowry tried to contribute as much as they could but they all had full-time careers elsewhere that provided secure income while we had to keep a constant eye on the wolf at the door. Then, too, Warren was in a rut, despondent, dragging his feet. He really wasn't sure which direction to move because of the failure of Operation Phips and his departure from the December Group. And while he still believed in me he had to carefully consider his next career move. So it was hard to get going. Not only that but it took months of delays and legal complications just to find the best way to structure the organization, how to raise money to stay alive in the interim by establishing a pre-Seaquest joint-venture fund with special stock considerations when and if the thing ever got off the ground. But finally in November 1977 we had completed and printed an offering circular for Seaquest International and went to work to find investors."

The circular was first rate and well argued but the initial reaction was discouraging. Stan Smith, who had happily worked eighteen-hour days administering Operation Phips, felt powerless: "I became more and more despondent, because for whatever else I knew how to do I was not the guy to raise a million one fifty-five. For one thing I didn't have the contacts. Plus Warren was in and out of the hospital with his back problem and it began looking to me as if I was destined . . . I mean one of my occasional paranoid fantasies at that time was that I would wind up on Skid Row."

By February 1978, Stearns had had time to assess the difficulties. "I saw that Seaquest International had three problems," he recalls. "Number one, we didn't have a specific target such as the *Concepción* to offer to potential investors. Instead, we were offering a company that would at some undetermined point go after a not-yet-specified target. Number two, since we were selling common stock there was no way an investor could write off his investment that year. And three, I'm sure investors were troubled by the fact that we had just come off a failure with Operation Phips.

"But surprisingly, Burt and I were still able to sell shares, particularly if we could pitch investors directly. But usually what happened was I could call an investment banker in Denver, for example, and he'd say the idea sounds terrific, then a month would go by and I'd never hear from him. So the fund raising was taking a lot of time."

During a meeting to discuss the matter, the would-be principals of Seaquest agreed to take advantage of an excellent working relationship with the Dominican Republic and begin looking for potential targets in its waters. For example, Santo Domingo, the oldest New World city, was at the mouth of the Ozama River which opens into an ancient harbor where literally hundreds of ships had sunk, many carrying treasure. If historian Jack Haskins were to research the wrecks of the Santo Domingo harbor at the archives in Seville, he was bound to come up with one or more likely targets. Webber liked the idea. Not only would Seaquest be able to obtain easily a lease for a new project that would help launch the corporation, but the search area would likely contain several pre-Columbian wrecks that would yield artifacts of far greater value than coins or specie.

Shortly after the conference, Webber called Haskins at his home in Islamorada, Florida, and explained the situation, adding that the researcher's expenses would be covered by money from the pre-Seaquest operating fund. Haskins readily agreed and by early March was on his way to Seville.

Webber in the meantime divided his time between helping Stearns with presentations to investor groups and conferring with Varian Associates about a special housing he was designing for their portable cesium unit:

"The ideas were starting to come together now. The portable cesium unit Varian had developed had a compact transistorized console unit that operated off a rechargeable battery pack that would be worn around the shoulder or waist, the same type of pack that TV film crews use. This was fine for land use but for underwater applications I designed a Plexiglas housing that would incorporate the console unit and the batteries in a complete package together with waterproof bulkhead controls and earphones. Then all you'd have to do is demagnetize the diver by exchanging all ferromagnetic fittings on his equipment with nonferrous ones. Properly designed, an underwater housing for the cesium could result in the entire unit having a neutral buoyancy—or adjusted to any degree of positive or negative buoyancy."

There was another feature of the Varian product that Webber liked: The cesium magnetometer was ten times more sensitive than its proton precursor and provided constant readings as opposed to the two-second cycling time of the proton unit. It would be six months or more before even a prototype housing would be constructed but at least Webber could look forward to solving the problem of precision depth control he encountered on the Silver Shoals. If he had had a portable underwater cesium during Operation Phips, he very likely would have found the *Concepción*. But Webber was not one to grieve over the past. His own search for the great galleon was over, all water under the reef, so to speak.

Standefer Aims at the Concepción

Or was it? Within a four-week period two events occurred that abruptly pushed the *Concepción* back onto center stage. The first began with a phone call to the Seaquest's corporate offices which at the time consisted of a filing cabinet and an extra phone at the kitchen table of Stan Smith's modest apartment. A potential Seaquest investor from Milwaukee asked Smith if he had seen the ad in the *Wall Street Journal* soliciting limited partnership investors for an expedition to Silver Shoals to find the *Concepción*. No, he hadn't, a surprised Smith replied. The caller said he had answered the ad and had received a prospectus. "It reads pretty well," he added. "Says here the name of the guy who's going to run the expedition is Dennis Standefer."

Curious to see the prospectus, Smith asked for a copy. When it arrived several days later he quickly read through the first few sections and immediately understood why the circular read so well: Entire paragraphs—and sometimes pages at a time—were direct lifts from the Operation Phips offering circular. Smith read on with some fascination, hoping to find somewhere evidence that Standefer and/or his researchers had come up with any documentation on the *Concepción* that Haskins had not found. On page 5 a paragraph stated that all the information available on the *Concepción* was a product of years of intensive research in Spain and the British Museum. Smith almost laughed. The paragraph was from page 11 of the Phips circular. Turning to the lengthy exhibits on the wreck of the *Concepción* and the historical background of the Spanish Main (some eleven pages in all) Smith was not surprised that both were practically word-for-word copies of the same sections of the Operation Phips circular.

Predictably, when Burt Webber and Warren Stearns saw the Standefer prospectus, they, too, were incensed. But there really was nothing much they could do. True, the Silver Shoals Expedition, Ltd. circular contained significant chunks of plagiarized material from the Operation Phips offering, yet the latter document was privately circulated and had not (and probably could not have) been copyrighted.

Attorney Tim Lowry, acting for Seaquest, wrote to the Chief of Staff of the Dominican Republic Navy, informing him of Standefer's apparent intentions, then wrote a second letter, this one to Standefer, advising him of the D.R.'s active exercise of its claim over the Silver Shoals and of the exploration lease that Webber had obtained. That done, the matter was dropped. Stearns continued his fund-raising efforts for Seaquest while Webber and Smith awaited word from Seville regarding possible treasure wrecks in the Santo Domingo harbor.

Professor Earle's Casual Remark

For his part, Jack Haskins, after nearly a week of snooping on behalf of Seaquest in the Seville archives, had not come across any promising wrecks in the Santo Domingo harbor or along the southern coast of the Dominican Republic. But while conducting his research he happened to meet in the scholar's room a young Canadian woman who knew a great deal about the *Concepción*.

Her name was Victoria Stapells-Johnson. An attractive articulate woman in her twenties, she had spent more than six months of nearly full-time research in behalf of Peter Earle, a professor of economic history at the University of London and the London School of Economics. For some time Professor Earle had been writing a book about the history of the *Concepción* and of the subsequent attempts to recover her—though he himself was not at all interested in her treasure. Haskins was delighted to meet another archivist who had also researched the *Concepción* and the two spent long hours talking familiarly about people and events from an era more than three centuries earlier. This chance meeting and shared interests would prove fateful.

Haskins returned home to Florida with a folder of photocopied documents relating to shipwrecks in the Santo Domingo harbor and the south coast. None, however, were in Haskins' opinion worthy of a serious salvage effort. When Webber received this report, he was despondent. How much longer could the agony last? He called Chicago and relayed the news to Stearns and Smith. Stearns tried to cheer his companions by saying he was slowly rounding up pledges of support. But the three men knew they were getting close to the end of their collective rope. A mood of quiet desperation set in. Webber spent several long evenings sitting glumly in the living room of his modest Annville home, surrounded by artifacts and coins, mementos of seventeen years of treasure hunting. Not even his wife Sandy could budge him from his grim meditation.

A man can take only so much failure before bitterness and cynicism begin to destroy his faith and goodwill. Burt Webber had had seventeen years of failure, yet he still hung on, fighting to survive with the same savage hope and tenacity as the *Concepción* herself. In a real sense Webber was like the Indian Andres de la Cruz who had floated for days toward Puerto Plata, holding on to a plank from the shattered galleon, watching his companions drift off into madness or become food for sharks. De la Cruz had prayed for deliverance and it had been granted. Burt Webber, whose long quest to realize a dream had itself become a kind of prayer, was likewise about to receive a helping hand from Providence.

When Haskins, on his return from Spain, had told Seaquest of Peter Earle and his book-in-progress on the *Concepción,* he was asked to get in touch with the professor with an eye toward establishing a useful research contact in England. Haskins did so and, in the course of a phone call, offered to share any data on the *Concepción* which the historian may not have. Earle was delighted to learn of Haskins' interest and promised to stay in regular touch. Some weeks later, in early April, Haskins received a letter from Earle in which he discussed the progress on his book manuscript and touched on several minor points concerning the salvage of the *Concepción*. Toward the end of his letter, Earle casually asked, "Incidentally, are you aware that the journal of the *Henry of London* exists in Maidstone here in England? I'd be happy to arrange for you to look it over if you'd be interested."

Haskins was thunderstruck. After years of searching for the log of the ship that actually discovered the *Concepción* forty-six years after her sinking, a logbook that very likely contained precise bearings and distances to the wreck, the Florida historian had found only tantalizing excerpts here and there. He had scoured the Archives of the British Admiralty, spent weeks in the Bodelian Library at Oxford, and probed deep in the British Museum—all to no avail. And now, in a chatty letter from a new acquaintance in England, he had learned that the vital document's whereabouts were known. Like the chance sea feather which Cotton Mather claimed had attracted the eye of the diver aboard the *Henry*'s longboat, which in turn led to the galleon's discovery in 1687, Peter Earle's letter seemed an unexpected signpost that would lead to the solution of the mystery. If so, this amounted to an utterly extraordinary stroke of good fortune.

Haskins immediately called Earle at his London apartment to say that, yes, he would be most interested to have a look at the logbook of the *Henry*. He was keenly aware he had just delivered the greatest understatement of his life. Earle offered more details: The log had apparently been turned over to Sir John Narbrough after Phips' triumphant first expedition. Subsequent to Narbrough's death in 1688, the logbook, together with many other books and documents of the Narbrough estate, had passed from one private library to another for many generations, eventually ending up in the hands of the sixth Earl of Romney. In 1965, the Earl donated much of the Narbrough collection to the library and archives of suburban Maidstone in Kent, about sixty miles southeast of London. Earle, with more than two decades experience as an English archivist, eventually tracked down the Maidstone repository. Of the logbook itself, Earle remembered that it did give details of the day the *Henry* found the *Concepción* but he couldn't recall if the descriptions would have any meaning for contemporary searchers. Haskins replied that it was worth a trip to England to find out and he would be in touch again soon.

Haskins next phoned Webber in Pennsylvania, reaching him late at night. The good news hit his companion like a bombshell. Possibly, just possibly, Webber's long night of darkness was about to end. Webber hung up and excitedly told Sandy of the discovery. She beamed, very happy to once again see the old spark in her husband's eyes.

"Look, Warren, if this is true, I've got to go there," Webber told Stearns on the phone the following morning. There was a slight pause on the Chicago end. A great deal hung in the balance. If Stearns agreed, it was tantamount to taking another look at the *Concepción;* it meant raising at least a thousand dollars from somewhere to pay Webber's expenses to England on a gamble that the logbook held the key. It meant that Stearns might be regarded as a fool for even toying with a wreck that had already proven a loser. It also meant that Warren Stearns believed in Burt Webber.

"Burt," he replied, "we're out of money but I'll raise it. Make reservations for a flight out of Boston and I'll arrange to have tickets waiting for you at the check-in counter."

Two days later Webber packed a bag, together with a package containing several charts of the Silver Shoals, and flew to London where he rendezvoused at Heathrow Airport with Haskins who had flown in from Miami hours earlier. This was Webber's first trip to England but so consumed with purpose was the visitor that he paid scant heed to Big Ben and bobbies, shrugged off jet lag, and together with Haskins immediately proceeded to an early evening appointment with Professor Earle.

"She Bears from Our Ship . . ."

Over pints of bitter the three men spent a long pleasant evening reminiscing about the story of the *Concepción,* sharing stories of the principal characters in the galleon's saga, comparing notes from obscure archival documents, and looking over various maps and charts. For Burt Webber, this was a time in his life in which each moment seemed to glow with special intensity:

"It was so rewarding for all of us to talk of events as though they had happened yesterday. And of course we talked of the journal. Peter said he would call the Maidstone Library first thing in the morning to make sure they would be expecting us. Before we left that evening he gave us the logbook's catalog number. The following day was very rainy and drizzly as we boarded our train to Kent. I can't tell you how exciting that ride was. I spent the entire time asking myself, 'What does the log have? What does it really say? Will it give bearings? Could the reef heads have changed since then?' Because Peter Earle couldn't remember what it had said since the data were of little interest to him.

"We got off the train and there up on a little hill two blocks away was the county courthouse and library. A few minutes later we walked in, trying very hard not to look too anxious. It wasn't a large library, but it was wood paneled and kind of cozy and quiet. We filled out a request card with the catalog number of the logbook and gave it to the young woman. She smiled and said Peter Earle had called earlier to advise of our coming. While she disappeared into the stacks to get the journal, Jack and I looked around us nervously. Suddenly, we both spied on the far wall a large sign showing a cartoon of some kind of parasite bug holding a metal detector. Beneath were the words 'Beware of Treasure Hunters! They rape the land and steal our precious heritage.' Jack and I looked at each other and tried not to laugh.

"A moment later the woman appeared with a large folio labeled 'The Narbrough Papers' and handed it to us. We took it to a large table in one corner and opened it. And there it was—the *Journal of the Henry of London*, dated 1687. It was almost incredible. Now Jack's very good with the old English, just as he is with the old Spanish. I can do the English but I'm slow, so right away he starts running through the log, glancing at the headings at the top of each page—'Voyage to Hispaniola,' 'Voyage to Samana Bay,' et cetera. Then suddenly there it is: 'From Puerto Plata to the North Bank.' Jack starts flipping through the log entries quickly, too fast for me to keep up. And I'm really getting mad, telling Jack to slow down so I could read the entries. I was really getting hot under the collar."

Abruptly, Haskins slowed down at an entry marked "Thursday the 20th." "Here it is, Burt." The two men read the entry in awed silence:

At 8 in the morning weighed with a fine small breeze at South-Southeast, running down Northwest and Northwest-by-North along the south side of the reef. After we passed those boylers from which we weighted, met with very few, and a constant depth from 15 to 16 fathoms, rocky ground and at 11 of the clock, having run down much about the same place where they left off searching, stood in with the reef, 'til our depth was ten fathoms and came to with our grapnel and chain South from the reef one and a half miles. Had a boyler east of us distance about three shiplengths. At noon observed and made latitude twenty degrees 37 minutes north. Soon after the boat and canoe went a searching and in two hours time our boat returned on board again bringing us happy and joyful news of the canoe finding the wreck, there being in her Mr. Covell, Francis Ingona and two divers, for which blessings we return praise and thanks to Almighty God. Our boat carried with her chain and grapnel and a new buoy rope and a new buoy with several wooden buoys and two long oars to fix upon the wreck that we might then better find her when we came upon the bank next. She lies in the midst of the reef between three large boylers, the tops of which are dry at low water. In some places upon her there is seven fathoms which is the largest depth, 6 and 5 the shallowmost part. Most of the timber is consumed away and so overgrown with coral that had it not been for her guns she would scarce ever have been found, it being at least 45 years since she was lost and the richest ship that ever went out of the West Indies.

With bounding hearts the two men next read the words which each for so long had prayed he would someday discover:

She bears from our ship East by South and a half South about three miles off and the westmost end of the reef in sight bearing West of us and the eastmost end Southeast by East and a half South. Fine fair weather all the 24 hours with small Southerly breezes. At sunset the boat and canoe returned on board having taken up: 3 sows, 1 champeine, one bar, 51 dollars, 21 half dollars [meaning pieces of 4], and ten pieces of two, in silver and coin money.

Burt Webber was ecstatic:
"When I finished reading the entry I felt like dancing on the table. Literally. Jack and I were jubilant. I understood immediately why the entry would make little sense to anyone who didn't know the reef very well. But as I read I could picture everything: Yes, that's the east end of the six-mile reef, exactly as they said. And when they moved up along the south side their anchorage would be right here. That's correct. Everything correlated perfectly and I felt in my heart right then and there, in that little library in Maidstone, that the *Concepción* had been found."

In the moments following the discovery Webber quickly converted the archaic compass headings into their modern degree equivalents and plotted the resulting bearing and distance lines on a chart drawn from the aerial mosaic. He penciled in an *X* on the chart. "There she is, Jack." The spot was slightly north of the mid-point of the Half Moon Reef and well within the perimeters the two men had plotted using the data from the Phips' expeditions.

Doing his best to maintain a scholarly composure, Webber managed to persuade the librarian to make an exception to library policy against photocopying bound documents. Somewhat puzzled by these two Americans, she copied the crucial page from the *Henry's* logbook, unaware that the information it contained was worth millions, perhaps tens of millions, of dollars.

Webber knew that a tremendous effort lay ahead of him before he would again return to the Silver Shoals, yet as he walked down the steps outside the Maidstone Library that dreary day he was euphoric. For once in his young life, the years of learning, his steady development of search procedures, his methodical approach, his technical innovations, his belief in himself—and all those years without a real success—seemed close to the brink of a total vindication. Returning to London the two treasure hunters immediately proceeded to Kings Row where they treated themselves by ordering elegant three-piece business suits.

"Dear Partners . . ."

There were those in the Chicago investment banking community who felt that Warren Stearns was nuts to have anything more to do with the search for the *Concepción* regardless of new information and search techniques. One could appreciate the argument: It is risky enough getting involved in a treasure hunt in the first place, but to take a proven loser like the *"De-cepción,"* which had defeated men and fortunes for centuries, and promote yet another attempt, is tantamount to professional suicide. Moreover, to come off a quarter-million-dollar loss and then turn right around nine months later to attempt raising another quarter million for the same venture would seem an impossible task. Stearns not only disagreed emphatically with the assessment but also vowed to raise even more for the second attempt.

"Any critics I may have had simply didn't know Burt Webber," Stearns recalled later. "Look, the guy *had* to be a winner from the day I first met him. I absolutely believed in him. So what do you do? Go out and lose one lousy round and say the fight's over? Or do you do what you believe? Generally, you do what you believe right up until you can't pay the rent anymore. Well, as long as we could pay the rent we were going for it all the way."

Despite the promising breakthroughs, the campaign to return to the Silver Shoals began slowly. Webber, Stearns, and Smith agreed to halt all fund raising for Seaquest International and instead launch Operation Phips II, an Illinois-limited partnership. The goal: thirty units of L.P. interest at $15,000 a shot for a total of $450,000. A new offering circular was needed quickly, a task which fell on Stan Smith at a time when his thoughts were less occupied with treasure than with a compound fracture of a broken heart:

"I had just broken up with my fiancée six weeks before we were to be married. But after five days of despondency I decided that now was the time in my life to take the bull by the horns. I was either going to take over and produce and create or waste away in self-pity. So for the next six weeks I worked full-time on the offering circular, bringing together chunks written by Burt and Warren, adding sections of my own, then getting it typed and finally printed. In many ways those six weeks were the most rewarding I'd had in a long time."

In the meantime, Webber wrote to the investors who had participated in Operation Phips (now referred to as "Phips 1"):

Dear Partners:

In April of this year, I learned for the first time of new material in Europe which we came upon during the course of Seaquest's on-going research efforts. It is most exciting! I immediately flew to Europe to read the actual *Log of the Ship Henry*, which discovered the *Concepción* 46 years after she sank, enabling Phips to earn his treasure and an enduring reputation. *The daily journal gives precise directions to, and bearings of, the sunken wreck to within a one-eighth-square-mile area*. She lies within the area originally searched. Despite finding 13 other wrecks, our surface-towed magnetometer did not detect her.

In my association with Varian Associates of Canada during the last 12 months, I have developed a completely submersible, diver-operated, hand-held cesium magnetometer that will allow a diver to position the sensor head to within a few feet of the base of the reef heads.

Given the *Henry* log and the new mags, I am convinced detection of the *Concepción* is virtually assured. We will be searching an area only ten to 15% as large as the original target area. . . . I am President and the largest shareholder of Seaquest. I recognize the importance to Seaquest and to me personally of having a success in the first expedition sponsored by it. Recognizing this, and having reviewed many other available targets in the "low-risk" category, I nevertheless enthusiastically recommend this new expedition *and believe chances of success are truly excellent . . .*

Webber's optimism was clearly evident in the letter but he had been through too many campaigns not to know that weeks of drudgery and very hard work lay ahead:

"Once we mailed out the offering circular to what seemed like everyone in the known universe, I started touring, appearing before small investment groups, luncheon meetings with two or three people at a time that Warren would set up. Oh it was a drag. The same pitch over and over, like selling encyclopedias, only I was going to places like Columbus, Indianapolis, Chicago, and Boston. In spite of the log of the *Henry*, the campaign was long and frustrating and at times depressing because each time I had to prove that the log was for real and that what it was saying was, 'This is where the wreck is.'"

Yet, for all his complaining and distaste for his role as traveling pitchman, Burt Webber, as Stearns knew, was nothing less than awesome as a salesman. No other treasure hunter, it seemed, could approach Webber in his mastery of facts, his command of every facet of his profession, and his intense, articulate, professional presentation. Investors who may have doubted the odds of finding the *Concepción* were nonetheless drawn to the project—they were investing in Burt Webber, this modern-day William Phips who talked with an enviable sincerity, who had a dream.

By early summer 1978 with indications that Phips II would become a reality by the fall, Webber flew to Canada with Dr. Pete Foose for a design conference with Varian engineers. Webber was particularly concerned with ensuring that the Plexiglas housing for the cesium electronics would maintain its fail-safe watertight integrity under the stress to be incurred in man-handling the unit from the salvage vessel to a reef boat in choppy seas. He also talked about possible field interference from ferrous equipment worn by the diver in the operation, for he knew that the cesium's super sensitivity necessitated dive gear that was all, or nearly all, ferrous free. To meet this requirement, Webber found an ally in the Dacor Corporation (a major manufacturer of scuba equipment) whose engineers provided him with components of the gear that would be worn under water.

During a field test, the interference (if any) on the cesium caused by each metal component was carefully measured. In the end Webber would ask Dacor to prepare several customized buoyancy vests, replacing all ferrous fittings with ones made of bronze. In another field test, Webber used several artifacts from his collection—cargo hooks, hull spikes and cannon balls—to evaluate the cesium's response to magnetic targets identical to those he would be looking for on the shoals. The mag was extraordinarily sensitive.

That Varian, a major corporation in the electronics industry, was agreeing to modify and package a cesium for underwater use was in itself quite remarkable, for its engineers were behind schedule on several military contracts. But Burt Webber's association and consulting work with the company had earned him professional respect and, on this occasion, a deserved favor.

Because the performance of the cesium would be critical on the shoals, Webber knew from experience he would need two units, one for back-up in case of an outage. But they didn't come cheap—each portable cesium plus battery pack, charger, and spare parts ran close to $17,000. Yet, considering the mags were keys that could unlock the door to a fortune, they were most definitely worth the price.

Returning home to Pennsylvania, Webber called Warren Stearns to report his encouraging progress with Varian. The Wizard of Oz in Chicago was very upbeat—the money was coming in steadily now. The conversation shifted to likely groupings of coral heads within the target area in which the wreck of the *Concepción* probably lay. There were three such candidates. Warren arbitrarily chose one group and bet Webber $100 that the wreck would be discovered there.

"Warren, I trust you won't be too upset if I find the wreck among one of the other two groups," Webber replied.

Stearns chuckled and allowed as he wouldn't mind at all. In fact if the *Concepción* was discovered as predicted, he wouldn't even mind if people blamed him for personally engineering the most successful "failure" of a tax shelter scheme in modern times.

8

Operation Phips II— the Long Wait Under Guard

Tony Garton and Samala

As Burt Webber now turned his attention to the nuts and bolts of outfitting a return expedition to the Silver Shoals, Seaquest learned of political developments in the Dominican Republic that could have ominous implications for Operation Phips II. In the elections held in that country in May, Joaquín Balaguer, the Dominican Republic's president since 1966, lost his bid to retain office to a relative newcomer, Antonio Guzmán, a businessman with rather more liberal leanings. For some time rumors of a coup had circulated around Santo Domingo amid fears that the productive stability that had accompanied Balaguer's years in office might soon end. Of prime concern to Seaquest was that, should such an event occur, its contract with the Dominican state might well be one of the first casualties. Weeks later, when it became evident that Guzmán would assume the reins of power without incident,

Seaquest could not rule out the possibility that the new administration might decide to renegotiate or even unilaterally cancel the agreement. Elsewhere, the Dominican Navy's Chief of Staff, Admiral Rivera, had recently retired (in part because of illness) leaving Seaquest uncertain as to whether his successor would be favorably disposed to an American expedition.

The Dominicans had already proved themselves worthy partners the year before by providing a patrol boat escort for the *Big G* after the Norman Scott encounter, and Webber knew their Navy's continued protection could well be critical in the months ahead. Not only were there Dennis Standefer's announced intentions to visit the shoals, but other rivals such as Scott might have another go at the *Concepción*. Actually, in the latter part of 1977 a Captain Ronald Becker, working out of Caicos Island, had probed the shoals aboard his 102-foot converted German patrol vessel. He, too, was hunting for the galleon but had reportedly rammed his vessel on a coral head, sustaining extensive damage. Reports indicated a Puerto Rico-based sea-going tug had to be dispatched to pull the stricken vessel off the reef and tow her back to the States for repairs. Whether or not that expedition had been well equipped for its task, what bothered Webber was that Captain Becker was the third treasure hunter (besides himself) in the past eighteen months to either visit the Silver Shoals or try to, or say he would in the near future. The fact that there would certainly be more attempts in the future was not comforting.

While Seaquest sought confirmation from the new government of the Dominican Republic regarding the lease, fund raiser Warren Stearns was kept busy answering questions from investors who had read a story appearing in several major newspapers concerning Dennis Standefer's announced expedition to search for the *Concepción*. Standefer's Seaborne Ventures, Inc. was apparently succeeding in its own goal of raising $500,000 and the outfitting of the *R/V James Bay* in Seattle was moving along on schedule. As part of an active media campaign, Seaborne had prepared a handsome, agency-created thirty-page brochure entitled "Seaborne Ventures, Inc.—Silver Shoals Expedition." Less an offering circular than a profile of the corporation and the historical background of the *Concepción*, the document, with its embossed cover, charts, photographs, and tissue overlays, was first rate and impressive. As a result of the publicity Seaborne had generated, both Stearns and Webber spent a good deal of time on the phone to magazine and newspaper editors explaining Seaquest's activities, stressing in particular the existence of an exclusive Seaquest lease arrangement with the Dominican Republic.

One periodical, *Sport Diver,* conducted phone interviews with both Webber and Standefer for an article in its July 1978 issue titled "Many Seek Silver Shoals Treasure." The magazine agreed with Seaborne Ventures that the Silver Shoals is in international waters but concluded that the Dominican Republic had both the guns and the inclination to make its claim of sovereignty stick. Hence anyone who found treasure there would have to divvy it up with the D.R., like it or not. The article described the *Concepción* as a very exciting wreck to work and suggested that potential investors exercise great discretion before buying in on any scheme to find her.

At this juncture Webber and Stearns flew to Santo Domingo for an introductory meeting with the new Navy Chief of Staff, Admiral Francisco Amiama. During a cordial meeting they learned that the admiral had been fully briefed on Webber's 1977 expedition to the Silver Shoals and was prepared to provide the Navy's full cooperation with Operation Phips II. Included were assurances to Seaquest that the exploration lease was very much in force and would be honored by the Dominican state. Burt Webber, it appeared, had a considerable reservoir of goodwill on which to draw. Doubtless his insistence on donating all the artifacts found on the first expedition (including the cross staff, valued in the tens of thousands of dollars) to the Naval Museum was a gesture that had not been overlooked. By way of further confirmation, Admiral Amiama, at Webber's request, assigned as the Navy's on-board liaison officer for Phips II, a young naval officer who spoke English fluently and whom Webber had befriended during Phips I.

Armed with these assurances, Webber for the most part relinquished further media-jousting tasks to Warren Stearns and Stan Smith and in August flew to Antigua in the British West Indies to line up a vessel for the expedition. A U.S. charter agent had highly recommended the *M/V Samala* not only for its accommodations but also for its remarkable owner-captain, Tony Garton. A strapping barrel-chested Englishman in his mid-fifties who wore imposing horn-rimmed glasses, Garton has the square-jawed determined good looks of an aristocratic admiral used to commanding men and ships. Moreover, his background was ideally suited for the task Webber envisioned.

Born into a prosperous family and educated in first-rate schools, Garton spent World War II in the Royal Navy, where for some time he served as an officer aboard a fleet oiler, later being rescued at sea after the ship was torpedoed by a German U-boat. After the war, he attended hotel school in Switzerland, then formed a highly successful hotel-management consulting firm, a venture that turned into an exhausting nonstop rat race, so much so that Garton cashed out in the early fifties and moved to the British West Indies. After a brief but scary bout with polio in 1956, Garton returned to England, bought a surplus coastal anti-submarine escort vessel, converted it to a motor yacht, christened it *Warrior Geraint* and by 1958 had begun a lucrative charter business out of Cannes, France, becoming a gourmet cook in the process. While there he met Jacques Cousteau. The two got along famously and soon thereafter Cousteau had chartered the *Warrior Geraint* for an eleven-week-long expedition to work on a sunken Roman galley in the Mediterranean. There followed two other Cousteau charters, one to the Red Sea to study sharks, the other to document Dr. John C. Lilly's work with dolphins.

In 1962 Garton shifted his home port to Antigua, and for the next decade enjoyed continued success as a top-rated charter operator, raconteur, and gourmet cook. When the *Warrior Geraint* was totaled in a 1973 freak fire caused by a faulty safety apparatus on a propane gas bottle, Garton went into partnership with two Canadian friends and purchased a beautiful ex-Royal Navy motor minesweeper built in 1958 and which for some reason had been mothballed a year later. Loading twenty tons of teak and mahogany aboard, Garton took the 112-foot vessel to a noted shipyard in Portugal where shipwrights and carpenters stripped her nearly to her hull and rebuilt her into a top of the line motor yacht. Rechristening her *M/V Samala* (after an obscure bay on the Yucatán peninsula with an easy-to-pronounce name), Garton returned to Antigua in 1975 and once again plunged into a busy schedule of charter cruises for a prominent and classy clientele. Among the *Samala*'s notable guests were ex-Beatle Paul McCartney, his wife Linda and their band Wings who in 1977 chartered the yacht in conjunction with a vacation and floating recording session. Garton and his crew received rave reviews for making the voyage, in McCartney's words, "The best recording session we ever had."

With business booming, one might ask why in August 1978 Captain Tony Garton would seriously consider chartering *Samala* to a treasure hunter who would need to convert her to a salvage vessel. Garton himself explains:

"Two reasons: the idea and the man. I was fascinated with the project and Burt Webber himself was really remarkable. He flew down to Antigua to discuss his plan and I knew immediately he was an utterly dedicated, sincere guy. And a powerful talker. His diction is good, he's aware and makes people aware of what he's saying. And he put everything in marvelous sequence—the event, the history, the past, and on up to the present. Burt lives history, absolutely lives it. By the time he was through, I was dead keen. We had a very good season coming up, however, and it took time to convince my partners that the charter was worthwhile but in the end I had my way."

Threats in Miami

While Garton made plans to bring the *Samala* to Miami by the second week of October for outfitting, Webber returned to the States to embark on a final round of business meetings, planning sessions, and phone calls with suppliers. While he remained in regular contact with Varian engineers in Canada (who'd promised a late-October delivery of the cesium mags), Webber stayed in frequent touch with the Dacor Corporation (the only company among the many Webber had approached that agreed to help) and its staff went all out to meet stringent demands. The company supplied aluminum scuba tanks and a number of plastic backpacks that were later modified with nylon straps that fastened not with metal buckles but with Velcro contact strips. Webber was, in fact, the vortex of a swirling energy field that was gradually gaining intensity and momentum, one that challenged his ability to stay on top of not only Velcro straps and delivery dates but also a host of "dry-side" developments out of Seaquest's Chicago office where Messrs. Stearns and Smith were working overtime in their own cyclone. Finally in early October, after a brief vacation home, Webber kissed Sandy and his four children goodbye and flew to Miami to await the arrival of Tony Garton and the *Samala*.

The vessel arrived on schedule October 12, crossed Biscayne Bay and proceeded a quarter-mile up the Miami River to a pre-arranged berth at the Miami Shipyard. When Webber stepped aboard he felt a special excitement—he was back aboard ship again. The *Samala* was the first physical evidence of a great quest that was beginning to materialize beyond the vaporous realm of contracts, phone calls, bank balances, and mountains of paper. Moving his gear aboard, including his battered, much-traveled attaché case full of research, Webber took one of the aft staterooms, ordered a telephone installed in the saloon topside, and proceeded immediately to supervise the delivery and installation of $101,000 worth of capital equipment. With any luck the job would be done in three weeks.

By now the veteran members of Phips I had begun to show up: dive master Bob Coffey, Duke Long, and Don Summers as well as durable Henry Taylor who in addition to his multiple expertise had agreed to handle the daily accounting responsibilities. Webber treated his four companions to a reunion dinner and shared with them the latest news, passing on details of the log of the *Henry,* and of the underwater housing for the new cesiums. His confidence was running high. "Gentlemen," he stated at one point. "We all know how tough it is out there, and I may be going out on a limb by saying this, but I frankly feel that if we have no problems with weather or equipment breakdowns, we'll find the *Concepción* in the first week."

Only those who had spent those grueling months in 1977 searching in vain for the galleon could appreciate the magnitude of Webber's remarks, yet there were three new faces joining the dive team who shared the excitement. Carter Leary, a diver in his mid-thirties from Washington, North Carolina, had already garnered some wreck experi-ence when in 1975 he discovered in the Pamlico River a Civil War Army picket boat from which he retrieved numerous artifacts for the State. A former member of the Army special forces who saw serious service in Vietnam, Leary also possessed a considerable knowledge of small arms and small-unit fighting tactics. Webber put him in charge of shipboard security.

On leave from Commercial Diving Services of Louisville, Ken-tucky, was Billy Fothergill, twenty-five, a ten-year pro and a factory-trained specialist in regulator repair and maintenance. Fothergill was also a certified emergency medical technician who would serve as the expedition's medical officer. Rounding out the dive team was Jim Nace, twenty-one, a husky former Air Force medic, a seventen-year resident of Lebanon, Pennsylvania, and an avid scuba diver. Nace was actually hired as a supernumerary and odd-job assistant who would take over diving chores only if one of the six divers were for any reason temporarily taken out of the line-up. Ironically, future events would cast Nace in a considerably different role.

Regardless of designated responsibilities out on the reef, all hands turned to shortly after eight each morning, divvying up each day's job list made up from Webber's meticulously prepared outfitting schedule. Soon the sound of hammers and drills aboard the *Samala* joined that from half a dozen other vessels nearby. Adding to the cacophony were frequent calls to employees over the shipyard public-address system, and the ringing bells of a drawbridge each time it rose to allow passage of a small freighter or harbor tug. The resulting sound mix would have been distinctively nautical were it not that the locale was three short blocks from downtown Miami and directly across the street from the beginning of Little Havana, a colorful bustling district settled years ago by Cuban expatriates.

For more than a week the outfitting proceeded smoothly. Then one morning Warren Stearns called Webber aboard the *Samala* with troubling news: Rumors had reached Seaquest that some party or parties may try to sabotage the expedition, possibly by damaging the *Samala*. There may even be some kind of contract out on Webber. During lunch Webber reported the conversation to the ship's company, refusing to disclose the source of the rumors or to speculate further. Any form of violence seemed far-fetched, and yet one could not deny that the stakes were high. In short, to ignore the reports might be a disastrous error. Accordingly, Webber ordered that during daylight hours someone would always be designated as an officer of the watch. Carter Leary was directed to install an alarm system that could be activated from either the bridge or saloon. To ensure security from 10 P.M. to 7 A.M., he hired off-duty Miami policemen (most of whom had S.W.A.T. training), instructing them to be on the lookout for swimmers, small boats, or even tell-tale bubbles from an underwater intruder. This done, Webber checked to make sure that his own personal protection—an H & K 9 mm automatic pistol in a shoulder holster—was in good working order should it be needed in an emergency. And finally, from that day on he never traveled alone. One could suggest that the precautions and increased vigilance were extreme reactions to mere rumors, but Burt Webber, a treasure hunter whose dedication was matched by a drive for perfection, whose entire career and professional reputation was on the line, was not about to take unnecessary chances.

The Outfitting of E/S 88

There was something of that drive, certainly an aura of command, in Webber's expression the afternoon I met him for the first time. I had just arrived by airport taxi and was admiring the *Samala*—not quite sure that such an elegant vessel *was* the *Samala*—when Webber appeared on the quarterdeck. We introduced ourselves and while someone helped bring aboard my dive gear, portable typewriter, and camera equipment he gave me a quick update on the outfitting

schedule. His voice was deep and resonant, and he spoke with a
military crispness. Though I had heard that voice on the phone
numerous times, its impact now was even more impressive. The man
defied easy classification. With his neatly trimmed short hair, khaki
safari shorts, white sport shirt and formidable dive watch, Webber
could have passed for a member of a Vietnam era Navy Seal Team
preparing for another night raid in enemy waters to rescue a downed
fighter pilot. The crow's feet around his eyes and the look of a long
defiant struggle they contained made him seem older than his thirty-
five years. Yet in an instant he could smile broadly, give out a
contagious laugh, his eyes popping wide with surprise, and suddenly he
was a zestful college kid full of mischief and adventure. In the days
ahead Burt Webber would by turns be stubborn, jovial, quick
tempered, brilliantly analytical, even patiently diplomatic, but behind
or beneath his every mood there always lurked a visionary intensity, a
sense of consuming purpose.

It was difficult for anyone aboard the *Samala* to escape feeling a
similar sense of mission, let alone the sheer drama of the project at
hand. Everywhere during working hours there was constant activity,
the ringing of phones, the dockside arrival of crates and boxes and
packages, people coming and going on errands, spot meetings and
repeated long distance calls to and from Seaquest in Chicago. Webber
was a man in constant motion, somehow in the thick of everything, yet
shrewdly delegating almost every task to lieutenants (which in this case
meant everybody). The *Samala*'s comfortable carpeted saloon, which
encompassed a bar and a galley table large enough to seat twelve,
served as headquarters. While Webber often sat at one end directing
and deciding, Henry Taylor sat at the other surrounded by stacks of
receipts, accounting journals, and checkbooks. Pecking away at an
adding machine, he seemed a calm and genial Buddha in the center of
the cyclone, keeping an all-seeing eye on the cash.

The weather on these busy days was idyllic—warm and not too
humid with a frequent afternoon on-shore breeze from Biscayne Bay to
temper that mid-day heat. The cool mornings were invigorating and by
7 A.M. most of the ship's company were up and headed across the street
to Nelson's, a coffee shop and grocery store. Amidst the din of Spanish
conversation and the crackling of ham and bacon on the grill, one could
enjoy a breakfast of Cuban bread, *café con leche*, scrambled eggs, and
orange juice—all for $1.75. The *Miami Herald* carried dreary stories of
inflation and a dollar slump but after a breakfast at Nelson's life never
seemed more full of promise.

By the end of October the work pace had begun to accelerate. The *Samala* had been moved onto the shipyard dry dock so that workmen could punch an eight-inch hole through the hull near the keel line to install a retractable horizontally scanning transducer. The unit was part of a Wesmar variable depth-ranging sonar which would provide a radar-type screen display as the *Samala* approached and maneuvered among the dangerous coral heads of the Silver Shoals. In addition to the radar, radio telephone, and other components on the *Samala*'s already-well-equipped bridge, Webber added a Nelco Auto Fix 500 Loran A & C unit, a Cobra 78X CB radio for communication with the reef boats, and a multi-frequency single sideband transceiver.

Once the sonar had been installed and the *Samala* moved back to her berth, the loading of equipment began in earnest. Everything was new and state-of-the-art. First on was an Innerspace 5000 p.s.i. (15 c.f.m.) diesel-powered air compressor, then two deep freezers, followed by two sixteen-foot Avon inflatable reef boats and repair kits. Among other items:

> Six complete sets of Dacor scuba equipment and twenty-two aluminum tanks
> Four Subsalve underwater lifting bags
> Two 35 HP Evinrude outboard motors with spare parts
> Two venturi excavation/air compressors, digging heads, hose, foot valves
> Four H & K 91 assault rifles, clips, cleaning kits, ammunition
> Two custom-manufactured lifting tongs and debris baskets
> And an enormous quantity of miscellaneous hardware, shackles, plywood, shock cord, epoxy glue, electrical and mechanical tools, ground tackle, mooring anchors, survey lines, buoys, weights, batteries, wet suits, weight belts, and medical equipment.

As if to authenticate the *Samala*'s change of status from luxurious charter yacht to luxurious treasure salvage vessel, artist Duke Long emblazoned her sides and top with large letter-numerals E/S 88 in bold red and black. The E/S stood for Exploration and Salvage.

For their part Captain Tony Garton and his four-man British crew were fully occupied with their own preparations for extended periods at sea. Not surprisingly, they were an experienced and congenial bunch. Navigator Jimmy Blackburn, an aristocratic and thoroughly knowledgeable yachtsman in his sixties, was an old friend of Garton and a much-decorated World War II R.A.F. pilot. The *Samala*'s mate, twenty-eight-year-old Frank West, was an experienced charter sailor who had skippered several Atlantic crossings. In charge of the *Samala*'s twin twelve-cylinder diesel engines was engineer Kevin Lawson, a twenty-year veteran of the Royal Navy submarine service, while "cookie" Chunky Cardwell, a Belfast-born Irishman in his mid-thirties, would be putting in long hours in the galley turning out remarkably varied meals (he had been advised that the fish on the Silver Shoals were toxic and thus inedible).

Contributing to the *esprit de corps* of what was an international team were white T-shirts and golf shirts on which had been silk-screened the expedition logo designed by Duke Long. The elegant emblem consisted of a shark swimming in front of a twin-fluked seventeenth-century anchor together with the words "Operation Phips II 1978–1979." From the outset, everyone wore his shirt proudly and for a while the golf shirts were the preferred attire for evenings on the town. The practice led to at least one amusing encounter on a Monday night when Webber and five others entered a German restaurant and bar, hoping to get a table without reservations. They were surprised to find the place packed with motorcycle gays in studded leather jackets, chain belts, and assorted iron cross ornamentalia. Webber's group was politely informed the restaurant was closed for a private party, but not before a half-minute of genuine confusion during which the quasi-uniformed visitors were asked if they were members of another motorcycle club whose arrival was expected.

Apart from occasional restaurant outings most expedition members congregated regularly at Tobacco Road, a comfortable tavern two blocks from the shipyard. There was nothing special about the place but it offered a good juke box, several pinball machines, and a needed respite from shipboard routine on warm muggy nights. Elsewhere, the bachelors on board early on discovered nearby the Bauder Fashion College (and its all-girl student body) and it wasn't long before the campus was buzzing with talk about the young treasure hunters and their motor yacht. This led to several informal parties aboard the *Samala*, but the proprieties were maintained—no female visitors were permitted belowdecks. The rule reflected an ongoing need for security at a time when the *Samala* was vulnerable.

Apropos security, on at least one occasion the off-duty policeman on the graveyard watch was a bit lax. Returning to the ship one midnight ex-special forces member Carter Leary noticed the guard on duty was sitting in his car watching a mini TV. Leary quickly climbed up onto the roof of an adjacent shed and lobbed an empty beer bottle onto the *Samala*'s afterdeck, hoping the shattering of glass would rouse the guard to action. The cop remained oblivious but the commotion attracted Webber who was in the saloon. When he went out to check on the noise, Carter stood up on the roof and raised his hand in a mock gesture of firing a pistol.

"Bang! Gotcha!" he yelled, adding, "Burt, you sure make an easy target in that white shirt you're wearing."

As the security guard quickly learned, Webber was not amused.

Big Foot and Final Countdown

By early November, the outfitting of the *Samala* was essentially complete, with the exception of the all-important cesium magnetometers. Webber was on the phone almost daily to talk to Varian engineers in Canada. There had been a leakage problem with one of the units, he was told, then a vexing signal-to-noise ratio on the other. Webber was getting irritated.

While he wrestled with these delays, Webber learned the *R/V James Bay* with Dennis Standefer in command had arrived in Key West after a long trip from Seattle to the Caribbean by way of Haiti and the Bahamas. There soon appeared an article in the *Miami Herald*. In it Standefer said his expedition was bound for the Silver Shoals to find the *Concepción* but that he had agreed to suspend operations for a one-week interlude during which he would use the *James Bay* to help Mel Fisher look for the *Atocha*'s treasure, 90 percent of which is believed to lie undiscovered deep beneath the sands west of the Marquesas Atoll. What puzzled Webber was that Standefer had apparently been in the Caribbean since late summer and had explored several wrecks in Bahamian waters without ever going near the Silver Shoals. The itinerary seemed odd. The *Herald* quoted Standefer as saying the *Concepción* would be the last of eight scheduled wreck excavations, that the Silver Shoals expedition would be in the black (through artifact recoveries) before it even went to the Silver Shoals. "*Concepción* is all in one place—it will take a month at most [to excavate]," Standefer claimed. He added—and this seemed rather far-fetched—that the venture had already recouped a quarter of its investment after working fewer than half the targeted wrecks.

Within hours of reading the news story, Webber received a call from the *Miami Herald* wanting his view of the Standefer expedition.

Before taking the call, Webber paused several seconds debating whether or not to launch a media broadside at the Standefer camp. At length he almost smiled, and reached for the phone.

"SECOND FIRM TAKES UP QUEST FOR SHIP'S TREASURE," headlined the Sunday *Miami Herald*, explaining that a confrontation appeared possible.

"We've known about Standefer's effort for quite some time, and the Dominican authorities are also aware of it," Webber was quoted in the story. "Our intention is not to get into a squabble with Mr. Standefer, and if we're interfered with the Dominican Navy will handle that." Elsewhere in the article: "Standefer has a very fine vessel, no doubt about it. If he wishes to venture to Silver Shoals and pulls it off with no problem, we wish him all the luck in the world, but I'm not concerned about it."

Burt Webber was killing 'em with kindness.

Later that day, when I happened to discuss with dive master Bob Coffey the intricate juggling act that Webber had been maintaining in order to pull everything together under pressure, Coffey laughed. "Just wait until we get out to the reef and into the water. You haven't even seen what Burt *does* yet."

No one, in fact, was more anxious to get out to the reef than Webber. On Friday, November 10, after yet another exasperating talk with Varian, which was now almost two weeks late delivering the two cesium mags, he was told the units were ready but that there were delays because of shipping and bonding problems. However, things looked good for the fourteenth. On hearing of yet another delay, one of the crewmen offered to phone Varian and impersonate a Brooklyn-accented hit man who was handy with concrete shoes. The spiel had possibilities: "Hallo, Varian? Dis is Doctuh Shoes. I think you need a pair. I'm a specialist in negative buoyancy problems, y' unnastand? I do good work. In fact I guarantee one-dive certification. Ain't had a floater yet." Webber opted instead to ask Dr. Pete Foose, who had flown down to assist with survey planning and mapping, to call the president of Varian and apply a bit of professional arm twisting upon returning home to Massachusetts.

Finally, on the fourteenth the first of the two mags arrived, packed in a bed of Styrofoam peanuts in an eight-foot-long shipping crate. As the crew gathered around, Webber supervised the unloading of this exotic arrival. The instrument, encased in shiny Plexiglas through which could be seen an impressive array of controls, display read-outs, lights, and assorted integrated gadgetry, was indeed wondrous to behold. Webber handled the mag gently with almost anthropomorphic respect. Indeed, it was a space-age creature of sorts and when he noticed embedded in the plastic cover plate a tiny collection of frozen bubbles shaped like a footprint, Webber nicknamed the mag Big Foot.

By 1:30 P.M. the *Samala,* with all hands aboard, cast off from her berth at the Miami Shipyard and proceeded out through Biscayne Bay and into the Atlantic, anchoring a mile offshore in twenty feet of water. Once the engines were secured Webber began a thorough checkout of essential expedition gear. The first inflatable reef boat was slid off the 01 level, and lowered by the two port-side davits into the water. The maneuver was a bit tricky owing to a running two-to-three-foot swell and fifteen-knot winds, but all went smoothly. An outboard motor was lowered and attached to the boat's transom and a minute later Duke Long got the craft under way for a five-minute test run. While the second reef boat and motor underwent a similar shakedown, Webber and Bob Coffey put on dive gear and prepared to test the electronic search instruments. Both men geared up with the practiced efficiency of old hands with many hundreds of hours of bottom time. Despite the seriousness of their purpose, both exuded an air of anticipation at the prospect of once more experiencing the special joy and sensations of diving. Coffey was the first in, executing a perfect shoulder roll entry from a height of six feet off the transom.

Webber followed a minute later, directed the placement of a descent line and a safety line, then went below to check out the bottom. There was a slight current and the visibility was poor—eighteen inches to two feet—but the site was sandy. When the two men returned to the surface, Jim Nace carefully lowered down one of the two Aquapulse II's, an underwater metal detector made in Erie, Ireland, which uses a pulse induction system that pumps a magnetic field into the floor bottom and can detect both ferrous and nonferrous metals. Seven minutes later, the pair surfaced and reported the unit had stabilized quickly and worked fine with a test target of scrap iron. After the second Aquapulse had passed the same test, Big Foot was very gingerly removed from its storage crate and carefully passed down to Webber. This time the divers were down more than fifteen minutes to allow for the mag to warm up and stabilize. Webber again returned to the surface and gave the thumbs-up sign. There were no leaks in the casing but he would follow up with a dry-land checkout.

By 5 P.M. all the gear had been restowed and the *Samala* returned to Miami, this time tying alongside the Dupont Plaza Hotel just off Biscayne Boulevard. The berth was a dramatic change from the shipyard, for the *Samala* now had access to the hotel's swimming pool, bar, and restaurant, not to mention being a block closer to the Bauder Fashion College. Webber was pleased with the sea trials but he was still worried about the arrival of the second cesium mag. The outfitting was now ten days behind schedule and the delay was costing Seaquest an average of $1,500 a day.

Beyond the cost overrun was the psychological stress that was getting on everyone's nerves. With each passing day life on the Miami River became less congenial. It was time to go treasure hunting and no one understood that more than Webber. He was clearly reaching the limit of his patience with waiting, with endless telephone calls, and with wondering whether or not he and/or the *Samala* was on some hoodlum's hit list. His tension showed in occasionally barked orders and brief temper flare-ups. Adding to his burdens was the strangely fickle behavior of Big Foot during a land test the following morning.

Shortly after breakfast I drove Webber and Carter Leary to a large grassy playground not far from International Airport where Webber intended to test the cesium's field response to various ferrous objects. After removing his watch and anything else that might register, Webber lay on the grass staring at the mag's console, flipped on the power, and waited for the gamma read-out total to stabilize to a steady five-figure reading. Instead, the reading kept fluctuating by eight to ten gammas. Webber figured this was merely the result of transient power surges associated with the warmup. When there was no change after more than fifteen minutes, Webber looked up grimly, his face fraught with tension.

"It's got to be the unit. Even an iron pipe under the grass around here couldn't cause the fluctuation." He looked into the distance. "Unless it's those high-tension wires over there. They might have a big field."

We carefully brought the mag to the station wagon, gently propped it in the back on blankets and Styrofoam bolsters, and drove ten miles down the south Dixie Highway. Webber was hiding his concern with difficulty. Clearly, if the mag was not working perfectly, nobody was going anywhere. Maybe it was the rain that fell early that morning, he theorized. Ground moisture might have carried the field current from underground power lines in the area. Moments later we entered a cane field that had been recently harvested. The ground was still slightly wet. Again Webber activated Big Foot and again the readings were dancing, this time by as much as twenty-two gammas. Webber seemed downright depressed. During the forty-five-minute trip back to the *Samala* we drove in silence while Webber catnapped.

The call to Varian was a long one. The engineers in Canada questioned him closely on the two test areas he had selected that morning. Their conclusion: Residual ground moisture from a light rainfall earlier in the morning had indeed caused the disturbance. In addition, the warmup time should be extended to a full thirty minutes. Varian suggested the mag be tested on a beach. Moments after the call Webber was on his way to a nearby stretch of shoreline, this time switching on the mag while en route. Arriving at an open stretch of sand, he again set up the unit, waited several more minutes until the thirty-minute mark had passed, then took a deep breath and activated the console. The gamma count immediately flashed on to display 46,654.01. For several tense seconds he watched as the .01 shifted to .09, then .04, finally to .03—and stayed there. Webber looked up with a wide grin on his face. Big Foot was ready to go treasure hunting.

And so was the rest of the expedition. Webber returned to the *Samala*'s berth at the Dupont Plaza and learned of yet more good news: The second cesium mag was on its way to Miami and would be delivered either late that night or early the following morning. Webber promptly conferred with Captain Garton and navigator Jimmy Blackburn, then announced that the expedition would depart for the Dominican Republic at 4:30 the following afternoon.

On hearing that cheering word most of the crew busied themselves with last-minute errands—mailing postcards, buying personal items, and in the case of most of the bachelors, heading for Bauder Fashion College. With the exception of those on watch, nearly everyone else went out for a last leisurely dinner with libation (while at sea each crewman would be limited to two beers or one glass of wine daily, and this only in the evening).

Sometime after 10 P.M. the second mag arrived and was carefully carried aboard to await an early morning checkout. Soon after that the few copies of *Playboy* and *Penthouse* that had been floating around the saloon mysteriously disappeared, leaving behind a dog-eared collection of old *Skin Diver* magazines. No one openly questioned the disappearance but the impression lingered that on this voyage a little sublimation would be the order of the day. The only female that would officially receive individual attention would be a ship named *Concepción*.

Thursday dawned warm and bright with promise. By noon Webber had returned from a successful checkout of the second mag while Captain Garton was still running about getting signatures on a dozen documents from a dozen different officials to clear the *Samala* for departure. Following a quick lunch all hands secured the ship for sea, closing portholes, and battening down any personal belongings that might come unglued in a beam sea. By 4 P.M. Captain Garton returned and engineer Kevin Lawson fired up the two diesels and the *Samala* throbbed with the loud drone of powerful machinery. Finally, as unmistakable proof that departure was imminent, the telephone was disconnected. At 4:30 P.M. on the button the *Samala* cast off and headed across Biscayne Bay toward the open Atlantic. For some time Webber remained on the bridge, his black beret at a jaunty angle, a look of satisfaction on his features. I shook his hand. He nodded, grinning. The outfitting had taken thirty-three days. It was Thursday, November 16. Operation Phips II was under way at last.

9

Assault on Silver Shoals: Triumph on Day Five

To Puerto Plata and the Shoals

As the *Samala* headed across the Florida Strait to North Bimini fifty miles to the east, Blackburn adjusted course to compensate for the northerly set of the Gulf Stream. Sometime after sunset we crossed the ghost wake of the *Concepción*, for it was in these same waters that the wrath of nature struck the 1641 fleet, marking the beginning of the galleon's tortuous odyssey. On this warm night the sea was docile and life aboard the *Samala* quickly settled into an underway routine.

There is something especially satisfying about standing on the darkened bridge of a vessel during an evening watch, taking a turn at the helm, keeping one eye on the ship's compass, the other peeled for a navigational light that should appear any minute off to starboard. An occasional bow wave sends a high arc of spray onto the wheelhouse glass, a tropic wind whistles gently, while inside one hears the whine of the radar display console over the low thrum of the engines. In between plotting fixes, log entries, and scanning the horizon with binoculars, there is time to sip mugs of hot coffee and talk to one's watchmate. It is at such moments that life has a special richness.

The following afternoon as the *Samala* headed southeast from Nassau down the Exhuma Sound, Webber spoke half seriously to Lawson.

"I wish you could put another two hundred RPM's on this vessel. This is the first time in months I've had nothing to do. I can't stay below in my cabin all the time reading and writing reports."

Webber grinned, his eyes gleaming with the same zest that must have imbued his predecessor Sir William. In fact, the only person who felt less than brisk was Captain Garton whose jaw had swollen following bungled dentistry before leaving Miami. Occasionally, he vented his minor agony by yelling at whatever poor soul was at the helm when the *Samala* took a roll through 60 degrees of arc.

"Dammit! Mind your helm!" he'd bellow. "Who's driving up there? Bunch of bloody tits!"

Moments later, when medic Billy Fothergill asked him about his jaw pain, Garton put on an aristocratic R.A.F. accent and replied, "Well, you see, nurse, it was this way. . . ." A day later Fothergill put him on antibiotics, admonishing the captain not to drink either milk or alcohol, two of the patient's favorite refreshments. Garton took the prohibition in good humor, managing at one point to whip up a brandy-laced chocolate mousse for the navigator and mate Frank West, remarking, "I've just invented a cure for which there is no known disease."

It was late Sunday evening as the *Samala* entered the calm lee of Hispaniola and approached the lights of Puerto Plata. The sky was overcast but the night was warm with a light offshore breeze. Captain Garton took care entering the narrow harbor channel, and by 11 P.M. we had tied up alongside a modern concrete wharf behind a small Dominican Navy corvette. After squinting at the ship's hull numbers, Leary reached for the *Samala*'s copy of *Jane's Fighting Ships*, then called out to Webber in his trademark southern drawl: "She could take us, boss. She's got twin forty millimeters, a three-inch fifty and four deck-mounted fifty caliber machine guns."

Dawn the following morning was heralded by the song of hundreds of sparrows feeding on unlucky cockroaches caught in the open on the wharf's broad cement expanse. As a glorious West Indian sunrise poured into the saloon, Chunky emerged from the galley with a huge plate of bacon and scrambled eggs, wearing a T-shirt that read "Another Bloody Day in Paradise." Indeed, the day seemed bursting with promise. Shortly after 9 P.M., a friendly delegation of Dominican Navy officers paid a visit. Among them was Navy Colonel (equivalent to a Commander) Manuel Montes Arrache who would join the expedition as the senior liaison officer. A close friend of Admiral Amiama, Colonel Montes is a thoroughly experienced UDT specialist and a bona fide national hero who successfully commanded the defense of Santo Domingo during the 1965 revolution. Also present was lanky thirty-year-old Lieutenant J.G. Ivan Diaz who would act as Montes' interpreter and assistant aboard the *Samala*. A ten-year Navy man, Diaz spoke fluent English by virtue of having lived several years as a child in Coral Gables, Florida. Like the other officers present, Diaz wore a summer dress khaki uniform with a short-sleeved shirt and a holster carrying a .45 caliber automatic. Wearing side arms is *de rigueur* for the officer corps in the Dominican Republic, but what fascinated the crew was the workmanship of Diaz's weapon. The pistol grips were of custom silver intricately engraved with florid designs while the holster and belt was a single piece of polished chestnut red leather onto which had been etched a pattern of rococo flourishes both elegant and masculine.

Webber warmly greeted Diaz and after the latter assisted with introductions the visiting American treasure hunter ordered the locks removed from the cesium storage locker. As the Dominicans peered down at the two magnetometers lying on a bed of white Styrofoam peanuts, Diaz translated his friend's description of their intended use on the reef. Webber was himself the apotheosis of poised spit and polish, wearing his Operation Phips golf shirt, pressed khaki pants and his black beret, and moving now from the magnetometers to the Aquapulse detectors and related search paraphernalia.

Later, while Webber and Garton drove to Santo Domingo for a meeting with Admiral Amiama, most of the crew wandered into town for a brief reconnaissance.

There was much about Puerto Plata that invited a leisurely inspection but everyone appeared too keyed up for the hunt to dally in port longer than necessary. Webber returned from Santo Domingo the following day, wearing an elegant spring business suit he'd used for his meeting with the admiral (which had been very cordial), but as soon as he had changed to his khakis and beret, he was again back in his car, this time testing a walkie-talkie. One could only imagine what the crowds of tourists from a visiting cruise ship thought as they saw in the back seat of a chauffeured sedan this chisel-jawed gringo in a black beret holding a Sony mini-transceiver with its aerial out the window while he ran through voice checks with Bob Coffey back aboard ship.

At 3:25 A.M. Friday, Leary sounded the general quarter horn alarm to awaken all hands. With her fuel tanks and stores topped off the *Samala* was ready to head for the Silver Shoals at last. Medic Billy Fothergill was a bit shaky as he helped cast off the bow line, having drunk more than a few beers hours earlier at a hole-in-the-wall night club known as Boite Danny's. As the ship caught the first swell coming out of the harbor he deposited the contents of his stomach over the port bow, then retired to his bunk to grab a few hours' sleep.

I had the 6 to 8 A.M. bridge watch with Garton and as we plowed a northeast heading through calm seas, we listened to the BBC world news on a portable shortwave radio and marveled at a splendid sunrise through pink thunderclouds.

By 10 A.M., as the vessel neared the vicinity of the reef, all hands were on deck. Morale was very high. By this time both Dominican Navy officers Montes and Diaz had changed from uniforms to T-shirts and swimming trunks. Montes clearly enjoyed being at sea. Understated and friendly (he insisted we call him Manuel), he was always ready to lend a hand. He had also installed aboard the *Samala* his own radio to communicate directly with the admiral in Santo Domingo in case developments on the reef required the Dominican Air Force to scramble a couple of combat planes to support Phips II. One sensed the Dominicans fully shared Webber's faith in the expedition's chances of success.

At noon Garton reduced speed to five knots and approached the northwest portion of the six-mile-long Half Moon Reef from the lee side, following predetermined loran bearings. I joined Coffey on the overhead of the bridge and saw for the first time the spooky beauty of the shoals. Across a distant horizon of calm deep-blue water a series of breakers, roughly two feet in height, arose out of nowhere and crested foamy white onto shallow invisible ledges, only to disappear. Here was indeed a sinister ship trap. I understood at once why Blackburn had timed our arrival to provide sunlight at our backs, for with the help of Polaroid glasses one could see deep into the water ahead as even now great columns of coral loomed in the distance off to port. Though there seemed no way of determining the configuration of the "boylers" ahead, Webber was on the bridge issuing directions with the utter assurance of one returning to his own backyard. He was guiding the ship into an anchorage area a quarter- to a half-mile from the actual lee reef line.

Once we were there, Webber directed the launching of reef boat No. 1 and sent a three-man team out to search for a suitable coral head that rose no higher than fifteen feet beneath the water's surface and to which the *Samala* could be moored and swing safely in a circle without hitting any adjacent heads. The search took nearly an hour but once a head had been chosen, dive master Coffey and two others geared up and dove down with hammers and hand picks to clear away coral projections from around the base of the column. Garton then deftly maneuvered the bow directly over the head and on signal paid out 150 feet of mooring chain from the bow locker. The divers then used lift bags to maneuver the chain around the head, secured the loop with a heavy shackle, and attached the free end to a specially constructed fifty-five-gallon steel drum through which had been welded a steel connecting rod. The floating drum, painted Day-Glo red and emblazoned with the words "*Gobierno Dominicana*—Operation Phips II," would serve as the expedition's permanent mooring. To finish the task, a heavy braided nylon mooring line was attached to the barrel, and assorted floats and chaffing gear set in place. Though the operation had never before been done (Webber had conceived the plan months earlier), the entire mooring had been briskly executed with spot-on seamanship.

It was sunset by the time the dive gear had been stowed. Dinner that night was sumptuous—flounder filets, mashed potatoes, string beans, and, to celebrate our arrival, an extra bottle of beer on each man's ration. After dinner Webber opened his attaché case and began reading selected passages from the old Spanish and English documents. Everyone, particularly the new members of the dive team—Jim Nace, Leary, and Fothergill—listened intently.

On Board the Electronic Roller Coaster

Over breakfast the following morning Webber recalled a dream he had during the night: "It involved Sir John Narbrough, the English admiral who died here on the reef during the last week of the second Phips expedition. They gave him a burial at sea with full honors. Anyway, last night Sir John appeared to me in a dream. He asked politely if there was a spare bunk aboard the *Samala*, that he'd very much like to get some sleep. Seriously! I guess the dream relates to all that's pent up mentally about the *Concepción* as far as the history and the people are concerned."

It was impossible not to sense pent-up feelings, for today was the last moment of preparation before actual search. Webber would test Big Foot at wrecksite seven where the cross staff had been discovered. If everything checked out, tomorrow would be Day One. The weather was cooperative for the first foray to the reef. By now both Avon reef boats had been put in service and, with the use of a hinged loading platform halfway between the waterline and the *Samala*'s deck, it was fairly easy to pass down equipment even with a two- to three-foot swell. Six men were required to gently pass Big Foot down to Webber's outstretched hands but it was done without a hitch. By noon boat No. 1 had returned from site seven with news that the cesium mag had worked perfectly.

As he removed his dive gear on deck, Webber explained to Garton that the one problem he had encountered was that the mag had been weight-compensated for fresh water instead of salt water, the result being the unit had a slightly positive buoyancy which made it a bit cumbersome to maneuver. The problem, however, could be easily overcome by attaching a few pounds of lead. During the afternoon, Webber supervised the checkout of the Aquapulse units, both of which passed their test probes. As the late afternoon sunset bathed the stern deck area, a crew filled all the scuba tanks from a cascade system hooked on to the big compressor. Wet suits and buoyancy vests were dunked in plastic garbage cans filled with fresh water, then hung out on overhead lines with clothespins like so much wet laundry. Finally, a small mountain of gear—regulators, fins, snorkels, masks, weight belts, knives, and wrist compasses—was given a thorough fresh-water rinse, then stowed in a large compartmentalized gear locker. Each man's equipment was color coded for identification, and absolutely everything from tanks to tweezers had its place. Masterful preplanning and scrupulous attention to detail were the hallmark of every step in dive team procedure.

After dinner that evening Webber once more drew out photocopies of English and Spanish documents, reading pertinent sections, reciting a litany of statistics. (Garton, who now referred to this postprandial exercise as "story time," was no less intrigued.) Taped to the side of the gun cabinet behind Webber was a chart of the reef section through which sliced the bearing line from the *Henry* to the wreck of the *Concepción*. Parallel lines 200 yards to each side of the line denoted a rectangle, roughly ⅛ of a square mile in area, containing about 150 coral heads, which had been gridded into thirty squares, designated A1, A2, B1, B2, et cetera. Of the thirty squares, fifteen contained coral-head groupings which corresponded with descriptions of the wrecksite. Inevitably, the grid numbers had been tossed into the hat and a pool established for $5.00 a shot. Webber repeatedly referred to the chart as he discussed the research.

One sensed this man would not stop his reviewing and rehearsing no matter how well prepared his expedition was. The bottom line was, after all, the discovery of the *Concepción*, not the search. And until it was found, every scrap of evidence and every procedure would be gone over and over again. Yet tomorrow was Day One of the actual search and, after Webber had completed his discussion of the research, I asked him how he felt on the eve of the hunt. He laughed as he reached down from his seat with a napkin to clean up a scrap of food:

"Well, I'm really so preoccupied in respect to answering that question that I'm cleaning mashed potatoes off the deck. No, seriously, I've been through the whole thing before but I can't truthfully compare this moment to others."

He paused briefly, as though wrestling with a host of ideas and impressions, then continued a somewhat eclectic line of thought, his speech voluble, now and then gesturing with his hands to emphasize a point:

"I'm not keyed up but at the same time I'm excited just to be here. Because no one else has been into this particular project to the depth I have—the research, the electronics, the money raising, the outfitting—and some of that energy is pent up inside. For me the greatest release will be actually locating the galleon and salvaging it. That's what I'm looking forward to, because I feel as though I'm carrying a one-ton weight on my back. When we find *Concepción* that weight will fall from my shoulders.

"Actually, today was probably one of the most exciting days of my life because we ran that cesium mag on the reef heads and seeing it work so beautifully was a tremendous thrill. Seeing Bob Coffey relieve me and watching him maneuver it in and out of coral heads, maintaining perfect depth control, spotting buried pieces of iron fifteen and twenty feet away, just watching the whole theory work was absolutely perfect. But the one thing that concerns me is that any time you work with highly technical prototype electronics you're always living on borrowed time. You're constantly thinking, 'How long is it going to keep clicking?' That's why we have two cesiums."

There was something in Webber's voice now, a rising undertone of warrior consciousness that any connoisseur of edgework would appreciate. The search would be rigorously routine and methodical but this could not disguise the fact that Webber, like everyone aboard, *was* keyed up. Webber, too, sensed it:

"This is probably one of the most tense moments in my life. Because it's all on the line. It's the night before battle and you're saying to yourself, 'Well, tomorrow, you're either going to win or lose. Either you'll be breathing or you'll be dead but tomorrow is the day. Naturally, you're filled with anxieties but if you have the confidence in your talents and training—and we have a very superb team here—you can't help but be positive. I think we're going to succeed, I really do."

It is an old belief that in every bird at sea there resides the ghost of a sailor, and that the appearance of such creatures over a vessel far from land is a kindly omen. Thus, when Burt Webber came on deck at sunrise to see a stately blue heron gliding past overhead he silently tendered greetings to Sir John Narbrough. By 8 A.M. the crew of reef boat No. 1—Webber, Coffey, and Leary—were donning their gear. Because of the shoals' 70-degree water temperature, one need only wear a wet suit jacket to prevent uncomfortable heat loss under water, but in addition everyone wore light gloves and long-sleeved cotton jump suits with Velcro fasteners for protection against coral cuts and the nettlelike stings of Firethorn coral (a constant annoyance to the unwary).

Once the reef boat was loaded with scuba gear I dove into the water with my Nikonos camera to take photos of the mag being lowered from the *Samala*. As I was adjusting the lens settings Webber called out, "Say, John, did you know about the twelve-foot tiger shark hanging around the boat last night?" I was a bit unnerved until he finally broke countenance and laughed at the joke. Actually, there *had* been a shark around the night before (Nace had chummed it to the side with table scraps) but it had barely topped two feet in length.

By 9:15 A.M. both reef boats departed for area B-5 and B-6 containing a large head dubbed Sea Horse Reef. Duke Long took command of boat No. 2, standing astride the forward seat holding in one hand the bow line while signaling with his other the path through the heads. The previous afternoon Webber had dropped several buoys around the circumference of Sea Horse and within minutes of his arrival this morning he was over the side and ready for action. The cesium, already warmed up, was carefully slipped into the water. Webber gave the high sign, then hit the exhaust valve of his buoyancy vest and slowly descended to the base of the head forty-five feet below. Coffey, acting as safety back-up man, followed Webber, staying above and behind him, keeping a watch out for any visible signs of wreckage. There was a degree of tidal surge against which both divers had to strain at times but Webber kept an even pace, maintaining the sensor staff in a horizontal position, his eyes riveted on the orange digital lights, listening through earphones for any shift in signal tone that accompanied an anomaly.

The Sea Horse Reef survey took less than an hour but produced no anomalies. As Webber and Coffey moved on to two other heads, nicknamed Buffalo and Clover, boat No. 2 tackled Sea Horse using a two-man team (one with the Aquapulse metal detector, the other as a safety back-up) to scour sand pockets for nonferrous metals such as bronze, silver, and gold which the cesium could not "see." To mark the site of any evidence found, the back-up diver on both teams carried a net bag containing several lead weights attached by a short length of string to pineapple–ring-shaped corks painted Day-Glo red and numbered.

Webber was just finishing the circumference of Clover without getting any readings when the audio tone in his headphones suddenly shifted higher—as did the gamma count. The anomaly came from the area between Clover and Buffalo. Moving out of his circumference pattern Webber swam toward a sand pocket as the readings grew stronger. Then he saw it—a ship's anchor, the shaft of which was projecting from a coral overburden. Directly adjacent to the shaft was a slightly curved piece of pottery about the size of a man's palm.

As soon as both boats returned to the *Samala* for a lunch break and tank refills, Henry Taylor examined the pottery shard. There appeared no possible way to identify such a nondescript artifact, but Taylor's expert eye immediately noticed a series of very shallow grooves made by a potter's fingertips as the vessel had been shaped on the wheel. Orienting the shard to its vertical axis, he next measured its concave arc, mathematically calculated the vessel's inside diameter, then projected the vertical curvature on paper and moments later advised Webber that the shard very likely belonged to a Spanish olive jar made around 1600. He added that a galleon such as the *Concepción* would most certainly have carried many such jars. Taylor's assessment was an impressive display of expertise.

During a quick lunch Webber was ebullient. It was too early to tell if they had found a wreck, but the finds might be evidence of salvage vessels that had once anchored adjacent to the wrecksite after Phips' second expedition. By 1:30 P.M. both boats were on their way back to the reef, having been advised by Chunky that he was "standing by to put the champers on ice." The *Samala* crew was staying in touch by CB radio, the reef boats having been designated Rubber Duck 1 and 2. At 3 P.M., boat No. 1 returned unexpectedly. Webber looked grim as he hastily came aboard and reported the mag had suddenly gone out on him. The unit was laid on a blanket atop the galley table while Webber began a systematic checkout. Within minutes he discovered that one end of the foot-long coaxial cable connecting the sensor shaft to the main console was slightly corroded, causing a short around a tiny gold-plated pin. Relieved that the problem was minor, Webber replaced the entire cable, then switched the mag on. But nothing happened. Tension ran high. The second cesium was brought out and two components swapped. Still nothing. Then Bob Coffey suggested the cable short may have caused Big Foot's battery pack to run down. Webber agreed and a freshly charged pack was installed. For the fourth time Webber flicked the switch on. Bang, the unit worked perfectly. Everyone let out an audible sigh. Webber looked up. "Welcome to Burt Webber's Electronic Roller Coaster!" he exclaimed.

By the time Big Foot had been repaired the day was too far gone for a return trip. Boat No. 2 soon returned, having found a portion of what might be a ballast stone and a heavy piece of iron that appeared to be part of definitely modern machinery. Dinner was accompanied by much speculation over the day's finds. Webber reported that before the mag had failed on the afternoon survey, he had encountered no new anomalies, adding, "We have to consider that we may only have perimeter scatterings from other ships that worked the wreck."

Into the Waters of B-9

The following morning, Day Two, Webber was anxious to get moving. On this foray he added Jim Nace to his team, directing the young diver to snorkle on the surface directly above the magnetometer operator and help the latter stay on the survey lines delineated by surface marker buoys. To do this Nace carried a small hammer and a short length of metal tubing. Striking the tube once meant move to the right while two taps signaled a need to move left. By 9:30 Webber's crew was on the reef, surveying areas B-5, C-5, and C-6. The results so far were negative but the mag was working beautifully. Webber and Coffey took turns behind Big Foot, both men straining against a somewhat stronger tidal surge through the reef. Even though wearing a mask and regulator, Webber exuded an aura of a man possessed, relentlessly probing the sensor shaft into every cave and cranny, struggling against the current to maintain orientation, ignoring every-thing around him except a narrow search area, the console display lights, and the steady tone in the phones. He paid little heed to a four-foot barracuda that began to follow him curiously at a distance. His concentration was understandable for no creature of the sea was more hungry than Burt Webber.

Noon passed and Webber remained beneath the surface working on his second tank change. By almost 1 P.M. he had crossed from area C-9 into B-9 and was on the upper windward side of Turtle Reef when he started to get hits: first one, then another, then more. They weren't large anomalies but they formed a distinct trail that led to the east. As Webber tracked in this direction he began to see scattered around the area ballast stones, pieces of pottery, iron straps and odd bits of what had to be ship's fittings fused into the bottom. While Bob Coffey and Jim Nace placed underwater marker buoys next to designated hits, Webber continued east 200 feet to the corner of the B-9 area, swimming through a narrow canyon. Here the readings grew stronger. Then he noticed at the base of one of the canyon walls a deep cavelike undercut. Hovering over the sandy floor of the cave entrance, Webber watched the read-out register tremendous readings from nearly every quadrant. A moment later, as he moved out from the canyon, a warning light began flashing on the console—the batteries were running down.

"Did you see it?" a beaming Nace exclaimed as Webber surfaced. "Man, there's junk all over the place down there."

That afternoon Long's crew secured their follow-up survey early and did a brief check of the sector in which Webber had recorded anomalies. Finding no evidence of precious metals, the team returned to the *Samala* with several small ballast stones, some iron ship's fittings and half a dozen pottery shards. The artifacts were definitely indicative of a shipwreck. Webber was pleased:

"This is exactly the kind of evidence I hoped to find—ballast stones, pottery, and fittings. And considering they're situated in between three reef heads, the area corresponds with the historical documentation."

The three in question were Duke's Reef, Turtle Reef, and Formosa Reef, all of which Henry Taylor and Duke Long named rather arbitrarily for the shapes they suggested. Each evening the two men would confer with Webber and Coffey regarding the next day's search area. Many of the larger heads which had not been designated during the Phips I survey, would be named at this time. What was remarkable about the area in which the artifacts had been found was its location deep in the middle of the reef, a site that truly seemed impossible for a galleon to have entered without following a kind of pinball machine route from the outer windward edge. Whatever the explanation may be, I myself tomorrow would have a firsthand look at the area while taking close-up photographs of artifacts *in situ* before divers removed them for cataloguing and identification.

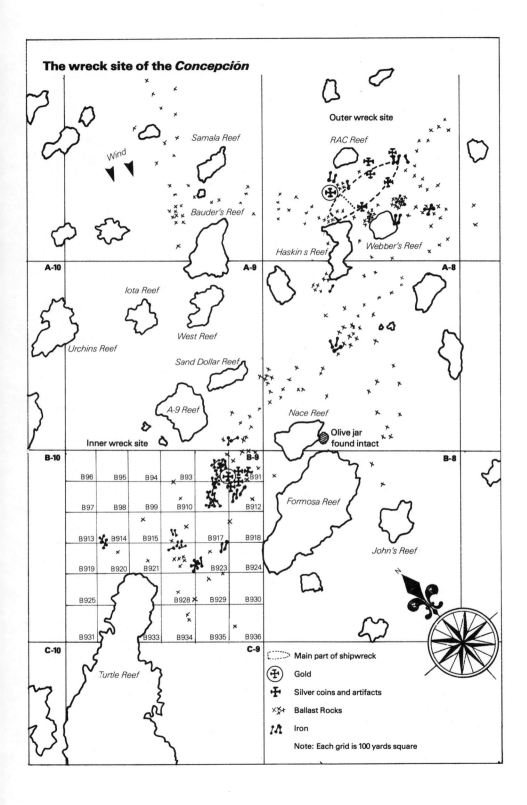

The wreck site of the *Concepción*

Outer wreck site

Samala Reef

RAC Reef

Wind

Bauder's Reef

Haskin s Reef

Webber's Reef

A-10   A-9   A-8

Iota Reef

West Reef

Urchins Reef

Sand Dollar Reef

A-9 Reef

Nace Reef

Inner wreck site

Olive jar
found intact

B-10   B-9   B-8

B96	B95	B94	B93	B91
B97	B98	B99	B910	B912
B913	B914	B915	B917	B918
B919	B920	B921	B923	B924
B925		B928	B929	B930
B931	B933	B934	B935	B936

Formosa Reef

John's Reef

C-10   C-9

Turtle Reef

·········· Main part of shipwreck

✦ Gold

✚ Silver coins and artifacts

×✶ Ballast Rocks

♫ Iron

Note: Each grid is 100 yards square

Day Three found the *Samala* rocking in a rather bothersome swell that a freshening wind had rustled up during the night but the less-than-ideal conditions did nothing to dampen the mood of growing excitement. Webber and his team left first for a thorough magging of the B-9 area. Boat No. 2, with a full complement aboard—Long, Summers, Fothergill, Colonel Montes, and I—headed for the reef twenty minutes later. Nearing Duke's Reef we encountered boat No. 1 on its way back to the *Samala*. Troubling news: the second cesium unit which had been brought out for a test had developed a tiny leak in the Plexiglas housing around the sensor staff and the salt water that entered had thrown the entire unit out. A tense-looking Webber directed us to proceed with mapping, detector and photo work. Long nodded and moved the boat over near Formosa Reef. Colonel Montes threw overboard an anchor which easily found a purchase in the coral outcropping. Long and Summers donned their scuba gear and within minutes had tumbled backward over the side, leaving only a trail of bubbles. After a quick check of my Nikonos and light meter I followed Fothergill into the water, deflated my buoyancy vest, and slowly descended into the waters of the Silver Shoals.

I have been fortunate in my travels to have glimpsed the submarine worlds of Hawaii, Indonesia, Fiji, the Florida Keys, and even the kelp forests of California. But I was nonetheless completely unprepared for the startlingly beautiful world I had entered. The sun pouring down through the shimmering canopy of water overhead suffused the landscape with a richness and color I had never before witnessed. Reaching a clearing of velvety sand at forty-five feet, I paused briefly to marvel at the incomparable blue of the watery horizon that stretched into the distance beyond and between the reef heads, while scant feet away a school of tiny neon tetras darted among the filigreed branches of some nameless coral blossom. I lingered a moment longer in this clear-light vision, rejoicing in nature's creation, then turned to the business at hand.

As I followed Billy Fothergill he swam over outcroppings and kicked slowly through canyons and across sand pockets, pausing at each of the Day-Glo markers, pointing to bits and pieces of pottery and iron, now and then placing his dive knife alongside the objects as an aid to scale measurements as I recorded the finds. Some of the granite ballast stones were the size of bread loaves yet they formed no apparent scatter pattern. Oddly, several of the rocks were perched atop coral shafts six to eight inches high, looking like golf balls on tees. How and why they got there was another mystery. Rounding the corner of a canyon wall, we looked up to see Duke Long sitting comfortably atop a giant mushroom-shaped coral colony, clipboard and grease pen in hand, busily sketching a diagram of the B-9 floor area.

We returned to the *Samala* at 1:30, bringing more ballast stones, several iron artifacts that appeared to be seventeenth-century ship's fittings, and an intact neck from an olive jar that was identical to the one Taylor had sketched. Webber was pleased but still frustrated by his electronics problems. No one needed reminding that the cesium mags were in a sense the whole ball game. While the second unit's sensor shaft dried in the sun, Webber called the Miami marine operator on the radiotelephone and patched a call through to Varian in Canada to make arrangements to air-ship them for repairs. In the interim, Big Foot would carry the load. Were it to fail, the entire expedition would come to a halt that would mean a delay of at least ten days. Webber had a short fuse that afternoon. When Summers returned to the reef after lunch, mistakenly leaving behind the Aquapulse detector, his boss fumed. "Well, just exactly what are you doing out there, taking a Caribbean dive vacation?" Webber barked into the CB microphone. The storm soon subsided, however, and by the end of working hours Webber was calmly stoic: "I've never had a piece of electronic gear that wasn't finicky, no matter how well made. It's just one of the things in this business you learn to put up with as best you can."

During the half-hour lull before dinner that evening diver Carter Leary moseyed up to the fo'c'sle to join engineer Kevin Lawson and me as we took in another splendid sunset. Nobody spoke much. Leary removed a beer from the ice chest, opened it, and sat down on the cushioned bench with the familiarity of a good ol' boy hitching up a chair on the porch of the country store. He took a slow pleasurable pull from the bottle, kicked one foot up onto a capstan, stared into the western sky, then broke the silence with his deep southern drawl: "Damn, I wonder what the poor people are doin'."

We were lucky blokes indeed.

From the Cave of Sand

If *Nuestra Señora de la Concepción* had been playing a centuries-long waiting game with the many who had courted her she was never more mischievous than she was on the very threshold of yielding to the boldest and most determined of her suitors. While his divers methodically probed every square foot of the B-9 sector, patiently marking every artifact and stone, Webber was again hit with an electronic outage that once more put his field expertise and patience to the test. It was Day Four and Webber once more had arrived at the site with the mag, only to find the battery pack dead. At 10:45 the reef boat returned to the *Samala* "with shit and feathers flying," as Chunky Cardwell later observed. Again the cesium was dismantled on the galley table. Newly charged batteries were installed, the housing clamped closed, and another anxious moment arrived. Would the mag function properly? Would it stabilize? Webber flipped the switch. A read-out instantly flashed across the console, fluttered briefly, then remained perfectly stationary. The unit worked fine.

By noon Webber was back on the reef, forgoing lunch to make up for lost time. Using Jim Nace for surface gridline control, Webber and Coffey worked the B-9 area, finding readings in a canyon area roughly 100 feet north of Formosa Reef. At times kicking hard against the tidal current, Webber pushed himself relentlessly, occasionally gesturing to Coffey to direct a marker placement on an anomaly. Some of the readings emanated from beneath coral debris, others beneath sand, still others from the walls of a cavelike hollow. Then, as Webber circled a small head adjacent to Formosa Reef, he spotted ahead of him an olive jar partially imbedded in coral at the base. Nace saw it, too, but mistook it for a large ballast stone. Diving down to the find, Nace was just about to tap on it with his hammer when his boss stopped him. Webber and Coffey immediately secured from magging to spend half an hour carefully chiseling the jar from its resting place. Back alongside the reef boat, they lifted it aboard. The artifact was a beauty—perfectly intact, barely encrusted, and free of discoloration. Moreover, the jar, being identical to Henry Taylor's earlier rendering, was of *Concepción* vintage. That night the small unnamed head was dubbed Nace Reef.

On this night Webber tried to piece together the evidence thus far uncovered, curious to know why some form of ballast pile had not yet turned up or at least indications of a dismantled ballast mound. Long and Summers wondered why their metal detector probes had not turned up any evidence of silver, given the many stories of silver chests dumped willy nilly overboard. Could it be the detector was malfunctioning, perhaps stuck on a low sensitivity setting? Webber agreed an on-site check of the detector should be done on the morrow. "What's gratifying to me so far," he concluded, "is that despite problems, my theory of depth control is proving to be correct. I think we'll soon be getting some hard answers."

On Thursday, November 30, the expedition awoke to find a three- to four-foot swell coming from the northeast, together with a steady fifteen-knot wind and 20 percent cloud cover. The sea state was vexatious but not unmanageable for experienced hands. This was also Day Five and at 9:30 A.M. Webber and his boat No. 1 team left with the mag hopefully to wrap up the B-9 survey. This morning Duke Long's crew remained behind to fit out boat No. 2 with a water pump/compressor unit operated by a two-stroke gasoline-powered motor bolted to the sturdy wooden bench seat in the forward section of the boat.

Connected to the motor by a V-belt pully were a rotary water pump and a simple but efficient air compressor. In operation the pump draws in seawater from a six-foot length of hose hanging over the side and sends it under pressure into a 150-foot length of 1½-inch-diameter hose connected to what marine salvors call a venturi excavation rig. The venturi is basically a J-shaped metal tube five inches in diameter and about three feet long coupled to twenty feet of open-ended hard-line hose of the same diameter. Water pumped from the surface enters the tube just above the elbow in a stream directed back into the attached hard-line hose. This flow generates enough suction in the open metal end to easily suck up sand and other light debris which a diver may push into it by hand. Thus, by positioning the metal mouth of the venturi rig in a narrow sand pocket a diver can virtually clean out the pocket while uncovering heavier objects such as coins and valuables (known in the profession as "goodies"). The sand and debris is in turn ejected from the open end of the hard line in a pile some distance from the actual dig.

Directly next to the water pump is an air compressor connected by a flexible coupling to a small holding tank, which in turn feeds two air hoses attached to second-stage scuba regulators. Because the air hoses are up to 200 feet long, a diver working directly in the vicinity may draw on the unlimited surface air supply provided by this system (known as a hookah rig) rather than rely on scuba tanks with their limited capacity—usually an hour. Safety-conscious Webber, however, insisted that all divers on hookah carry scuba on their backs as an emergency back-up in case of a failure of the surface air supply.

The venturi compressor system is not new to marine excavation; however, Webber had carefully chosen the components and tested the assembly to ensure it did not exceed the carrying capacity of the reef boats, even when the craft was loaded with divers, tanks, and gear. When put to use out on the reef, the venturi rigs would allow Webber to quickly remove the sand that had accumulated over more than three centuries on the scattered debris of a wreck.

By 11 A.M., as Duke Long's crew completed its outfitting of boat

No. 2 with the venturi-compressor assembly, Webber unexpectedly returned. Everyone was prepared to learn of another mag malfunction. Instead Webber announced he was through magging for the time being, because the tidal surge around the heads made survey work difficult. As important, the time had come to open up a few likely looking sand pockets. Moments later boat No. 2 pulled away from the *Samala* and set up on the site. An hour later boat No. 1 with Webber, Coffey, Nace, and me aboard arrived, and the assault on B-9 began in earnest.

Swimming once more through the lush wonderland of the Silver Shoals, I followed Webber, watching him as he supervised the placement of the venturi rig, conversing easily with the divers by using hand signals, now taking the Aquapulse to probe into a low-ceilinged sand cave that opened onto a rather narrow corridor between two large coral heads that rose some thirty feet from the floor (which itself was composed of sand and coral boulders). The cave seemed an unlikely place for debris of any kind to collect, let alone treasure, but moments later he emerged and handed the Aquapulse to Coffey, indicating he had picked up strong readings and directing the venturi to be moved into the cave.

While this was taking place, Nace, swimming fifty feet away over a low coral head, spotted a ballast stone about ten inches in diameter. There were others like it scattered about but this one was quite free of marine growth and thus seemed a good choice for a souvenir. Nace reached down, grabbed the stone, and pulled it away from the coral. Turning it over he noticed a strange object stuck to the underside—a dark-gray, roughly circular disc about two inches across. He pried the object from the rock and examined it closely. It bore no markings but it felt rather heavy. Nace wasn't sure but this just might be some kind of coin. He went over to Webber and showed it to him.

Had Nace handed his boss the end of a high-voltage wire the impact could not have been more electrifying. Webber knew in an instant that he was holding a heavily sulphided silver coin, very likely a piece of eight. A sudden burst of air bubbles flew out of his regulator, surrounding his head as they floated upward in a great cloud of exultation. As Webber nodded his head excitedly, shaking hands with Nace, I shot several pictures, then tapped Webber on the shoulder. He turned to face the camera with coin in hand, his eyes wide with elation and astonishment, then seconds later shot upward to the surface. He could be forgiven if his ascent may have been slightly faster than the diving manuals recommended.

Radioing Henry Taylor to stand by, Webber returned to the

Samala as fast as safety would permit and fairly leaped aboard and handed over the find. Taylor immediately dropped the object into a bowl of muriatic acid, a solution which quickly removes all sulphur oxide from heavily sulphided coins. For several long minutes the two waited, surrounded now by Captain Garton and his four-man crew, everyone staring at what appeared to be an Alka-Seltzer tablet bubbling in a cup of weak tea. At last Taylor, wearing rubber gloves, removed the object, wiped it clean with a cotton rag, and held up a gleaming silver piece of eight on which were stamped a shield with the letters *OMP,* to identify the coin as being from a Mexican mint. There was no date but Taylor quickly confirmed that this was exactly the kind of coin that the *Concepción* had carried.

Almost immediately Webber jumped into the reef boat and roared back to B-9 to report the findings to his dive team. The news had a wondrous effect and everyone worked now with the certainty they were closing in on something big. While Coffey and Leary worked the Aquapulse in the narrow canyon between the two heads, Webber and Nace moved into the darkened cave and began pushing sand into the mouth of the venturi from a spot that had given strong readings. The hole gradually grew deeper and wider as Webber gently pawed handfuls of sand away. Then something fell from the side of the hole. It was a piece of eight, charcoal-gray but only lightly sulphided. Then another, then two, then a half dozen. Nace put the coins into a meshed-nylon goodie bag. The coins fell in a steady trickle now, falling into the growing pocket in threes and fours, then in handfuls.

While the treasure had begun to pour from the sands of the cave, Bob Coffey scanned with the Aquapulse the bottom of the narrow canyon. Coral rubble was piled high in places and he set the detector to the most sensitive of its three scales to maximize the depth of its penetration. Nearing the end of the north wall the meter suddenly jumped from zero to ten. It stayed pegged at ten for nearly a dozen feet. Not sure whether this was a true reading or merely a transient power surge from the detector's batteries, Coffey shifted to a less sensitive scale and made a second pass. Again the needle pegged. Shifting to the least sensitive scale Coffey made a third pass and still the needle pegged. As he hovered along the wall a moment considering the implications of the readings, Coffey noticed a six-inch hole in the wall occupied by a spiny sea urchin. Right next to the creature on the lip of the hole, looking as though they had been put there by a sloppy casino croupier, sat a stack of five pieces of eight, heavily sulphided and coated with a yellowy slime. As he reached with his diving knife to pry the stack loose Coffey let out a gurgled whoop of joy. The conclusion was inescapable: Underneath the rubble beneath him there must be one hell of a lot of Spanish silver.

All was happy confusion, for it seemed that everyone now was making similar discoveries, each diver trying to drag his nearest companion over to view yet another cluster of coins, or another wild reading on the Aquapulse. Amid the underwater handshaking and backslapping, Webber continued to reap a joyful harvest. As the coin count mounted past seventy, a speck of pale blue suddenly appeared in the sand. An instant later a five-inch-high porcelain cup tumbled noiselessly from the sand into Webber's hands. The cup, devoid of any chips or cracks, glowed with extraordinary beauty even in the dim light of the cave. Webber examined its graceful shape, the delicacy of the hand-painted design, and the small Chinese inscription on the base. He immediately guessed what he held in his grasp—a pristine example of Ming dynasty china that had been shipped to the Philippines, taken by Manila galleon across the Pacific to Acapulco, carted to Mexico City, carried by burro train across the Sierra Madre Mountains to Veracruz, and taken aboard the *Concepción*, only to find a watery grave in the desolate reaches of the South Atlantic.

When Webber broke the surface alongside reef boat No. 1 he handed the cup to Summers and raised his voice to the heavens:

"Praise God! She is found!"

As the rest of the dive team surfaced alongside, the air filled with cheering, whoops, and laughter. Webber reached for the walkie-talkie to call Tony Garton and crew.

"Captain, you can put the champagne on ice. We have found the *Concepción!*"

"Bloody marvelous, Burt!" came the crackling reply several times over. "That's bloody marvelous!"

By 3:30 P.M. both boats had returned to the *Samala*. Amidst much handshaking and hugs and congratulations, Henry dumped the first handful of coins into a container of muriatic acid. Within an hour a small pile had accumulated—shiny, eight-*real* Spanish pieces of eight in uncirculated mint condition, the very stuff of legendary treasure. The day's haul: 128 coins. Webber radiated an aura of triumph and enormous relief. Truly, a great weight had begun to slip from his shoulders. Moments later Taylor discovered a coin with a date—1639— and one rare eight-*real* dated 1620. But the one Webber valued the most that moment was the one which lucky Jim Nace had chanced upon beneath a ballast stone in B-9.

Chunky Cardwell outdid himself in serving a splendid feast that night. The entrée of breaded veal cutlet made a wonderful side dish for the case of iced Moët champagne. After a glass of bubbly almost everyone, Webber included, confessed the day's triumph was so overwhelming that it had yet to really sink in. But the festive meal was rife with toasts and benedictions. Everyone stood and raised his glass to the Dominican Republic, following which Garton toasted the hope that the *Samala* would soon be so laden with treasure that he would be forced to return to port early. Henry Taylor toasted his coming fatigue from cleaning coins, following which Webber presented Jim Nace with a $100 bonus for finding the first coin.

"We found over a hundred coins today," he proclaimed. "Tomorrow we'll find a thousand!"

All hands raised their glasses and cheered.

Z-One-Z. Green. Major.

Later that evening Webber went to the bridge and called the Miami-based international marine operator, instructing her to dial the Seaquest office number in Chicago. It was just past 6 P.M. in the midwest, but Webber hoped Warren Stearns or Stan Smith might still be at work. By arrangement Webber called Chicago with field reports at least every other day. Because the radio frequency was not secure from eavesdropping, he had devised a code which allowed the transmission of essential information on the progress of the search which would be indecipherable without the key. When there was no answer at the office, Webber tried Stearns' home number. No answer. Nor did Stan Smith answer his phone. As a last resort he called the Palm Beach, Florida, home of his attorney Ken Beall who was just about to sit down to dinner. Beall quickly fetched a paper and pen and listened carefully.

""Z-one-Z. Green. Major," Webber announced with military precision. "I repeat: Z-one-Z. Green. Major."

Beall jotted down the transmission but, alas, he couldn't remember what he'd done with his own code sheet. He had no clue to what it meant but he could sense by Webber's tone of voice that something momentous had happened.

"Ken, do you copy transmission? Over," Webber asked.

"Yeah, right, Burt, I read you," Beall answered quickly. Then: "Ah, Burt, I don't have the . . . ah, information sheet with me right now, but . . . Oh hell, Burt, did you find it?"

There was a brief pause on the other end, then a guarded laugh.

"Yes, Ken, we found it. We found it. Please notify all concerned and I will be in touch with home office tomorrow."

Indeed, Burt Webber, Jr., had found the *Concepción*. The fabled lady of the good and pure had finally yielded to the man who more than any other deserved to win her hand—and her bountiful dowry. After 338 years, Burt Webber's ship had finally come in.

10

Further Mysteries, Further Finds

Celebration in Puerto Plata

The two days following the recovery of the first coins from the *Concepción* were memorable. As diver master Bob Coffey proclaimed, "We're no longer treasure hunters, we're treasure finders." To prove his point, Coffey returned the next morning to remove the coral overburden from the site where he had obtained strong readings and discovered hundreds of coins fused together in great clumps. Many bore the clear markings of the cross-weave from the gunny sacks in which they had been stored. Other blocks retained the roughly square configuration of the wooden chests that once contained them (the wood had long since rotted away). Regardless of size, the fused clumps would later be chemically treated to separate the coins which would be cleaned and polished.

As Coffey carefully worked his treasure loose with a chipping hammer, Webber and Nace were twenty feet to the east filling their goodie bags with coins at an increasing rate. Along with the cascade of silver came bits of wood, musket balls, iron spikes, broken pottery and porcelain, splashes of silver, a holy water container and several more fine examples of Ming dynasty cups. As the venturi removed more and more sand, Webber began tunneling out from the cave and underneath the coral debris that lay in the narrow canyon. Eventually, the rubble would be cleared away down to the level where the treasure had originally been scattered, but for the time being there was enough to do just scooping up handful after handful of pieces of eight, plus some pieces of four, and even a few copper maravedi coins.

During the morning hours I photographed both the general area and the dig in progress but as the dust clouds from the venturi gradually decreased visibility, I put aside my camera and helped Bob Coffey by carrying treasure to the surface as he broke off large chunks of coins from his underwater mother lode. To actually hold in my hands these legendary pieces of eight and to know that the last person to touch them had died centuries ago was an extraordinary feeling. But to be doing so in fifty feet of water in the lush coral reef canyons of the Silver Shoals rendered the experience almost beyond comprehension. There was, in fact, little time to ponder the significance of the setting for the flurry of activity required teamwork. One massive clump of coins, for example, weighed nearly 200 pounds and required three men and an air bag to raise it to the surface and into the reef boat. Not until later when the find was aboard the *Samala* did anyone pause long enough to consider that he was gazing on something that was easily worth over six figures.

Nor were the most precious treasures the heftiest. Jim Nace discovered this that afternoon as he removed coins from the ceiling and walls of the shallow tunnel dubbed the Money Hole. Using a powerful underwater flashlight to illuminate the gloom, Nace reached up to pluck a coin when suddenly a thick stream of sparkling gold wafted right in front of his face mask and straight into the mouth of the venturi underneath his right elbow. Before he realized what had happened, the contents of what had once been an intact pouch of gold dust had passed before his eyes like a gossamer veil, and vanished into oblivion.

"The thing I don't understand," Webber remarked to me during lunch as he looked at several cannon balls on the deck of the *Samala*, "is why we've found cannon balls but no cannons—or anchors?" He retained a puzzled face for an instant, then burst into laughter. Had we found either of those artifacts there would be reason to suspect the identity of the wreck since the *Concepción* had lost all her anchors and all but a few of her bronze cannons (English salvors very likely found what remained of the latter). Still, even as coins by the thousands were now being fetched from B-9, there were unanswered questions. The sector producing the treasure represented a canyon area roughly twenty feet in length by twelve feet wide between two reef walls which rose to within twenty feet of the surface. True, the area was between three coral heads but the absence of significant amounts of ballast rock—or a ballast pile—strongly suggested the area we were excavating did not represent the main wrecksite. The character of treasure and artifacts discovered there might indicate that we may have found some other portion of the ship that had drifted away from the wrecksite.

Webber was confident that further cesium survey work in adjacent areas would provide answers in the days ahead but for the moment he was content to tap into the richness of the canyon. To facilitate mapping, he divided the 100-square-yard B-9 area into thirty-six smaller sectors of fifty square yards each. The canyon was contained in sector B9-#1.

Saturday, December 2, was the third and last treasure-digging day before the expedition headed back to Puerto Plata. The return would be a few days ahead of schedule, but Colonel Montes, seeing the treasure pile up aboard the *Samala*, was anxious to establish the necessary links for immediate military support, including the use of fighter planes on standby-alert status.

While Webber and Nace continued to harvest the Money Hole, a four-man crew began loading coral debris from the canyon into a four-foot-square metal debris basket attached to a Subsalve lifting bag. When the basket was full Billy Fothergill would partially inflate the lifting bag with air from a scuba tank, just enough to float the basket off the canyon floor, following which Coffey, Summers, and Long would push the basket to a dumping ground some distance away. While this work was in progress the venturi rig continued to suck away· sand to uncover coins by the hundreds, porcelain, pottery, small pieces of timber, a silver incense jar, and parts of ship's rigging.

After lunch Summers and Long returned to the site to remove all buoy markers from the reef heads, hide the venturi rigs under coral overhangs, and otherwise cover traces of the expedition's visit. Back on the *Samala* the rest of the afternoon was spent loading aboard the pump-compressor rigs, and stowing gear for the trip to port. Webber was in an ebullient mood, while expedition medic Fothergill was no less glad his boss would be out of the water a few days; Webber had worked so hard during the mag survey that he had sustained coral cuts on his lower legs and developed fin blisters on the top of his feet which in turn had become infected by coral grit. As long as Webber was spending hours daily under water the open cuts and blisters had no chance to heal. Yet this seemed a small price to pay for a professional obsession. No doubt William Phips had endured his own special discomforts to gain his prize.

Indeed, there were interesting parallels between both treasure hunters and their expeditions to the shoals. Webber was thirty-six, the same age as his predecessor when he first discovered the *Concepción*. Both men were Americans, both had chartered English ships with English crews, and both had found the wreck early in the afternoon on a Thursday. There may have been other similarities but as the *Samala* headed through a following sea to Puerto Plata, no one aboard had yet put events of recent days into perspective. Nor would they for some time to come.

All hands were proudly wearing Phips II golf shirts as the *Samala* tied up at 7:30 P.M., ready to greet a very excited group of investors, principals, wives, and one or two children—perhaps fifteen in all—who had flown that morning into Santo Domingo, thence by car or chartered plane to Puerto Plata. Among the first to board were Warren Stearns, Stan Smith, and Ken Beall, all of whom hugged Webber and shook hands in triumph. There to share the victory was Sandy Webber, a petite blond woman who kissed her husband and beamed with pride. While Chunky poured the first of many drinks from the saloon bar, the visitors gathered around the afterdeck as Webber, resplendent in his beret and his hour of victory, opened a small carton and spilled out onto the top of the cesium storage box a score of beautifully cleaned and polished pieces of eight. As he narrated his story, more artifacts appeared, Instamatics and Polaroids flashed every few seconds, and the air was full of laughter, ahhs, and questions. Elsewhere, even as Captain Tony Garton bedecked the saloon table with a spread of hors d'oeuvres, rumors of Señor Webber's astounding treasure find were spreading throughout Puerto Plata, relayed by a dozen boys who habitually hung out on the wharf to earn a few centavos running errands for crewmen on visiting boats.

By midnight the party aboard the *Samala* had only just started to slow. At that juncture all the members of Phips II had autographed someone's hundred-dollar bill as a souvenir, told several high adventure stories to fascinated listeners, and celebrated the good news with many a lifted glass. As the guests finally began leaving, steady-going veteran Bob Coffey summed up his impressions: "I think the excitement of treasure hunting is the excitement other people have talking to you about it." Moments later a military sedan pulled up alongside the *Samala*'s berth, followed by a small convoy truck with half a dozen soldiers in camouflage fatigues carrying automatic rifles. The sedan's door opened and out stepped Colonel Manuel Montes, no longer wearing a T-shirt, shorts, and sandals, but dressed in trim summer dress khaki uniform and very much in charge, issuing orders to the platoon petty officer to station his men around the *Samala* and her treasure. Peeling a twenty-peso note from a roll of bills, he handed it to one soldier, directing him to fetch food and coffee from somewhere in town. The soldier snapped to attention and saluted. For one more night at least the *Samala* would again be under guard.

A Surprise Private Showing

An hour before sunrise the calm of a warm night was disturbed by the arrival of two sedans and the convoy truck. Webber, Sandy, and lawyer Ken Beall stepped out of the lead car and boarded the *Samala* for a cup of coffee. As Colonel Montes and Lieutenant J.G. Diaz appeared from the second vehicle the guards on duty snapped to attention. Several more soldiers, also armed with M-16's, jumped from the back of the convoy truck which a minute later backed up to the *Samala*'s gangway. As Webber and company watched, the soldiers hefted several heavy metal lockers full of treasure onto the convoy truck. Colonel Montes, who fairly barked his orders, was clearly anxious to transfer the treasure to the safety of the naval base in Santo Domingo. With the chests and soldiers aboard the truck, Montes signaled to Webber and a minute later everyone was back in his car and headed for the main highway across the island.

The ride to Santo Domingo was a wild three-hour dash at speeds as high as 70 and 80 MPH. The treasure truck (Montes in command) made remarkable time, assisted by a string of hair-raising near misses as it passed buses and farm trucks at speed, honking loudly at intersections and paying scant heed to road courtesy. When the convoy ran into a minor slowdown at a traffic circle in the picturesque city of Santiago in the middle of the island, Diaz, his M-16 at his side, simply held out his hand and frowned authoritatively at two lanes of green-light cross traffic, effectively bringing it to a standstill.

The caravan arrived intact in Santo Domingo shortly before 10 A.M. and wheeled through the guarded portals of the Navy base en route to a modern three-story headquarters building topped with a forest of communication antennas. Moving around to the rear of the building, the convoy truck came to a halt next to a columned portico under which was parked a silver four-door Chevrolet with window curtains bearing the insignia plates of a three-star admiral. Colonel Montes hopped down from the passenger side of the truck, briefly adjusted his gun and holster, then signaled to Webber and party to wait while he went inside. He was gone more than fifteen minutes, time enough for one to imagine the no-nonsense line of questioning Admiral Amiama had followed with his old friend Colonel Montes: "You're sure Webber's really found the *Concepción*? How many coins? Thousands? And he's not hiding anything?"

Eventually Montes reappeared outside the portico to invite Burt and Sandy Webber into the Chief of Staff's office. Admiral Amiama was a tall, robust man, slightly balding with executive glasses and a warm ingratiating manner. Sandy Webber, who not two days earlier had her hands in dishwater cleaning up after four children, was utterly charmed by the admiral's respectful attention. He ordered his steward to bring her coffee and pastries, then asked her to make herself comfortable while he and Señor Webber went on a short errand.

Attorney Ken Beall and I were sitting in our car as Admiral Amiama, Webber, and Colonel Montes emerged from the building. We watched as they got into the admiral's limousine and pulled away from the portico, followed closely by the convoy truck with the soldiers—and the treasure. I got out and stood alongside the car to stretch my legs, feeling the rising heat of the day and a slight twinge of paranoia. The more I looked at the high-walled interior courtyard and the gun-wielding guards in camouflage, the more I felt I was on a stage set for "Mission Impossible." For a brief instant I contemplated a matching scenario: "They've got Webber, they've got the treasure, they know where the wreck is, and there's been no press releases on the find," and finally, "I'd prefer a wall with southern exposure and, yes, thanks, I would like a blindfold."

Actually, Webber himself wasn't sure at first where he was headed. As the limousine left the naval base something thudded to the floor at his feet. Apologizing, Admiral Amiama picked up the exotic machine pistol and replaced it in the fast-draw scabbard from which it had fallen. Moments later the limousine pulled off the coastal road into a long gravel driveway lined with stately palm trees and almost as many commando sentries toting Israeli-made Uzi machine guns. Only then did the smiling admiral reveal that Webber was about to meet Antonio Guzmán, the President of the Dominican Republic.

It was a replay of the Phips legend: the treasure hunter meeting the King. Webber wished he'd worn something more than his Phips II golf shirt, khaki pants, beret, and desert boots (laced loosely to ease the pain of his wounds), but the victorious American, his face red and cracked from the sun, his hands covered with myriad coral cuts, could not have appeared more dashing and adventurous in his moment of triumph. Inside a spacious and lovely beach cabaña, Webber and the admiral were cordially greeted by President Guzmán accompanied by the president of the Central Bank of the Dominican Republic. A tray of rich Dominican coffee was produced just as Colonel Montes appeared with a work party of soldiers carrying the treasure. The heavy padlocks were removed from the lockers and the chests opened to reveal the splendid treasure of Silver Shoals. As the Dominicans gazed at each artifact, Webber reached for a specially wrapped packet containing the first coin they had found from the *Concepción*. Through interpreters he told the story of how diver Jim Nace had turned over a ballast stone to find it. Webber then asked the President if he might reserve this singular find for Nace. Guzmán quickly agreed, requesting that the coin be conveyed to the diver with his personal congratulations. He then accepted the American's invitation to choose a coin for himself, shook Webber's hand warmly, thanked him for the wonderful work he had done, and wished him good hunting in the months ahead.

Hardly had Webber returned to the base when Admiral Amiama insisted his friend immediately go to sick bay where his personal physician would examine Webber's infected cuts and blisters. Webber agreed and within minutes of experiencing the pinnacle of elation found himself fighting back tears of excruciating pain as the base doctor peeled away the festering scabs to thoroughly clean and bandage the sites of infection. Returning to the admiral's office (with a prescription for antibiotics and a warning not to go in the water until new scabs had formed), Webber pushed aside lingering pain and concentrated on the next moves he would make together with the Dominicans. It was agreed that Henry Taylor would come to Santo Domingo to supervise the identification, cataloguing, and cleaning of all coins and artifacts, this to be done in a spacious work area directly above Admiral Amiama's office. The Central Bank of the Dominican Republic would store the treasure in its vaults and ensure accountability with inventory sheets bearing several signatures. In this way every coin and artifact would be carefully authenticated by an unbroken chain of verification and control that began as the treasure was brought aboard the *Samala* and would eventually extend to the showrooms of the world's coin auction houses. Paralleling this effort would be an elaborate on-site procedure by which each artifact would be carefully cleaned, tagged, inventoried, and photographed (or illustrated), after which it would be preserved in special boxes of foam "peanuts" or, in some instances, salt water. On arrival in Santo Domingo, the finds would be examined by curators of the national museum and, eventually, appraised by world experts specializing in rare collectibles.

Elsewhere, Admiral Amiama promised a Dominican corvette would be stationed on the reef to protect the wrecksite from intruders during the expedition's two-week Christmas break. As for publicity, he desired to play the *Concepción* as low key as possible, particularly regarding the potential value of its treasure, so as not to encourage any parties to attempt a foray to the shoals which might result in an encounter and, heaven forbid, gunplay. Both men realized the impossibility of keeping such a sensational story under wraps for very long, especially after the expedition members had spent Christmas with their families. Accordingly, the admiral agreed to make an announcement to the Dominican press corps shortly before the holidays while Webber would wait until just after the New Year before releasing anything to the U.S. media. That evening during a long dinner with investors at El Bodegon restaurant, Webber explained the need for a temporary press blackout. Still, no one present realized the explosive worldwide impact that the *Concepción*'s discovery would have four weeks later.

In the meantime, there was another ten days of salvage work to do out on the reef. The *Samala* got under way from Puerto Plata before dawn on December 19, carrying aboard Jack Haskins who had flown down immediately upon learning of the discovery. A rugged handsome man with curly red hair, a freckled smile, and black bifocal glasses that somehow look racy, Haskins has the affable air of a man essentially at peace with himself, able to look for whimsy as well as treasure. Also aboard for the first time to beef up the dive team was Harry Weiman, a thirty-five-year-old ex-submariner and a native of Lebanon, Pennsylvania, with extensive scuba experience and a gift for fixing anything from giant compressors to small light meters.

Once the *Samala* was again tied to her permanent mooring, the reef boats were launched and sent to area B9-#1 to buoy the reef heads. The job took longer than usual when both boats were temporarily lost in the maze of heads. A slightly chagrined Duke Long radioed the *Samala* for a bearing and soon afterwards the dig was under way.

After closely examining the immediate area around the B9-#1 sector, Haskins agreed with Webber that the site certainly did not have the appearance of a wreck, regardless of the treasure it was yielding. Could it be that the sector contained a portion of the *Concepción* that had broken away from the ship and drifted still farther into the reef? If so, the two men reasoned, a visual search of the reef heads to windward might turn up evidence of the main wrecksite. That evening, Haskins checked the chart position of a large stockless anchor that had been discovered by Phips I in 1977 several hundred yards to the northeast of area B-9. If that anchor had come from the *Concepción*, there was reason to believe the wreck may lie on or near a line connecting the two finds.

The following morning Haskins and Duke Long donned scuba gear and pushed away from the reef boat anchored over B9-#1, moving at a leisurely pace on a northeast heading. They remained only fifteen feet beneath the surface to keep a wide visual perspective, their practiced eyes noting with interest the few ballast stones scattered here and there. For twenty minutes the pair kicked along, straining a bit against a stronger tidal surge. Then, as they rounded the corner of a large head 130 yards from B-9 they saw something that charged them with excitement. Resting on top of a coral pedestal below them was a large mound of ballast stones, some weighing hundreds of pounds. Nearby was another, smaller pile of stones. His heart pounding, Haskins kicked down to examine the mounds closely, quickly running through his mind the mass of data on the wreck he had long since memorized. Yes, everything seemed to fit: the east-west orientation of the keel line, the cavelike configuration of the large coral head that loomed over what would figure to be the stern section, the slight forward pitch of the ballast mounds, even the positioning of the three coral heads in which the hull was locked.

As the certainty of his find grew stronger, Haskins reveled in the moment. For this self-taught marine historian who had labored so long in the archives of Europe in search of a legendary ship, destiny had granted him the privilege of being the first person in 338 years to lay eyes on the crumbling grave of the *Nuestra Señora de la Concepción*.

As wonderful as the discovery of the main wrecksite was, there was still so much treasure pouring from the B9-#1 site (it would later be dubbed the Silver Trench) that the start of a full-scale excavation of the new find would have to be postponed. Burt Webber had an embarrassment of riches. Hardly an hour went by that word did not arrive of some new artifact discovery: a silver candle snuffer, a batch of wooden cocoa stirrers, a candle holder, several silver dinner plates, or one of many examples of contraband silver in the form of splashes, plugs, cupcakes, and wedges. All fell from the sandy sides of ever-widening holes as divers probed deeper into what seemed to be a bottomless Christmas stocking.

Two days before this second trip to the reef came to a close, Jack Haskins, at Webber's direction, moved a venturi rig to the main wrecksite in an area now designated 08 (the "0" standing for the outside or windward portion of the reef). With Fothergill and me assisting, he began hand-fanning sand from a pocket that had given strong readings on the Aquapulse. I took the first turn as safety back-up and watched in fascination as Haskins dug gently into the sand and within minutes began finding pieces of pottery and odd bits of wood. At the one-foot level he came across scattered coins, mostly pieces of eight which he handed to me with tea-finger elegance. At two feet he found more pottery shards and the leather sole of a shoe, the latter of which he handed me. While he continued digging I studied the still pliable fragment, noticing the stitching holes around its edges, trying to imagine what its owner had looked like, wondering if he had been wearing the shoe at the time it had made its way to its resting place fifty feet under water. Strange, but this remnant of clothing, this tattered piece of leather, more so than coins and porcelain, brought home to me the reality of the dramatic events that had taken place here. It was as if we were opening a watery time capsule that carried us deeper and more intimately into its past with each artifact it yielded to the present.

As the *Samala* made her way back to Hispaniola, this time to the naval base in Santo Domingo where she would remain for the Christmas break, I began to realize for the first time the magnitude of Burt Webber's accomplishment—and of the timeless appeal of his story. Just how universal that appeal was could not be anticipated for to a degree that would be determined by how Webber and Seaquest presented the discovery to the news media. Not surprisingly, a scenario had been outlined months earlier and would be finalized in the days ahead. The approach was straight-forward: On January 3, Webber, accompanied by Jack Haskins and Dr. Pete Foose, would hold a press conference at the New York Sheraton and use a slide presentation in lieu of actual treasure to substantiate the find. The story would be approached in a dignified professional manner with less emphasis on the romance and more on the businesslike and scientific approach that led to the discovery. Yet not even Webber could anticipate the excitement the announcement would generate.

Breaking the News

"An American announced today he has discovered a sunken treasure worth millions of dollars, maybe forty million," said David Brinkley on the NBC network news on the evening of January 3, 1979.

"He found the wreck and the cargo of a Spanish galleon, the *Concepción*. It sank with a cargo of treasure the Spanish had looted from Mexico in 1641. Here's Robert Hager."

Reporter Hager, in an account that ran nearly two minutes (and using backdrop slides provided by Seaquest), described how "Today an adventurer, a treasure hunter from Pennsylvania named Burt Webber, came to New York to tell reporters how he had found the wreck. He's only the second man ever to find the *Concepción*. The first lived 300 years ago and the quest for its treasure has become legendary among modern divers." The report continued, describing how divers came across clues such as ballast stones and hull fittings, then "finally, this photograph was made just as a diver discovered the first coin, a Spanish piece of eight." Then a quote from Webber: "When we saw that piece of eight, we came to the surface for we knew that must be the wreck. It was still inconclusive but excitement was running high, the adrenaline was really pumping . . ."

Hager continued: "The Dominican Republic gets to keep half of the treasure, and some of the rest must be shared with financial backers, but Webber and his men have been celebrating. It looks as though there may be plenty of treasure to go around."

Watching the broadcast from the living room of his Chicago home, a proud and happy Warren Stearns found himself wiping a tear from his eye.

At the press conference earlier that day, Burt Webber, wearing a vested suit, had been razor-sharp and self-possessed. Standing before a microphone-clogged rostrum in a banquet room of the Sheraton Hotel, he faced a bank of TV cameras and fifty members of a press corps widely known as the toughest and most skeptical in the business. From the outset he was peppered with the bottom-line question: How much money is the treasure worth? When he replied to the query with a "no comment," his questioners immediately fired back with, "Why no comment?"

"Well, gentlemen," Webber answered, "there's any number of reasons, from security reasons to marketing reasons to contract agreements with a foreign government but basically the answer is very speculative. Not only do we not know precisely how much treasure remains but its actual profit potential depends on how well it is marketed. For example, if we find 50,000 coins and through poor marketing procedures flood the market with them, the value of the treasure would diminish drastically. Also, we don't wish to do what other organizations have done, that is escalate this wreck up to the hundreds of millions when we haven't finished working it. We could go on finding treasure for months to come, or the next handful could be our last. But this is not a glory-seeking expedition, it's a carefully planned-out business venture."

He scored points on the reply, but now the questioning turned to the *Concepción*. Why was it so important? he was asked. Why so historically significant? His answers were interrupted once or twice, then finally one woman reporter, sounding impatient, asked, "Look, why exactly have you come here to New York to hold this press conference?"

Webber bristled slightly and glared back at the reporter and answered with a resonant voice of unarguable authority:

"Because we found a legend!"

With that, Burt Webber won over his audience and the mood changed. Questions suddenly turned friendly. Whoever this young man was, he was to be respected. As one reporter later remarked, "I wouldn't want to try changing his mind." New York, or for that matter, the world, had never met a treasure hunter quite like Burt Webber, Jr.

Death Stalks the Reef

When he returned to the Silver Shoals in early January, Webber was anxious to get into the water again—and be free of the deluge of phone calls, queries, offers, and requests for interviews that had besieged him from the moment the story had broken. The finding of the *Concepción* had made the front page of nearly every major newspaper in the U.S. as well as many others overseas, making Webber not only the biggest anomaly in Annville, but also an overnight celebrity. Even Sandy was the subject of a page-one feature profile in the *Philadelphia Inquirer*. All the world, it seemed, loves a treasure story. For its part the Dominican government was enjoying the exposure given the country by the international media. When an NBC-TV news film crew accompanied Webber to Santo Domingo, Admiral Amiama and several staff aides showed up at dockside for on-camera handshaking and best wishes as the *Samala* left for the Silver Shoals. The Chief of Staff even assigned a patrol boat to take a gaggle of reporters out to the reef for a one-day visit.

As anticipated, the B9-#1 canyon continued to yield a cascade of silver and artifacts, among the latter of which were silver dinner plates and utensils and more Chinese porcelain and intact ceramic bowls. And adding a touch of magic to an already splendid setting was the arrival of the great herds of humpback whales who came each January to the Silver Shoals area for several months of breeding and calving. These gentle and magnificent creatures, broaching the surface, at times leaping nearly entirely out of the water, were a source of ceaseless wonder and a reminder of the great richness and diversity of life in these waters.

As further magnetometer surveys continued to produce additional anomalies in the area around the main wrecksite, together with seemingly countless Aquapulse readings, Webber concluded that a complete excavation of both wrecksites could take another six to nine months. To handle the task, he would add a third reef boat, then later a fourth, and recruit several more divers. The *Samala* would continue to remain on the reef for ten days to two weeks at a time; however, for supply and security reasons the base of operations was changed from Puerto Plata to Santo Domingo. The salvaging of the *Concepción* would, in fact, be more or less a routine undertaking from this point on. Webber understood, of course, that nothing is ever routine in a profession which has inherent risks. What he didn't know was that he would soon come very close to proving it with his life.

It happened on a dead calm morning in February. While a venturi rig and hookah hoses were being set up over B9-#1, Webber and diver Harry Weiman went below with tanks and together moved a large coral boulder weighing half a ton to a dumpsite, after which Webber examined the cleared area with a metal detector. He now switched to the hookah air supply and began working with the venturi rig while Weiman went back and forth to the surface carrying equipment. Unbeknownst to anyone on or under the water, exhaust fumes from the two-stroke gas engine on the reef boat were, in the absence of a breeze of any kind, being sucked up by the intake manifold of the air compressor. As a result air mixed with lethal carbon monoxide fumes was being pumped down to Webber.

Moments later as Weiman, still on tank air, swam down to go on hookah, he saw Webber suddenly switch back to his tank and begin kicking up to the surface. As the latter passed him he made a sign of some kind but Weiman, thinking his boss needed something from the boat, continued on down, switched to hookah, and began working. Webber surfaced in a semi-conscious condition.

"Shut off the compressor! Harry!" he yelled at Jim Nace.

As he was being pulled into the boat Webber said, "Get me back to the *Concepción*." He meant "*Samala*" but at that moment lost consciousness.

Fifty feet under water Weiman was puzzled when he felt the

hookah shut down after he'd been on it for only a couple of minutes. As he shifted back to his tank regulator he felt a bit light headed but shrugged it off as a passing side effect of repeated trips to the surface. Then Nace appeared and signaled him to surface immediately.

A second reef boat came out to the site and quickly brought Webber back to the *Samala*. He was still unconscious when carried aboard and according to cookie Chunky Cardwell, "It looked like we had a dead treasure hunter on our hands." In the absence of diver-medic Fothergill who had remained ashore for treatment of a broken finger, ex-Air Force medic Jim Nace put Webber on oxygen. He regained consciousness but his vital signs remained erratic. Bob Coffey, well aware of the dangers of carbon monoxide poisoning, wasted no time deciding his boss should be evacuated to a hospital as soon as possible. Colonel Montes radioed Admiral Amiama directly on his private frequency and the latter in turn called the U.S. embassy and explained the emergency to Colonel Stanley Houston, the military attaché. Houston, who knew Webber as well as the urgency of the situation, phoned the U.S. Coast Guard in Puerto Rico and requested a helicopter evacuation. At first he was turned down with an explanation that a trip to Silver Shoals would put the aircraft into an emergency fuel zone. But minutes later, doubtless following a word with top brass, orders were issued to fly the mission anyway.

A rescue helicopter was already in the air by the time Harry Weiman returned to the *Samala*, having remained on site long enough to secure the venturi-compressor. Though he had been on the contaminated hookah for only a short time, he now had a splitting headache and felt none too steady.

Shortly after noon the Coast Guard rescue helicopter appeared on the horizon and within minutes had lowered hospital corpsman Ed Wilson onto the afterdeck of the *Samala*. After a quick examination Wilson declared Webber should be evacuated immediately to the Rio Piedres Hospital in San Juan and Weiman should come along for a thorough checkout. Without further delay Webber was placed in a wire "corps basket" and hoisted up into the hovering helicopter. Wilson and Weiman followed in lift chairs. During the hour-and-forty-five-minute trip to San Juan, Webber, still on oxygen, momentarily lost his pulse but medics restored it and gave him an intravenous infusion of a sugar solution. By dinner time that evening in San Juan, Weiman's headache had nearly vanished while hospital doctors, after monitoring and blood tests, told Webber he would soon recover. However, lab tests had shown Webber to be so saturated with carbon monoxide that there was a danger of his coming down with chemical pneumonia during the next forty-eight hours. Fortunately, he did not. A few days later he was pronounced fit and ready to return to work.

In retrospect, the mishap belonged in the category of accidents whose probability of occurrence was extremely remote, particularly since normal precautions had been taken to position the air compressor away from the motor's exhaust manifold. Yet even the most meticulously executed operations are subject to Murphy's Law (i.e., if something can go wrong, it will). That Burt Webber did not die that calm February morning is the result once again of across-the-board professionalism. His insistence on the availability of scuba back-up for all divers on hookah (a procedure all too often ignored elsewhere) was a crucial life-saving factor which, coupled with prompt medical treatment, prevented a tragedy. Then again, the incident demonstrated the value of experience—Webber had made the right moves under crisis conditions and had got himself back up to the reef boat under circumstances that would cause the drowning of anyone other than a veteran water man.

Actually, Webber had shown similar cool only two days earlier while he was resting alone for five minutes at a depth of ten feet to decompress from a prolonged dive to fifty-five feet. As he did so a mammoth twelve-foot tiger shark made two "what's-for-lunch?" passes before Webber was able to negotiate a slow, back-pedaling, deceitful retreat to safety.

By the end of February the excavation of sector B9-#1 was still producing a remarkable yield of coins and artifacts. Nace, who had found the first coin, kept his lucky streak alive by finding another singular artifact. At first the object appeared to him to be worthless modern-day junk, perhaps some kind of metal pully wheel off an old compressor. The "wheel" turned out to be a bronze astrolabe dated 1619 and worth many thousands of dollars. The remarkable instrument, one of few ever retrieved from sunken wrecks, was doubtless one of those used to determine the *Concepción's* latitude in the days preceding her demise. On the scene to photograph this and other discoveries was a film crew for East-West Productions headed by noted underwater cinematographer Stan Waterman whose credits include the underwater footage for *The Deep* and the much-acclaimed shark documentary *Blue Water White Death*. Waterman and his crew reveled in the reef's lush surroundings while shooting footage for a CBS-TV network special, "The Lost Treasure of the *Concepción*."

It was March before the expedition had begun to shift its attention to the outer main wrecksite. Here Webber confronted a task requiring the removal of many tons of coral rock and debris before he could reach a level four to eight feet below the surface that constituted the reef bottom at the time the *Concepción* wrecked. He was also aware that this sub-bottom floor would have been gleaned of obvious treasure by Phips' divers as well as subsequent visitors. The sand pockets at this level, however, held great promise since their contents were beyond the reach of seventeenth-century technology.

During an examination of the main site, it soon became obvious that the Narbrough expedition in 1688 had been in error. Phips and Narbrough claimed they could not penetrate the *Concepción*'s stern section because of what they presumed to be great amounts of coral rock grown over it. In fact, what had actually happened was the stern section, which had remained above water after the ship sank, had broken off and relocated itself. Webber concluded that the wreckage and treasure discovered in sector B9-#1 represented a portion of the wandering stern section. The finding of a pilot's astrolabe in this area, plus the fact that all recoveries were of silver coins, worked silver, and quality porcelains (shipped merchandise) substantiated the opinion. Moreover, this same sector had not yielded common earthenware items that would normally be in the ship's bow or midships section.

This conclusion led to further questions, however. Since the stern of the ship was roughly 60 × 30 feet, only a small portion of that section could have become lodged in the B9-#1 sector. Where the rest of the stern had come to rest remained a mystery. Quite possibly it could have gradually disintegrated as it bounced from reef to reef along the circuitous 125-yard path to B-9; however, a thorough magnetometer and Aquapulse survey of the corridors between the two wrecksites produced no significant anomalies or evidence of a treasure spill. Beyond this mystery, Webber was unable to explain how a stern section containing substantial amounts of silver would have had the buoyancy to float the distance it did.

By mid-May, despite slow going, Webber had found on the main wrecksite several thousand silver coins, silver plates, spoons, forks, candlestick holders, earthenware cups and plates, large amounts of indigo dye with scant remains of their wooden shipping boxes, wooden goblets, portions of hull planking, a musket barrel, iron barshot, and clay pipes. But the most exciting finds of all came from a sand pocket that at first had shown no great promise. Lucky Jim Nace, to no one's surprise, found here a long, lovely chain necklace of gold, as pure and untarnished as the day it fell into the sea. Soon thereafter Bob Coffey found a second, this one a spectacularly ornate necklace of the most delicate gold filigree links intertwined to form an exquisite chain weighing more than ten ounces. Coffey's gleaming discovery would be the single most valuable artifact recovered from the *Concepción*.

Later that month, while Coffey took charge of the expedition in his absence, Webber flew to England to re-enact for documentary cameras his first reading of the *Log of the Henry*. While there he again visited Dr. Peter Earle, the discoverer of the log, and learned from him of research that may partially explain the stern section mystery. During a review of Spanish documents, Earle came across an account of the Spanish capture of an Englishman and several others on the north coast of Hispaniola in January 1642. The English captive testified that he had been aboard an English ship that had robbed two large rafts containing 120 survivors from the *Concepción*, along with gold and silver valued at 500,000 pesos.

Half a million pesos seemed a rather extraordinary amount to have taken aboard the rafts since it would have weighed more than fifteen tons in silver alone. But since the stern was the only portion not under water after the sinking, it remained the only repository from which treasure could have been removed. Webber and Earle agreed that the treasure put on the raft would logically be the more valuable items such as ornate jewelry and worked gold and silver. Moreover, the removal of such a large amount of weight would explain why the stern was light enough to float away.

This same Spanish account also mentioned that a great amount of silver had been placed on top of one of the reef heads close to the wrecked galleon. The report corroborated several others which historian Jack Haskins had found.

What all this suggested was that Operation Phips II would find less treasure than originally thought (although in consequence the substantial amount already found would become more valuable) while there appeared to be a strong possibility of finding a sizable quantity of treasure atop one of the surrounding reefs. To assist him in his hunt, Webber ordered a very powerful experimental ferrous/nonferrous metal detector with a four-foot-diameter search coil. In a report to investors, he declared his intention to undertake an exhaustive and wide-ranging electronic and visual survey of a large area surrounding the wrecksite. Before the expedition was through, Webber vowed, he would leave no ballast stone unturned in the search for the galleon's riches.

As the hot summer weather came to the South Atlantic, the expedition settled into the hard business of removing tons of coral from the main wrecksite. Progress was slow and with no whales or camera crews around to provide a break in the routine, the work lost some of its glamour. To increase efficiency, Webber tried several underwater tools with mixed results. A hydraulic jackhammer (powered by hydraulic fluid pumped from the surface) proved impractical when it was discovered that the operator had to be anchored to the ocean floor with weighted lead boots. A chain saw (also hydraulic) showed promise but cut too slowly through coral. Later, specially ordered carbide cutting tips proved more effective. By far the most useful was a "Porta-Power" hydraulic fragmentation tool. This portable, self-contained device looks like a caulking gun connected by a flexible hose to a flat waffle-sized pad or an extending piston rod which can be slipped into cracks and fissures and pumped full of hydraulic fluid. The expanding pad or piston rod exerts up to three tons of pressure against the sides of a fissure, enough to dislodge large coral boulders. With the use of a Porta-Power, divers were able to break away boulders weighing as much as 1,800 pounds and air-bag them to a nearby dump site. Such an undertaking, however, could only be done during slack tide periods (two to four hours daily) since the tidal surge in the 08 area made even normal movement difficult. Still, Webber and his team were now making recoveries in deep sand pockets at sub-bottom depths of eight and twelve feet.

Along with artifacts from the *Concepción,* divers were finding everywhere around the wrecksite remnants of Phips-period salvors including grappling hooks, iron ramrods, crowbars, English clay pipes and numerous glass onion bottles, the latter suggesting the boatmen of yesteryear did a fair bit of drinking on the job. Elsewhere, evidence of less congenial times regularly turned up in the form of human bones deep beneath the sands. Still later, divers found fused in the upper level of some coral rocks fragments of what appeared to be an exploded mortar. Very likely the explosive had been used by salvors who had fished the wreck either before or shortly after Phips' second expedition. Though the device was probably of limited use, it was one more example of the ingenuity and thoroughness of the many seventeenth-century visitors to the *Concepción*'s gravesite. What was also clear was that until Burt Webber's arrival, no one had previously discovered the treasure that had found its way to the Silver Trench of sector B9-#1.

It was late July when Webber, at the suggestion of Colonel Montes (and with the concurrence of a special government commission) first used small underwater explosives to enable him to penetrate through the fused coral shielding that completely covered several sand pockets rich in artifacts—a task otherwise beyond the reach of the tools used to date. The whales had long gone and the reef's scant fish population would be minimally affected. Moreover, Webber's intention was not to blast holes in the reef but merely to fracture the coral, after which divers would remove the fragments in debris baskets to a nearby dumping ground.

The procedure worked well and in fact led to the discovery of one of the expedition's most intriguing and valuable finds. Using fragmentation explosives with almost surgical finesse Webber removed nearly fifteen tons of fused coral over a sand pocket that was too deep for a metal detector survey. At the bottom of the pocket eight feet below were the remains of a two-by-four-foot wooden chest. Covering its bottom were contraband pieces of eight stacked four high in perfect rows, over which was a false bottom. In the main compartment were beautifully crafted silver plates stacked neatly in rows, together with twenty Chinese porcelain tea cups, only three of which were broken.

Before the *Samala* returned from this visit to the reef, the dive team had removed with the aid of explosives more than forty-five tons of coral, more than the combined total of all the previous voyages. The principal objective had been the massive coral overburden that had covered the spillage area created when the *Concepción*'s stern section broke away. Indeed, when that sector had finally been cleared, divers found many coins and artifacts that were exactly the same as those found in the B9-#1 sector.

The matching relationship of artifacts from these two sectors was one more piece of evidence confirming Webber's hypothesis of what really happened to the *Concepción* during her final days. The stern section, by virtue of being above the waterline after the ship sank, was almost completely dismantled by survivors to fashion rafts. And, as Peter Earle's research suggested, those aboard the larger rafts very likely took with them as much treasure as they could safely manage, all of which could only have been pilfered from the storerooms above the waterline—i.e., the stern. Finally, the *Concepción* broke in half below the waterline just aft of the mainmast, and the stern section—what was left of it (along with the treasure it contained)—drifted farther into the reef until it sank in the B9-#1 sector some 125 yards to the west. Thus, Webber concluded he had found not just a portion of the stern, but virtually all of what was left of it—and its treasure.

With the exception of the silver that survivors dumped on top of a reef head near the galleon (and which would now be locked in coral overgrowth), there was mounting evidence that the expedition would very likely not discover a new and highly productive source of treasure. Having already salvaged a considerable fortune, Webber could afford to regard this likelihood with equanimity. Indeed, the discovery of that fortune had already begun to change Webber's role as a treasure hunter. As president of Seaquest International, he was now required to attend board of directors' meetings, strategy sessions, and a host of land-side conferences, all of which cut into his time out on the reef. Success, it seemed, would remove Webber from the water and ensconce him in the corporate business world where he would plan and develop future expeditions to go after other lucrative shipwrecks. The change was not altogether unwelcome after seventeen years of hunting. Webber would have more time to be with his family—more time to enjoy a spacious new home that even now was being built in a rural valley not far from Reading, Pennsylvania. He looked forward to wrapping up Operation Phips II in the near future and in the process solving one last mystery: that of the silver on the reef top.

The Most Valued Treasure of All

It was mid-September when the expedition, following a reprovisioning break, geared up for a final assault on the Silver Shoals. Everything was ready, but the weather was brewing up the biggest Sunday punch ever to hit the Dominican Republic. August and September are hurricane months, and as a precaution, Webber had chosen a storm anchorage in the small well-protected Luperon Harbor some fifty miles west of Puerto Plata. The precaution proved timely for while the *Samala* lay at anchor there, Hurricane David struck the south coast causing the greatest devastation in the country's history. In the aftermath the *Samala* returned to the shoals for what would turn out to be a lengthy twenty-one-day visit. While divers finished excavating the deep holes which permeated the coral bottom of the main wrecksite like Swiss cheese, Webber began a survey of the reef tops with an experimental prototype metal detector, only to be stymied by repeated electronic failures. Abandoning the prototype, he turned to his Aquapulse metal detectors but obtained no readings on any of the heads. Either the heads contained no treasure or it was locked too deep within the coral to be detectable. Finally, Webber surveyed the same heads with the cesium mag and obtained ferrous readings on Haskins Reef against which the galleon's stern section had once rested.

Research suggested this head was also the most likely candidate as a dumping ground for treasure.

Late one afternoon after the divers had secured, Webber, together with Colonel Montes and Billy Fothergill, placed charges on the top and along the wall just below the waterline of Haskins Reef. Retreating a safe distance in a reef boat, the team detonated the charges. Early the following morning Webber returned to the scene and saw monstrous boulders lying at the base of the reef, leaving exposed large deep notches going into the reef head some five feet below the water's surface. Exploring these with a detector Webber soon found hundreds, then thousands, of silver coins, including a second astrolabe to which several coins were fused. So the legend of treasure stacked on a reef top was true—and Webber had found it.

At the end of every working day for the next week, Webber and Colonel Montes placed charges on the reef and detonated them, gradually slicing away the head until they had taken it down fifteen feet below the waterline. Each time they found more coins, plus silver candlestick holders, a statuette in the Greek style carved out of an elephant's tusk, a gold perfume vial, even a third astrolabe (found by Duke Long and dated 1632). Yet the total yield was not a king's ransom, amounting as it did to only a very small fraction of the mother lode that legend said once lay atop the head. The explanation for the disparity was obvious: between William Phips' two expeditions to the shoals some lucky salvor had found the treasure and plucked it from its perch. What had remained were silver and artifacts that had slipped beyond reach into the cracks and fissures of the head.

Though the yield was not as much as hoped, Webber was nonetheless gratified. With the finding of treasure within Haskins Reef, he had solved the final mystery of the *Concepción* and her fabled cargo. To be sure, the expedition would not end until one last survey had been completed along an expanded perimeter of the wrecksite, but there was little doubt that the long months of salvage were about to come to a triumphant close.

One morning during those final days, as he swam with the cesium mag through the canyons of the reefs he had come to know so well, Burt Webber had to remind himself that he no longer had to push quite so hard. He had found the *Concepción*. And Big Foot was clicking along nicely, no longer quite as fickle as in times gone by. He had time now to reflect on the extraordinary events of the last year, events that had catapulted him into an international limelight, conferring upon him instant celebrity status. To the few of his new acquaintances who had commented on that overnight transformation, Webber had more than once smiled and replied, "Try seventeen years."

Webber sensed that millions who had learned about his successful search for a legendary galleon would conclude that he had it made, that he was now a rich man. Another American dream come true. It didn't bother him that some viewed his good fortune in that light, because Webber, too, believed in the American dream, had fought for it, and he was proud to live in a society where that dream was still possible. Yet as he swam through the canyons of the Silver Shoals, Webber's mind (at least that part not glued to the console read-out) was less occupied with his new status than with recent memories that flashed before him in freeze-frame increments.

He remembered those long hot exhausting days in 1977 when he and the crew of Phips I endured months of failure, suffering from nerve-shattering fish poisoning. He recalled the fear in the eyes of the men gathered around Don Summers as he struggled to regain consciousness after a near drowning. He could still feel the memory of that bleak Chicago meeting with Warren Stearns and Stan Smith, a meeting in which each man felt himself to be a failure. And he would long remember those moments at home when he stared at a declining bank balance, knowing that a check was *not* in the mail, wondering in his heart of hearts if maybe he *was* on the wrong track, that maybe he should abandon his dream.

But he didn't give up. Nor did the people around him who shared his dream abandon Burt Webber.

In a real way that was the treasure he valued most of all.

Epilogue

It was mid-November 1979 before leaden skies and falling temperatures heralded the first snowfall that would provide Chicago with its winter wardrobe. In contrast to the dreary weather outside, the atmosphere in the offices of Seaquest International at 8 South Michigan Avenue was warm and bustling. The expedition had ended more than a month earlier but there had been no slackening of the pace. The *Samala* was back in Miami to off-load equipment and be refurbished; a prestigious New York public relations firm was coordinating an extensive media campaign; and the schedule for a tour of the treasure was being finalized. Apropos this latter development, museums and major aquariums in at least ten U.S. cities (Chicago, Boston, Dallas, and Tampa to name four) would showcase an elaborate exhibit of artifacts for three-month stints over a thirty-six-month period.

Elsewhere, plans were under way for the first coin auction, this one in London. Among the bidders expected at the event were several U.S. dealers who would acquire coins in lots for later marketing to the general public in the States. Added to the mix was the premier telecast of the CBS TV documentary special "The Lost Treasure of the *Concepción*." In all, Seaquest's offices, with meetings, ringing phones, and daily parade of visitors, showed the unmistakable momentum of success.

Inevitably, the degree of Seaquest success—one level anyway—will be measured in dollars and cents. Just what that total dollar figure will be cannot be predicted with any certainty at this writing. But there would seem to be no doubt that the treasure of the *Concepción* will ultimately be worth many millions and represent a total substantially greater than that realized from the discovery of any previous galleon since the days of Sir William Phips.

Aside from the understandable interest in the eventual worth of the treasure, there remains another, equally significant, facet to Burt Webber's singular achievement, one which he shares with his Seaquest associates. Not surprisingly, it has been largely overlooked.

At a time in history when there seems to be no patch of water or land or air space on the planet that has not been staked out, claimed and/or declared sovereign territory by some country, tribe, or business entity, Burt Webber succeeded in not only finding a great treasure but also in actually bringing it back home completely unscathed by any challenge to his claim that it was *his*. This accomplishment, as prosaic as it may appear, is nearly as stunning as the finding of the *Concepción* itself.

To anyone familiar with events in the treasure hunting world in recent years, the probability of legal challenges stemming from the discovery of valuable shipwrecks has been so great as to be virtually a foregone conclusion. Time and again Burt Webber had watched as other treasure hunters, after considerable sacrifice and with great ingenuity, had found a mother lode, only to be driven to bankruptcy and sometimes nervous breakdowns by the ensuing struggle for possession with bureaucratic pirates, federal and state governments, disgruntled partners and others out for what they could get. Webber and Seaquest avoided this pitfall by expending a great deal of time and effort to secure all necessary contracts and agreements long before anyone got his toes wet. In so doing they also established an unbroken chain of accountability and verification for every item of treasure, thus rendering its authenticity above suspicion. To be sure, none of this paper chasing was as glamorous as scooping up coins from the Silver Trench of B9-#1 but without it the expedition would have been an exercise in futility.

For Burt Webber the prime personal satisfaction derived from seeing the whole venture come together as a unity: "That was the greatest part of the experience—the coordination, the organization, putting people together, assembling the research, the electronics, the staffing of a first-rate team of professionals—and going out and doing it, finding the *Concepción*. Seeing the whole thing come together like a fine watch gave me a tremendous feeling of accomplishment."

Echoing these sentiments during a leisurely conversation one afternoon, Warren Stearns appended his own insight: "The fact that it is still possible for a group of people to come together on a project like this, to invest their energy and money, and to share in the rewards of success says a great deal that is good and true about America and the free enterprise system."

No less true is that Burt Webber, Warren Stearns, and Stan Smith may claim responsibility for giving treasure hunting a respectability that occupation has not enjoyed since the days following Phips' triumphant return to England. In the months and years ahead one may expect to find men and women of means soberly discussing the merits of limited partnerships aimed at recovering yet another fabled wreck. Because of Burt Webber and Seaquest, corporate treasure hunting as a fully legitimate high-technology profession has come of age.

Yet for all the earnestness and zeal with which Webber and his associates strive to overcome the traditional swashbuckling pirate image of the treasure hunter, there seems little likelihood that they will eradicate all of the less-bankable aspects of the stereotype, least of all its inherent romance (which has never been known to detract from an otherwise viable project). For all the talk of search parameters and esoteric equipment, there will still be the blue waters of the Caribbean, the heat of the tropic sun, and the siren call of history's great galleons.

Nor, I think, would Burt Webber himself entirely deny the claim, for he is the embodiment of the quintessential treasure hunter. The truth of this was borne out one cold January morning in New York City. Less than a day had elapsed since Webber had announced at a press conference the finding of the *Concepción* and already he was caught in a whirlwind of appointments and interviews. He was front page news in *The New York Times* and had given six interviews to reporters for other major periodicals. I was accompanying Webber, acting as press liaison while he ran the media gamut. At one point, following his appearance on the "Today" show, the two of us were standing in the lobby of the NBC headquarters at Rockefeller Center waiting for a network-supplied limousine when Webber suddenly turned to me.

"John, there's something very important I want you to do."

He reached into his attaché case and pulled out what appeared to be several pieces from a broken flower pot that had been worn smooth by water. I suspected they may have come from the site of yet another treasure galleon disaster. He handed them to me.

"Take these and send them to Dr. Pete Foose at Amherst College. I want him to have them put through a thermal luminescence test for dating. If the results are what I think they'll be, we could be on to a really big one."

I saw that far-away gleam in his eyes as he talked and instantly realized that on that cold day in Manhattan, Burt Webber, for all his sudden fame and recognition, was already anxious to begin the search anew. Whether or not he would ever articulate the essence of his professional being to talk-show hosts, reporters, or friends matters not at all. For Burt Webber, like his peers through all ages, knows and lives a great secret: The hunt itself is the treasure, the journey is the destination.